Workbook to Accompany Understanding

Health Insurance

A Guide to Billing and Reimbursement

2021 Edition

Workbook to Accompany Understanding

Health Insurance

A Guide to Billing and Reimbursement

2021 Edition

Michelle A. Green, MPS, RHIA, FAHIMA, CPC

Technical Collaborator

Lucreia B. Bennett, MA, RHIA, CCS, CPC

⁂ Cengage

Australia • Brazil • Canada • Mexico • Singapore • United Kingdom • United States

Workbook to Accompany Understanding Health Insurance: A Guide to Billing and Reimbursement: 2021, 16th edition
Michelle A. Green

SVP, Higher Education & Skills Product: Erin Joyner

VP, Higher Education & Skills Product: Michael Schenk

Product Director: Matthew Seeley

Senior Product Manager: Stephen G. Smith

Product Assistant: Dallas Wilkes

Learning Designer: Kaitlin Schlicht

Senior Content Manager: Kara A. DiCaterino

Senior Digital Delivery Lead: Lisa Christopher

Marketing Manager: Courtney Cozzy

IP Analyst: Ashley Maynard

IP Project Manager: Kelli Besse

Production Service: MPS Limited

Designer, Creative Studio: Angela Sheehan

Cover Image Source: T.Sumaetho/Shutterstock.com

The 2021 versions of CPT, HCPCS Level II, ICD-10-CM, and ICD-10-PCS were used in preparation of this product.

CPT publications are published by the American Medical Association and CPT is a registered trademark of the American medical Association. The American Medical Association is not affiliated with Cengage and has not sponsored, endorsed, or licensed this publication.

For product information and technology assistance, contact us at
**Cengage Customer & Sales Support, 1-800-354-9706
or support.cengage.com.**

For permission to use material from this text or product, submit all requests online at **www.copyright.com.**

ISBN: 978-0-357-51559-4

Cengage
200 Pier 4 Boulevard
Boston, MA 02210
USA

Cengage is a leading provider of customized learning solutions with employees residing in nearly 40 different countries and sales in more than 125 countries around the world. Find your local representative at **www.cengage.com.**

To learn more about Cengage platforms and services, register or access your online learning solution, or purchase materials for your course, visit **www.cengage.com.**

Notice to the Reader
Publisher does not warrant or guarantee any of the products described herein or perform any independent analysis in connection with any of the product information contained herein. Publisher does not assume, and expressly disclaims, any obligation to obtain and include information other than that provided to it by the manufacturer. The reader is expressly warned to consider and adopt all safety precautions that might be indicated by the activities described herein and to avoid all potential hazards. By following the instructions contained herein, the reader willingly assumes all risks in connection with such instructions. The publisher makes no representations or warranties of any kind, including but not limited to, the warranties of fitness for particular purpose or merchantability, nor are any such representations implied with respect to the material set forth herein, and the publisher takes no responsibility with respect to such material. The publisher shall not be liable for any special, consequential, or exemplary damages resulting, in whole or part, from the readers' use of, or reliance upon, this material.

Printed in the United States of America
5 6 7 8 9   26 25 24 23 22

CONTENTS

PREFACE

INTRODUCTION

The Workbook is designed to help learners apply the concepts presented in the textbook. This is accomplished through application-based assignments that are directly related to the content of the textbook. This edition of the Workbook is updated and redesigned for maximum effectiveness.

This Workbook can be used by college and vocational school programs to train health insurance specialists, medical assistants, medical office administrators, and health information technicians. It can also be used as an in-service training tool for new medical office personnel and independent billing services, or independently by insurance specialists who wish to increase their skills and scope of knowledge.

OBJECTIVES

After completing the assignments in each chapter, the learner will be able to:

1. Contact and interview a health insurance specialist (or similar professional) and explore career opportunities.
2. Create a professional cover letter and résumé.
3. Conduct an effective job search utilizing the Internet and local resources.
4. Access networking sites for professionals, such as listservs.
5. Interpret health insurance statistics.
6. Explain the effects of managed care on a physician's office.
7. Interpret remittance advice and explanation of benefits documents, and appeal denied claims.
8. Differentiate between fraud and abuse and HIPAA's privacy and security rules.
9. Accurately assign ICD-10-CM, CPT, and HCPCS level II codes, and differentiate among reimbursement methodologies according to health care setting.
10. Accurately enter required information on CMS-1500 claims according to individual payer requirements.

ORGANIZATION OF THE WORKBOOK

- All workbook chapters contain a multiple choice review at the end of each chapter.
- Chapter 1 contains assignments about interviewing a professional in your field of study; creating a resume and cover letter and interviewing for a job; preparing a professional journal abstract; learning about professional credentials; learning how to be a professional; and taking telephone messages.
- Chapter 2 contains assignments about interpreting health insurance coverage statistics, researching major developments in health insurance, calculating reimbursement, navigating the health insurance marketplace, and reviewing data for the quality payment program/merit-based incentive payment system.

- Chapter 3 contains assignments about interpreting the National Committee for Quality Assurance's health plan report card, explaining managed health care federal legislation, describing The Joint Commission (including its performance initiative), summarizing components of the Fairview Health Services integrated delivery system, and creating a managed care contract quick reference sheet.

- Chapter 4 contains assignments about interpreting the use of an encounter form, a remittance advice, and an explanation of benefits; writing appeal letters; calculating patient coinsurance, deductible, and provider reimbursement amounts; maintaining a current chargemaster; and monitoring the revenue cycle.

- Chapter 5 contains assignments about creating a student confidentiality statement, preventing health care fraud and abuse (HIPAA), following HIPAA privacy and security rules, identifying HIPAA covered entities, processing telephone call requests for the release of patient information, and explaining the purpose of the Hospital Inpatient Quality Reporting Program and the Hospital Compare website.

- Chapter 6 contains assignments about interpreting a general equivalence mapping, comparing ICD-10-CM to ICD-9-CM, interpreting ICD-10-CM coding conventions, using the ICD-10-CM Index to Diseases and Injuries, using the ICD-10-CM Tabular List of Diseases and Injuries, and interpreting the Diagnostic Coding and Reporting Guidelines for Outpatient Services.

- Chapter 7 contains assignments about using the CPT Index; assigning CPT Evaluation and Management (E/M), Anesthesia, Surgery, Radiology, Pathology and Laboratory, and Medicine codes; assigning CPT modifiers; coding patient cases; verifying CPT codes; and interpreting relative value units.

- Chapter 8 contains assignments about using the HCPCS Level II index, assigning HCPCS Level II codes, assigning codes to administered drugs using HCPCS level II, assigning HCPCS level II modifiers, coding patient cases, and verifying HCPCS level II codes.

- Chapter 9 contains assignments about interpreting data analytics for reimbursement; calculating and interpreting the case-mix index, relative weights, and MS-DRG payments; calculating Medicare Physician Fee Schedule payments; interpreting DRG decision trees; entering data to calculate Medicare Severity DRGs; and interpreting Ambulatory Payment Classifications data.

- Chapter 10 contains assignments about choosing the first-listed diagnosis, linking diagnoses with procedures/services, interpreting National Coverage Determinations, coding from case scenarios, coding from SOAP notes and operative reports, and completing a DRG coding validation review.

- Chapter 11 contains assignments about discussing the National Provider Identifier (NPI) standard, discussing the purpose of the Medically Unlikely Edits (MUE) project, identifying CMS-1500 claims completion errors, and completing the UB-04 claim.

- Chapter 12 contains assignments about completing commercial primary CMS-1500 claims, commercial primary/secondary same payer CMS-1500 claims, commercial secondary CMS-1500 claims, and group health plan CMS-1500 claims.

- Chapter 13 contains assignments about completing Bluecross Blueshield primary CMS-1500 claims, Bluecross Blueshield primary/secondary payer CMS-1500 claims, and Bluecross Blueshield secondary CMS-1500 claims.

- Chapter 14 contains assignments about completing Medicare primary CMS-1500 claims, Medicare as secondary payer CMS-1500 claims, Medicare/Medigap CMS-1500 claims, Medicare/Medicaid (Medi-Medi) CMS-1500 claims, and Medicare roster billing claims completion.

- Chapter 15 contains assignments about completing Medicaid primary CMS-1500 claims, Medicaid as secondary payer CMS-1500 claims, Medicaid mother/baby CMS-1500 claims, and CHIP CMS-1500 claims.

- Chapter 16 contains assignments about completing TRICARE primary CMS-1500 claims and TRICARE secondary CMS-1500 claims, and determining standard time and military time.
- Chapter 17 contains assignments about completing workers' compensation primary CMS-1500 claims and completing a workers' compensation intake form.

NEW TO THE 2021 EDITION WORKBOOK

- In Chapters 1–5, websites and and assignment instructions were updated.
- In Chapter 6, ICD-10-CM coding assignments were updated.
- In Chapter 7, CPT coding assignments were updated.
- In Chapter 8, HCPCS level II coding assignments were updated.
- In Chapter 9, assignment instructions were updated.
- In Chapter 10, CPT, HCPCS level II, and ICD-10-CM codes were updated for all coding cases.
- In Chapter 11, assignment instructions and CPT, HCPCS level II, and ICD-10-CM codes were updated.
- In Chapters 12–17, CMS-1500 answer keys for all case studies were updated.

Workbook to Accompany Understanding

Health Insurance

A Guide to Billing and Reimbursement

2021 Edition

Health Insurance Specialist Career

## CHAPTER 1

INTRODUCTION

This chapter familiarizes students with interviewing a professional, creating a résumé and cover letter, interpreting (and understanding) information from professional journal articles, networking with other professionals via professional discussion forums, and interpreting professional codes of ethics. This chapter is placed in the front of the workbook to allow students time to create or revise their résumé, build networking skills, and prepare for job interviews. Often it takes several weeks for a job search to be conducted and interviews to be scheduled. Practicing in these areas is important before you complete this course or graduate from a program of study in this field.

ASSIGNMENT 1.1 – INTERVIEW A PROFESSIONAL

Objectives

At the conclusion of this assignment, the student should be able to:

1. State the responsibilities of a professional employed in this field of study.
2. Explain whether this position would be one the student would be interested in obtaining.

Overview

Health insurance specialists often have similar educational backgrounds. However, their job responsibilities and roles vary greatly depending upon the organization by which they are employed. This assignment will familiarize the student with specific job responsibilities of a professional employed in this field.

Instructions

1. Prepare 10 questions that you would like to ask of a professional employed in your field of study.

 NOTE:

> Your instructor might devote classroom time to brainstorming such questions (or use a discussion board forum if you are an Internet-based student). This will allow you to share questions with other students in your course and obtain additional questions to ask of the professional.

2. Identify a credentialed professional in your field of study (e.g., CCS, CPC, and so on), and contact the professional to schedule an onsite interview. When you contact the professional, conduct yourself in a professional manner, and explain that you are a student completing a required assignment.

NOTE:

If it is not possible to schedule an onsite interview, check with your instructor to determine whether a telephone or e-mail interview would be acceptable.

3. Prepare for the interview by reviewing and organizing the questions you will ask of the professional.

4. Dress appropriately (as if for a job interview), and arrive 10 minutes early for the interview.

5. Adopt a professional and respectful manner when asking interview questions, and be prepared to answer questions asked of you. Be sure to take notes as the professional responds to the interview questions. If you choose to tape-record the interview, be sure to ask the professional for permission to do so.

6. After the interview, thank the professional. Request a business card and e-mail address. Be sure to follow up the interview within 10 days by mailing a handwritten thank-you note.

7. Prepare a three-page, double-spaced, word-processed document summarizing the interview, as follows:
   a. Identify the professional's name, position, and facility.
   b. Writing in the third person, summarize the professional's responses to your interview questions. Be sure to organize the interview content in logical paragraphs. (A paragraph consists of at least three sentences.) Do **not** prepare this paper in a question/answer format. If you have questions about how to write this paper, ask your instructor for clarification.
   c. In the last paragraph of the paper, summarize your reaction to the interview and state whether you would be interested in having this professional's position (along with why or why not). Also, predict your future by writing about where you will be in 10 years (in terms of employment, family, etc.).
   d. Check and double-check spelling, grammar, and punctuation. Have at least one other person review your document (e.g., college writing lab, English teacher, family member or friend who has excellent writing skills, and so on).

ASSIGNMENT 1.2 – READY, SET, GET A JOB!

Objectives

At the conclusion of this assignment, the student should be able to:

1. Conduct a job search using local resources and the Internet.
2. Create a professional career résumé and cover letter.
3. Research organizations in preparation for a job interview.
4. Determine personal worth to an organization, to facilitate salary negotiation.
5. Anticipate questions that could be asked during a job interview.
6. Describe appropriate follow-up to be performed after a job interview.

Overview

Begin your successful job search by creating a professional career résumé and cover letter. Prepare for a job interview by practicing for the interview, researching the organization, and determining your worth. Follow up after the interview by mailing a handwritten thank-you note to the interviewer.

 NOTE:

Some facilities require students to submit a cover letter and résumé for consideration by the clinical supervisor prior to placement for professional practice. This assignment will assist in that process.

Searching for a Job

To conduct a successful job search, you must assess your skills, establish goals, plan your job search, and understand the job market (Figure 1-1). Because it can take six to nine months to complete a successful job search, be sure to contact your school's career services department at least three months before graduation. Be prepared to complete the job search approximately six months after graduation. (Some job searches can take longer!) Consider following these steps to conduct your job search:

1. Perform a self-assessment by identifying your accomplishments, experience, goals, interests, skills, and values. (You have to figure out what you want from a job before you can determine what you have to offer prospective employers.)

2. Research career options and employers. Completing an internship or obtaining part-time or summer employment in your field of study will allow you to network with professionals in that field, leading to job opportunities. Researching prospective employers helps you decide which ones to contact for possible employment.

3. Plan your job search by establishing a target date for obtaining a position, remembering that it can take several months to find a job. Decide how much time you can devote to your job search, get organized, and spend time each week working on your search. Consider using multiple strategies (Figure 1-1) to seek employment; the more contacts you make, the more interviews you will get.

4. Document your job search by keeping a record of résumés mailed, interviews scheduled, and thank-you notes sent. This process allows a job seeker to easily follow up with contacts and increases credibility with prospective employers.

5. Searching for a job is very hard work, and you must be persistent because it can be discouraging. Treating the search like a job will help you produce results. (After your successful job search, establish an action plan for career progression that includes continuing education and professional networking.)

 NOTE:

It is acceptable to submit your résumé to a prospective employer more than once. Some employers maintain résumés for only 30 days, so if your job search takes months, it is possible that you will need to submit your résumé more than once. Such persistence also demonstrates your enthusiasm and interest in that employer.

CLASSIFIED ADS. The "Help Wanted" ads in newspapers list numerous jobs. You should realize, however, that many other job openings are not listed, and that the classified ads sometimes do not give all of the important information. They may offer little or no description of the job, working conditions, or pay. Some ads do not identify the employer. They may simply give a post office box to mail your résumé to, making follow-up inquiries very difficult. Some ads offer out-of-town jobs; others advertise employment agencies rather than actual employment opportunities. When using classified ads, keep the following in mind:

- Do not rely solely on the classifieds to find a job; follow other leads as well.

- Answer ads promptly because openings may be filled quickly, even before the ad stops appearing in the paper.

- Read the ads every day, particularly the Sunday edition, which usually includes the most listings.

(continues)

FIGURE 1-1 Job search methods.

FIGURE 1-1 *(continued)*

- Beware of "no experience necessary" ads, which may signal low wages, poor working conditions, or commission work.

- Keep a record of all ads to which you have responded, including the specific skills, educational background, and personal qualifications required for the position.

COMMUNITY AGENCIES. Many nonprofit organizations, including religious institutions and vocational rehabilitation agencies, offer counseling, career development, and job placement services, generally targeted to a particular group, such as women, youth, minorities, ex-offenders, or older workers.

EMPLOYERS. Through your library (e.g., local yellow page listings for physicians and clinics) and Internet research, develop a list of potential employers in your desired career field. Employer websites often contain lists of job openings. Websites and business directories can provide you with information on how to apply for a position or whom to contact. Even if no open positions are posted, do not hesitate to contact the employer and the relevant department. Set up an interview with someone working in the same area you wish to work. Ask them how they got started, what they enjoy or dislike about the work, what type of qualifications are necessary for the job, and what type of personality succeeds in that position. Even if they don't have a position available, they may be able to put you in contact with other people who might hire you and they can keep you in mind if a position opens up. Make sure to send them your résumé and a cover letter. If you are able to obtain an interview, be sure to send a thank-you note. Directly contacting employers is one of the most successful means of job hunting.

FEDERAL GOVERNMENT. Information on federal government jobs is available from the Office of Personnel Management through the Internet at **www.usajobs.gov**.

INTERNET NETWORKS AND RESOURCES. The Internet provides a variety of information, including job listings and job search resources and techniques. However, no single network or resource will contain all of the information available on employment or career opportunities, so be prepared to search for what you need.

Remember that job listings may be posted by field or discipline, so begin your search using keywords. When searching employment databases on the Internet, it is sometimes possible to send your résumé to an employer by e-mail or to post it on-line. Some sources allow you to send e-mail free of charge, but be careful that you are not going to incur any additional charges for postings or updates.

LABOR UNIONS. Labor unions provide various employment services to members, including apprenticeship programs that teach a specific trade or skill. Contact the appropriate labor union or state apprenticeship council for more information.

PERSONAL CONTACTS. Your family, friends, and acquaintances may offer one of the most effective ways to find a job. They may help you directly or put you in touch with someone else who can. Such networking can lead to information about specific job openings, many of which may not be publicly posted.

(continues)

FIGURE 1-1 *(continued)*

PRIVATE EMPLOYMENT AGENCIES AND CAREER CONSULTANTS. These agencies can be helpful, but they are in business to make money. Most operate on a commission basis, with the fee dependent upon a percentage of the salary paid to a successful applicant. You or the hiring company will pay a fee. Find out the exact cost and who is responsible for paying associated fees before using the service. Although employment agencies can help you save time and contact employers who otherwise might be difficult to locate, the costs may outweigh the benefits if you are responsible for the fee. Contacting employers directly often will generate the same type of leads that a private employment agency will provide. Consider any guarantees the agency offers when determining if the service is worth the cost.

PROFESSIONAL ASSOCIATIONS. Many professions have associations that offer employment information, including career planning, educational programs, job listings, and job placement. To use these services, associations usually require that you be a member of their association; information can be obtained directly from an association through the Internet, by telephone, or by mail.

SCHOOL CAREER PLANNING AND PLACEMENT OFFICES. High school and college placement offices help their students and alumni find jobs. They set up appointments and allow recruiters to use their facilities for interviews. Placement offices usually have a list of part-time, temporary, and summer jobs offered on campus. They also may have lists of jobs for regional, nonprofit, and government organizations. Students can receive career counseling and testing and job search advice. At career resource libraries they may attend workshops on such topics as job search strategy, résumé writing, letter writing, and effective interviewing; critique drafts of résumés and watch videotapes of mock interviews; explore files of résumés and references; and attend job fairs conducted by the placement office.

STATE EMPLOYMENT SERVICE OFFICES. The state employment service, sometimes called Job Service, operates in coordination with the U.S. Department of Labor's Employment and Training Administration. Local offices, found nationwide, help job seekers find jobs and help employers find qualified workers at no cost to either. To find the office nearest you, look in the state government telephone listings under "Job Service" or "Employment."

- *JOB MATCHING AND REFERRAL.* At the state employment service office, an interviewer will determine if you are "job ready" or if you need help from counseling and testing services to assess your occupational aptitudes and interests and to help you choose and prepare for a career.

  After you are "job ready," you may examine available job listings and select openings that interest you. A staff member can then describe the job openings in detail and arrange for interviews with prospective employers.

(continues)

FIGURE 1-1 *(continued)*

- ***CareerOneStop.org***, sponsored by the U.S. Department of Labor, is a source for career exploration, training, and jobs.

- **SERVICES FOR SPECIAL GROUPS.** By law, veterans are entitled to priority for job placement at state employment service centers. If you are a veteran, an employment representative can inform you of available assistance and help you deal with problems. States have One-Stop Service Centers that provide various special groups and the general public with employment, training, and related services available under the Workforce Investment Act of 1998.

Instructions

1. Go to **www.monster.com**, and click on Career Advice to begin your research process about résumé writing, interviewing, salary and benefits, and more.

2. Go to the *Occupational Outlook Handbook* at **www.bls.gov/ooh**. This "is a nationally recognized source of career information, designed to provide valuable assistance to individuals making decisions about their future work lives. Revised every two years, the *Handbook* describes what workers do on the job, working conditions, the training and education needed, earnings, and expected job prospects in a wide range of occupations."

3. Go to **www.hoovers.com** to access its database of 12 million companies and research information on prospective employers.

4. Select one or more of the following health care websites to research available positions:

AAPC	**www.aapc.com**
Allied Health Careers	**www.alliedhealthcareers.com**
American Association of Medical Assistants	**www.aama-ntl.org**
American Health Information Management Association	**www.ahima.org**
For the Record	**www.fortherecordmag.com**
Health eCareers™ Network	**www.healthecareers.com**
H.I.M. Recruiters	**www.himjobs.com**

5. Write a cover letter and create a résumé, referring to the samples in Figures 1-2 and 1-3.

6. Write a thank-you letter, referring to the sample in Figure 1-4.

7. Contact five prospective employers that currently have available positions and complete a job search log. (Submit the log to your instructor for review.)

JOB SEARCH #1

Title of job posted: _____

Date prospective employer contacted: _____

Name and address of organization: _____

Phone number of organization: _____

Fax number of organization: _____

E-mail address of organization: _____

Name of person contacted at organization: _____

Application method: ❏ Fax   ❏ In person   ❏ Online   ❏ _____

JOB SEARCH #2

Title of job posted: _____

Date prospective employer contacted: _____

Name and address of organization: _____

Phone number of organization: _____

Fax number of organization: _____

E-mail address of organization: _____

Name of person contacted at organization: _____

Application method: ❏ Fax   ❏ In person   ❏ Online   ❏ _____

JOB SEARCH #3

Title of job posted: _____

Date prospective employer contacted: _____

Name and address of organization: _____

Phone number of organization: _____

Fax number of organization: _____

E-mail address of organization: _____

Name of person contacted at organization: _____

Application method: ❏ Fax   ❏ In person   ❏ Online   ❏ _____

```
JOB SEARCH #4
Title of job posted:                        _____
Date prospective employer contacted:       _____
Name and address of organization:          _____
Phone number of organization:              _____
Fax number of organization:                _____
E-mail address of organization:            _____
Name of person contacted at organization:  _____
Application method:        ❏ Fax      ❏ In person     ❏ Online      ❏ _____
```

```
JOB SEARCH #5
Title of job posted:                        _____
Date prospective employer contacted:       _____
Name and address of organization:          _____
Phone number of organization:              _____
Fax number of organization:                _____
E-mail address of organization:            _____
Name of person contacted at organization:  _____
Application method:        ❏ Fax      ❏ In person     ❏ Online      ❏ _____
```

Creating a Résumé and Cover Letter

A résumé won't get you a job; however, it can eliminate you from the pool of candidates if unprofessionally prepared. Employers often identify interview candidates by reviewing résumés to eliminate those unqualified. Résumés or cover letters that contain typographical errors or evidence of poor communication skills are discarded because employers are unwilling to spend valuable time interviewing such candidates.

Carol Woughter

Placement & Transfer Expert

Your cover letter (Figure 1-2) is actually a marketing tool because it focuses on your qualifications as a prospective employee. It should be well written so that the employer will review your résumé. When creating your cover letter, be sure to consider the following:

- Research the prospective employer's organization to personalize the letter. Your knowledge of the organization demonstrates your interest in the employer.

Street Address
City, State Zip
Current date

> Call the human resources department at the prospective employer to find out to whom the cover letter should be addressed.

Name
Title
Company
Street Address
City, State Zip

Dear Mr./Ms.:

Paragraph 1—Explain why you are writing, and identify the position and your source of information. Summarize your strongest qualifications for the position using a series of phrases (e.g., I am applying for the Coding & Reimbursement Specialist position as advertised in *The Alfred Sun*, October 9, YYYY. My coding/insurance processing skills and attention to detail are my strongest qualifications for this position.).

Paragraph 2—Detail your strongest qualifications and relate them to the position requirements. Provide evidence of related education and employment experiences. Refer to your enclosed résumé (e.g., I will graduate in May YYYY with a Certificate in Insurance and Reimbursement Specialist from Alfred State College, where I completed extensive coursework in coding and insurance processing. My 240-hour professional practice experience allowed me to perform coding and insurance duties at Alfred State Medical Center. The completed evaluation of this experience documents my attention to detail, excellent work ethic, and superior coding and insurance processing skills. My education also included general education courses, which has provided me with an excellent background in computer applications and human sciences. I plan to take the C.C.A. certification examination in June YYYY, after I graduate. Please refer to the enclosed résumé for additional information.).

Paragraph 3—Request an interview and indicate how and when you can be contacted. Suggest that you will place a follow-up call to discuss interview possibilities. Thank the employer (e.g., Please contact me at (607) 555-1234 after 4 PM, Monday through Friday, to schedule an interview at a mutually convenient time. I will contact you next week to ensure that you received my cover letter and résumé. Thank you for your consideration.).

Sincerely,

[*handwritten signature*]

Your typed name

Enclosure

FIGURE 1-2 Sample cover letter.

- Briefly explain several special abilities or significant accomplishments so the employer will be interested in you. Be sure you do not misrepresent your experience or skills. If you do not meet every job qualification, emphasize your strengths.
- Group similar information within the same paragraph, and organize paragraphs logically so the cover letter is easy to read. Use action verbs to make the cover letter interesting and display energy.
- Write in a formal style. Be clear, objective, and persuasive (as opposed to just describing your education and experience background).
- Do not include any information that might cause the employer to question your ability to do the job. (Everyone has weaknesses, but there is no sense pointing them out to a prospective employer in your cover letter! Save this information for the interview, where it will allow you to appear modest about your professional skills.)
- Check and double-check spelling and grammar. Consider having at least one other person review your cover letter (e.g., school career services professional, English teacher, and so on).

If you are a recent graduate, your career résumé (Figure 1-3) should probably be limited to one page; however, if you have extensive work experience in a health-related field, a two-page résumé is acceptable. Because the purpose of your résumé is to get an interview, the résumé should contain information appropriate to the position you wish to obtain so that it convinces a prospective employer that you have the skills necessary for the available position. In addition, when preparing your résumé, be sure to focus on the prospective employer's needs. This may mean revising your résumé each time you apply for a position (e.g., rewrite the job objective in the résumé).

EXAMPLE: You see an advertisement for a position that seems perfect for you, and along with plenty of others you send the employer a cover letter with your résumé. By the application deadline, human resources personnel are ready to review hundreds of résumés. (A job notice routinely pulls in between 100 and 1,000 résumés.)

The cover letters and résumés are reviewed quickly, with those containing any errors immediately discarded to narrow the applicant pool. Your résumé, however, is not only perfectly written but also well organized and pertinent to the available position. Thus, it is carefully reviewed and placed on the small stack of résumés that will be used to schedule interviews.

The Interview Process

An interview gives you the opportunity to demonstrate your qualifications to an employer, so it pays to be well prepared.

Bureau of Labor Statistics

During a job interview, you are evaluated on how well suited you are for the available position. Therefore, when preparing for a job interview, be sure that you have a good understanding of the organization, job responsibilities and duties, corresponding skills required, and how your experience relates to the position.

Job Interview Tips. (Reprinted according to Bureau of Labor Statistics reuse policy.)

Preparation

- Learn about the organization.
- Have a specific job or jobs in mind.
- Review your qualifications for the job.
- Prepare answers to broad questions about yourself.

SALLY S. STUDENT

| 5 Main Street | Alfred, NY 14802 | (607) 555-1111 |

JOB OBJECTIVE An entry-level insurance and coding specialist position.

EDUCATION STATE UNIVERSITY OF NEW YORK, COLLEGE OF TECHNOLOGY AT ALFRED, Alfred, NY. Candidate for Associate in Applied Science, Coding & Reimbursement Specialist, May YYYY.

HONORS & AWARDS: Dean's List, Fall YYYY, Spring YYYY, and Fall YYYY.

Recipient, Outstanding Coding & Reimbursement Specialist Student Award, May YYYY .

CERTIFICATION C.C.A. eligible, June YYYY.

PROFESSIONAL AFFILIATIONS Student Member, American Health Information Management Association. Member, Alfred State College Health Information Management Club.

WORK EXPERIENCE Coding and Insurance Professional Practice, Alfred State Medical Center, Alfred, NY. Assigned ICD-10-CM, CPT, and HCPCS level II codes to inpatient, outpatient, and emergency department records. Abstracted inpatient cases using MediSoft abstracting software. Generated CMS-1500 and UB-04 claims. Processed denials by correcting claims and resubmitted for payment. Summer YYYY.

Cashier, Burger King, Hornell, NY. Assisted customers, operated cash register, and opened/closed store. August YYYY – Present.

AVAILABILITY May YYYY.

REFERENCES Available upon request.

FIGURE 1-3 Sample career résumé.

- Review your résumé.
- Schedule a mock interview with your school's career services office.
- Arrive before the scheduled time of your interview.

Personal Appearance

- Be well groomed.
- Dress appropriately (e.g., professionally).
- Do not chew gum or smoke.

NOTE:

Avoid smoking prior to the interview, because the smell of tobacco can be obvious and offensive to a nonsmoking interviewer.

The Interview

- Relax and answer each question concisely.

 NOTE:

It is acceptable to ask that a question be repeated. You can also bring a pen and paper to the interview to record questions and take notes.

- Respond promptly.
- Maintain eye contact and good posture.
- Use good manners.
- Do not interrupt the interviewer.
- Highlight ways in which you can be an asset to the organization based on your experience, education, skills, and knowledge.

 NOTE:

Be absolutely truthful. Do not misrepresent any information about yourself.

- Learn the name of your interviewer and shake hands as you meet.
- Use proper English; avoid slang.
- Be cooperative and enthusiastic.
- Ask questions about the position and the organization (e.g., salary range, working hours, clarification of job functions, working environment, and when the interview results will be available).
- Do not speak negatively about a previous place of employment.
- Thank the interviewer verbally when you leave and, as a follow-up, in writing.

Testing. Some organizations require applicants to complete an exam onsite to demonstrate proficiency (e.g., coding, medical terminology, and so on).

- Listen closely to instructions.
- Read each question carefully.
- Write legibly and clearly.
- Budget your time wisely and do not dwell on one question.

Information to Take to an Interview

- Social Security card
- Government-issued identification (e.g., driver's license)
- Evidence of certification if professional certification is required for the job (e.g., coding credential)
- Résumé

NOTE:

Although an employer may not require applicants to bring a résumé to the job interview, you should be able to furnish the interviewer with information about your education, training, and previous employment. Because you may become nervous during the interview, it is helpful to have your résumé available to prompt you for this information.

- References

NOTE:

Employers typically require three professional references. Be sure to obtain permission before using anyone as a reference, and make sure the person will give you a good reference. Avoid using relatives and friends.

INTERNET LINKS

The following websites contain more information about preparing for an interview:

Job-Interview   **www.job-interview.net**

Following Up After the Interview. Be sure to send the interviewer a handwritten thank-you letter (Figure 1-4) after an interview. The letter indicates that you are considerate and polite, and it also allows you to reemphasize your positive attributes to the interviewer. The thank-you letter should be written the same day of

Dear [name of interviewer]:

Thank you for interviewing me for the [name of position] position at [name of organization]. After meeting with you, I am convinced that my background and skills will meet your needs.

I appreciate that you took the time to familiarize me with the organization. I believe I could learn a great deal from you and would certainly enjoy working with you.

In addition to my qualifications and experience, I will bring excellent work habits and judgment to this position. With the countless demands on your time, I am sure that you require people who can be trusted to carry out their responsibilities with minimal supervision.

I look forward to hearing from you concerning your hiring decision. Again, thank you for your time and consideration.

Sincerely,

[your signature]

FIGURE 1-4 Sample thank-you letter.

the interview and mailed that night. Be sure to thank the interviewer and mention something that happened or was discussed to remind the interviewer of who you are.

Evaluating a Job Offer. (Reprinted according to Bureau of Labor Statistics reuse policy.)

Once you receive a job offer, you are faced with a difficult decision and must evaluate the offer carefully. Fortunately, most organizations will not expect you to accept or reject an offer immediately. There are many issues to consider when assessing a job offer. Will the organization be a good place to work? Will the job be interesting? Are there opportunities for advancement? Is the salary fair? Does the employer offer good benefits? If you have not already figured out exactly what you want, the following discussion may help you develop a set of criteria for judging job offers, whether you are starting a career, reentering the labor force after a long absence, or planning a career change.

The Organization

Background information on an organization can help you decide whether it would be a good place for you to work (Figure 1-5). Factors to consider include the organization's business or activity, financial condition, age, size, and location. You can generally get background information on an organization, particularly a large organization, by telephoning its public relations office. A public company's annual report to the stockholders tells about its corporate philosophy, history, products or services, goals, and financial status. Most government agencies can furnish reports that describe their programs and missions. Press releases, company newsletters or magazines, and recruitment brochures also can be useful. Ask the organization for any other items that might interest a prospective employee. If possible, speak to current or former employees of the organization.

Does the organization's business or activity match your own interests and beliefs? It is easier to apply yourself to the work if you are enthusiastic about what the organization does.

How will the size of the organization affect you? Large firms generally offer a greater variety of training programs and career paths, more managerial levels for advancement, and better employee benefits than small firms. Large employers may also have more advanced technologies. However, jobs in large firms may tend to be highly specialized. Jobs in small firms may offer broader authority and responsibility, a closer working relationship with top management, and a chance to clearly see your contribution to the success of the organization.

Should you work for a relatively new organization or one that is well-established? New businesses have a high failure rate, but for many people, the excitement of helping create a company and the potential for sharing in its success more than offsets the risk of job loss. However, it may be just as exciting and rewarding to work for a young firm that already has a foothold on success.

Does it make a difference if the company is private or public? An individual or a family may control a privately owned company, and key jobs may be reserved for relatives and friends. A board of directors responsible to the stockholders controls a publicly owned company and key jobs are usually open to anyone.

Is the organization in an industry with favorable long-term prospects? The most successful firms tend to be in industries that are growing rapidly.

Reprinted according to Bureau of Labor Statistics reuse policy

FIGURE 1-5 Questions to ask before you accept the position.

Background information on the organization may be available at your public or school library. If you cannot get an annual report, check the library for reference directories that may provide basic facts about the company, such as earnings, products and services, and number of employees. Some directories widely available in libraries include:

- *Dun & Bradstreet's Million Dollar Directory*
- *Moody's Industrial Manual*
- *Standard and Poor's Register of Corporations*
- *Thomas' Register of American Manufacturers*
- *Ward's Business Directory*

Stories about an organization in magazines and newspapers can tell a great deal about its successes, failures, and plans for the future. You can identify articles on a company by looking under its name in periodical or computerized indexes in libraries. However, it probably will not be useful to look back more than two or three years.

The library also may have government publications that present projections of growth for the industry in which the organization is classified. Long-term projections of employment and output for more than 200 industries, covering the entire economy, are developed by the Bureau of Labor Statistics and revised every two years—see the *Monthly Labor Review* for the most recent projections. The *U.S. Industry and Trade Outlook*, published annually by the U.S. Department of Commerce, presents detailed analyses of U.S. industries. Trade magazines also may include articles on the trends for specific industries.

Career centers at colleges and universities often have information on employers that is not available in libraries. Ask a career center representative how to find out about a particular organization.

Nature of the Job. Even if everything else about the job is attractive, you will be unhappy if you dislike the day-to-day work. Determining in advance whether you will like the work may be difficult (Figure 1-6). However,

Where is the job located? If the job is in another section of the country, you need to consider the cost of living, the availability of housing and transportation, and the quality of educational and recreational facilities in that section of the country. Even if the job location is in your area, you should consider the time and expense of commuting.

Does the work match your interests and make good use of your skills? The duties and responsibilities of the job should be explained in enough detail to answer this question.

How important is the job in this company? An explanation of where you fit in the organization and how you are supposed to contribute to its overall objectives should give you an idea of the job's importance.

Are you comfortable with the hours? Most jobs involve regular hours—for example, 40 hours a week, during the day, Monday through Friday. Other jobs require night, weekend, or holiday work. In addition, some jobs routinely require overtime to meet deadlines or sales or production goals, or to better serve customers. Consider the effect the work hours will have on your personal life.

How long do most people who enter this job stay with the company? High turnover can mean dissatisfaction with the nature of the work or something else about the job.

Reprinted according to Bureau of Labor Statistics reuse policy.

FIGURE 1-6 Additional questions to ask before you accept the position.

the more you find out about the job before accepting or rejecting an offer, the more likely you are to make the right choice. Actually working in the industry and, if possible, for the company, would provide considerable insight. You can gain work experience through part-time, temporary, or summer jobs, or through internship or work-study programs while in school. All of these can also lead to permanent job offers.

Opportunities Offered by Employers. A good job offers you opportunities to learn new skills, increase your earnings, and rise to positions of greater authority, responsibility, and prestige. A lack of opportunities can dampen your interest in the work and result in frustration and boredom. The company should have a training plan for you. Be sure to ask the following questions:

- What valuable new skills does the company plan to teach you?
- What promotion possibilities are available within the organization?
- What is the next step on the career ladder?
- If you have to wait for a job to become vacant before you can be promoted, how long does this usually take?
- When opportunities for advancement do arise, will you compete with applicants from outside the company?
- Can you apply for jobs for which you qualify elsewhere within the organization, or is mobility within the firm limited?

Salaries and Benefits. Wait for the employer to introduce the subjects of salaries and benefits. Some companies will not talk about pay until they have decided to hire you. To know if an offer is reasonable, you need a rough estimate of what the job should pay. You may have to go to several sources for this information. Try to find family, friends, or acquaintances recently hired in similar jobs. Ask your teachers and the staff in placement offices about starting pay for graduates with your qualifications. Help-wanted ads in newspapers sometimes give salary ranges for similar positions. Check the library or your school's career center for salary surveys, such as those conducted by the National Association of Colleges and Employers or various professional associations.

If you are considering the salary and benefits for a job in another geographic area, make allowances for differences in the cost of living, which may be significantly higher in a large metropolitan area than in a smaller city, town, or rural area.

You also should learn the organization's policy regarding overtime. Depending on the job, you may or may not be exempt from laws requiring the employer to compensate you for overtime. Find out how many hours you will be expected to work each week and whether you receive overtime pay or compensatory time off for working more than the specified number of hours in a week.

Also take into account that a starting salary is just that—the start. Your salary should be reviewed on a regular basis; many organizations do it every year. How much can you expect to earn after one, two, or three or more years? An employer cannot be specific about the amount of pay if it includes commissions and bonuses. Benefits can also add a lot to your base pay, but they vary widely. Find out exactly what the benefit package includes and how much of the cost you must bear (e.g., health insurance).

If You Do Not Get the Job. If you do not get the job, consider contacting the organization to find out why. Ask the following questions:

- What was your general impression of me during the interview?
- In what ways could I improve the way I interview?
- What were my weaknesses, and how can I strengthen them?
- What things did impress you, and why?
- What suggestions do you have for improving my cover letter or résumé?

- Is there anything else you would advise me to work on?
- What were the characteristics of the successful candidate?
- Do you have any other positions available for which I might be suitable?
- Finally, is there anything else I should ask you?

Remember that there will be additional opportunities for job interviews. Try not to get so discouraged that you discontinue your job search. Although it is hard to be turned down, it is part of the search process. Keep looking, and you will find the right job with the right employer.

INTERNET LINKS

Occupational Employment Statistics available as a link from **www.bls.gov**.

The National Compensation Survey is available at **www.bls.gov/ncs**.

Occupational Employment Statistics data are available at **www.bls.gov/oes**.

ASSIGNMENT 1.3 – JOURNAL ABSTRACT

Objectives

At the conclusion of this assignment, the student should be able to:

1. Identify the name of the professional association's journal.
2. Write a journal abstract of an article from a professional association's journal.

Overview

Professional association journals communicate information about health care advances, new technology, changing regulations, and much more. This assignment familiarizes students with the contents of professional journals in their fields and requires students to prepare an abstract (summary) of a selected article.

Instructions

1. Locate the name of your professional association's journal in Table 1-1.
2. Locate a journal by:
   a. Going to its website (many journals are posted online).
   b. Borrowing a journal through interlibrary loan (e.g., college library, local library).
   c. Contacting a professional in your field of study or your instructor to borrow a journal.

 NOTE:

Borrowing a journal from a professional in your field of study is an excellent way to start the networking process that will lead to employment. If you borrow a journal, be sure to return it promptly, and include a thank-you note. (Student members of professional associations do receive their profession's journal. Because it can take eight weeks to receive your first journal after joining your professional association, your best option is to go to the library or borrow a journal.)

3. Select and read an article from a recent edition (e.g., within the past year) of your professional association's journal.

4. Prepare a one-page, double-spaced, word-processed document that summarizes the journal article. Be sure to include the following information:
   a. Name of article
   b. Name of author
   c. Name of journal
   d. Date of journal
   e. Summary of journal article

 NOTE:

Do *not* include your opinion about the article's content.

5. Check and double-check spelling, grammar, and punctuation. Have at least one other person review your document (e.g., college writing lab, English teacher, family member or friend who has excellent writing skills, and so on).

TABLE 1-1 Professional Journals for Coding and Reimbursement Specialists

Professional Journal	Professional Association	Website
CodeWrite	American Health Information Management Association	**www.ahima.org**
Healthcare Business Monthly	AAPC	**www.aapc.com**

ASSIGNMENT 1.4 – PROFESSIONAL DISCUSSION FORUMS (LISTSERVS)

Objectives

At the conclusion of this assignment, the student should be able to:

1. Explain the value of joining professional discussion forums.
2. Join a professional discussion forum.
3. Review discussion forum contents to identify topics relevant to a particular field of study.
4. Participate in a professional discussion forum.

Overview

Networking, or sharing information among professionals, is a valuable professional activity. The Internet has made it much easier to network with other professionals by using web-based professional forums. This assignment familiarizes the student with the value of Internet professional discussion forums.

Instructions

1. Go to **https://list.nih.gov**, and click on "About NIH Listserv" to learn the purpose of a listserv. To access the listserv forums, register for an account and login.
2. Select a professional discussion forum from Table 1-2, and follow its membership instructions.

 NOTE:

Joining professional discussion forums is usually free!

3. Access archived forum discussions and observe current discussions for the period designated by your instructor (e.g., one to three weeks), noting topics that are relevant to your field of study.

4. Post a discussion comment or question on the forum and observe responses from subscribers.

5. At the end of the period of observation and participation, determine whether the forum would be helpful to you on the job.

TABLE 1-2 Discussion Forums and Internet Sites for Professionals

Professional	Name of Forum	Internet Site
AHIMA members	Communities of Practice	**engage.ahima.org**
Reimbursement specialists (Medicare)	Medicare Prospective Payment Communication	**https://list.nih.gov** Click "Search Public Lists," enter "PPS-L," scroll down, click on "PPS-L," and click "Subscribe or Unsubscribe" to join.

ASSIGNMENT 1.5 – LEARNING ABOUT PROFESSIONAL CREDENTIALS

Objectives

At the conclusion of this assignment, the student should be able to:

1. Access professional association websites to locate information about insurance and coding credentials.

2. List available credentials and describe eligibility requirements for each.

3. Determine annual continuing education requirements for maintaining professional credentials.

Overview

Credentialing examinations are offered by the AAPC, American Association of Medical Assistants (AAMA) and the American Health Information Management Association (AHIMA). Educational requirements, examination fees, and required or recommended experience vary for each credential, depending on association requirements. Becoming credentialed is an important achievement. This assignment will allow you to compare credentials offered by professional associations, so you can determine which is best for you!

Instructions

1. Go to the appropriate professional association website indicated in Table 1-3.

2. Locate information about professional credentials offered by each professional association. (Be sure to review the professional association's examination application booklet to obtain all of the information needed to complete Table 1-3. This will require the use of Adobe Reader software, which is available as a free download from **www.adobe.com**.)

3. Complete the table.

 NOTE:

Navigate each website to locate information needed to complete the table. This will help you learn how to locate information at a professional association website, which often requires using tool bars and pull-down menus.

TABLE 1-3 Professional Association Credentials

AAPC www.aapc.com					
Credential Abbreviation	Meaning of Credential	Education	Experience	Exam Fee	Continuing Education Units (CEU) Requirements
CPC					
COC					
CPB					

American Health Information Management Association (AHIMA) www.ahima.org					
Credential Abbreviation	Meaning of Credential	Education	Experience	Exam Fee	CEU Requirements
CCA					
CCS					
CCS-P					

ASSIGNMENT 1.6 – PROFESSIONALISM

Objectives

At the conclusion of this assignment, the student should be able to:

1. Explain the importance of professionalism.
2. Discuss qualities and skills that characterize a professional person.

Overview

The *Merriam-Webster Dictionary* defines professionalism as the "conduct, aims, or qualities that characterize a professional person." Health care facility managers establish rules of behavior so employees know how to behave professionally. Employees are expected to develop certain skills to demonstrate workplace professionalism, which results in personal growth and success.

Instructions

Match the definition in column A with its corresponding skill in column B, entering the appropriate letter on the blank line for each.

Column A

_____ 1. Ability to differentiate between technical descriptions of similar procedures.

_____ 2. Ability to be friendly, helpful, and positive while performing their job duties.

_____ 3. Having the ability to be confident, have better relationships, self-respect, and a successful career.

_____ 4. Ability to provide excellent service when addressing questions and concerns to patients and colleagues.

_____ 5. Someone who motivates team members to reach their goals.

_____ 6. A person who is motivated to increase their knowledge by participating in continuing education and certification.

_____ 7. Ability to work alone, or pitch in and help coworkers when needed.

_____ 8. Ability to be flexible and try new ideas.

_____ 9. Ability to resolve issues with positive outcomes.

_____ 10. Ability to know the difference between right and wrong.

Column B

a. Attitude
b. Conflict Management
c. Critical Thinking
d. Customer Service
e. Leadership
f. Managing Change
g. Productivity
h. Professional Ethics
i. Self-Esteem
j. Team Building

ASSIGNMENT 1.7 – TELEPHONE MESSAGES

Objectives

At the conclusion of this assignment, the student should be able to:

1. Explain the importance of documenting complete telephone messages.
2. Determine the information to be obtained from callers.
3. Accurately prepare telephone messages.

Overview

The telephone can be an effective means of patient access to the health care system because a health care team member serves as an immediate contact for the patient. Participating in telephone skills training and following established protocols (policies) allow health care team members to respond appropriately to patients.

When processes for handling all telephone calls are developed and followed by health care team members, the result is greater office efficiency and less frustration for health care team members and patients. It is essential that health care team members accurately and completely document information from a caller, promptly deliver messages to the appropriate team member, and maintain confidentiality about the content of all messages.

Instructions

1. Review voice message case scenarios, which were recorded as voicemail on Dr. Al A. Sickmann, M.D.'s office telephone during lunch.
2. Enter key elements on each telephone message form, including:
   a. Name of person for whom the message was left.
   b. Caller's name (obtain correct spelling), company or department, and return telephone number.
   c. Date and time of the call.
   d. Message for the health care team member.
   e. Action to be taken (e.g., please call ..., will call back, urgent, and so on).
3. After reviewing voice message data, complete a blank message form to communicate each telephone message to Dr. Al A. Sickmann, M.D.

   a. Case 1

   Mrs. Faye Slift, an established patient, called at 12:15 PM on 9/8/YYYY to let us know that a refill of high blood pressure medication is needed. The patient's phone number is (123) 934-6857. The patient would like us to call the pharmacy to have the prescription refilled. The patient states that we have the pharmacy number on file. The patient would also like us to call to verify that we got the message. The patient only has enough medication for the rest of this week.

DATE _____	TIME _____
TO _____	

WHILE YOU WERE OUT

MR./MRS. _____

FROM _____

PHONE (____) ____ _____

TELEPHONED _____	PLEASE CALL BACK _____
CALLED TO SEE YOU _____	WILL CALL AGAIN _____
RETURNED YOUR CALL _____	URGENT _____

MESSAGE:

_____

_____

_____

_____

_____

TAKEN BY _____

b. Case 2

Ed Overeels, a new patient, called at 12:40 PM on 9/11/YYYY to request that a local doctor close to his home to treat chronic lower back pain. Ed works evenings and is available anytime in the morning for an appointment, and would like to get in as soon as possible because of currently experiencing a flare-up due to the recent move from Ohio. His number is (123) 212-6588.

DATE _____   TIME _____

TO _____

WHILE YOU WERE OUT

MR./MRS. _____

FROM _____

PHONE (_____) _____

TELEPHONED _____   PLEASE CALL BACK _____

CALLED TO SEE YOU _____   WILL CALL AGAIN _____

RETURNED YOUR CALL _____   URGENT _____

MESSAGE:

_____

_____

_____

_____

_____

TAKEN BY _____

c. Case 3

Tristan N. Shout, a returning patient, called at 1:00 PM on 9/20/YYYY to let us know of a recent job change and new insurance coverage. Tristan can now return to our office since Dr. Sickmann is a participating provider in the new insurance network. An annual exam needs to be scheduled before the year is up. Tristan would like to make an appointment for the latest appointment that we have available on a Friday. Please call (123) 319-6531 as soon as we get the message.

```
DATE  _____        TIME _____

TO    _____

                          WHILE YOU WERE OUT

MR./MRS.      _____

FROM          _____
              (            )
PHONE         _____

TELEPHONED          _____        PLEASE CALL BACK  _____

CALLED TO SEE YOU   _____        WILL CALL AGAIN    _____

RETURNED YOUR CALL  _____        URGENT             _____

MESSAGE:

_____

_____

_____

_____

_____

                                            TAKEN BY _____
```

ASSIGNMENT 1.8 – MULTIPLE CHOICE REVIEW

1. The concept that every procedure or service reported to a third-party payer must be linked to a condition that justifies that procedure or service is called medical
   a. condition.
   b. necessity.
   c. procedure.
   d. requirement.

2. The administrative agency responsible for establishing rules for Medicare claims processing is called the
   a. Centers for Medicare and Medicaid Services (CMS).
   b. Department of Education and Welfare (DEW).
   c. Department of Health and Human Services (DHHS).
   d. Office of Inspector General (OIG).

3. When answering the telephone at a provider's office, you must
   a. place the patient on hold without asking.
   b. say the name of your office clearly.
   c. take a message on scratch paper.
   d. use health care jargon.

4. Which organization is responsible for administering the Certified Coding Specialist certification exam?
   a. AAPC
   b. AHIMA
   c. AMBA
   d. NHA

5. Which clause is implemented if the requirements associated with prior approval of a claim prior to payment are not met?
   a. eligibility
   b. hold harmless
   c. no fault
   d. nonparticipation

6. The ability to motivate team members to complete a common organizational goal display is called
    a. autonomy.
    b. collegiality.
    c. leadership.
    d. management.

7. Patients with health insurance may require _____ for treatment by specialists and documentation of posttreatment reports.
    a. billing
    b. coding
    c. electronic data interchange
    d. prior approval

8. Which protects business contents (e.g., buildings and equipment) against fire, theft, and other risks?
    a. bonding insurance
    b. business liability insurance
    c. property insurance
    d. workers' compensation insurance

9. Which is another title for a health insurance specialist?
    a. coder
    b. health information manager
    c. medical assistant
    d. reimbursement specialist

10. If a patient is seen by a provider who orders a chest x-ray, which diagnosis should be linked with the procedure to prove medical necessity?
    a. abdominal distress
    b. heartburn
    c. shortness of breath
    d. sinus pain

11. The principles of right or good conduct are known as
    a. bylaws.
    b. ethics.
    c. rights.
    d. standards.

12. The notice sent by the insurance company to the provider, which contains payment information about a claim, is the
    a. claim form that was submitted.
    b. electronic data interchange.
    c. explanation of benefits.
    d. remittance advice.

13. When an individual chooses to perform services for another under an express or implied agreement and is not subject to the other's control, the individual is defined as a(n)
    a. casual employee.
    b. dependent contractor.
    c. independent contractor.
    d. statutory employee.

14. Employers are generally considered liable for the actions and omissions of employees as performed and committed within the scope of their employment. This is known as
    a. the chain of command.
    b. errors and omissions.
    c. *respondeat superior*.
    d. the scope of practice.

15. Third-party payer _____ review CMS-1500 claims to determine whether the charges are reasonable for payment.
    a. claims examiners
    b. coders
    c. providers
    d. remitters

16. Which type of insurance should be purchased by health insurance specialist independent contractors?
    a. bonding
    b. errors and omissions
    c. medical malpractice
    d. workers' compensation

17. ICD-10-CM codes are assigned to _____ on inpatient and outpatient claims.
    a. diagnoses
    b. procedures
    c. services
    d. treatments

18. Some health insurance companies require _____ for treatment provided by specialists and documentation of posttreatment reports.
    a. authentication
    b. cost-reduction campaigns
    c. prior approval
    d. retrospective review

19. High blood pressure is an example of a
    a. code.
    b. diagnosis.
    c. procedure.
    d. service.

20. The patient receives a report detailing the results of processing a claim (e.g., payer reimburses provider $80 on a submitted charge of $100). The provider receives a notice sent by the insurance company, which contains payment information about a claim; this is called a(n) _____.
    a. explanation of benefits
    b. insurance claim
    c. remittance advice
    d. scope of practice

Introduction to Health Insurance

## CHAPTER 2

INTRODUCTION

This chapter familiarizes students with health insurance coverage statistics and major developments in health insurance. Students will interpret health insurance coverage statistics and create an Excel chart to display health insurance data. Students will also perform a literature search to evaluate resources appropriate for preparing a research paper that explains major developments in health insurance and their impact on health care access, delivery, quality, reimbursement, and technology.

ASSIGNMENT 2.1 – HEALTH INSURANCE COVERAGE STATISTICS

Objectives

At the conclusion of this assignment, the student should be able to:

1. Interpret U.S. health insurance coverage statistics.

2. Compare U.S. health insurance coverage from one year to another.

3. Create a pie chart to display U.S. health insurance coverage statistics using Microsoft Excel.

Overview

The ability to properly interpret health insurance statistics and effectively communicate findings is a valuable skill for the health insurance specialist. This assignment requires students to interpret statistical data and display it by creating a pie chart using Microsoft Excel.

Instructions

1. Refer to Figure 2-1 in this workbook chapter to answer the following questions:
   a. Which type of health insurance coverage decreased for the U.S. population?
   b. What was the percentage change in Medicaid coverage from Year 1 to Year 2?
   c. Which type of health insurance coverage remained statistically the same?
   d. Which two factors could explain the increase in the number of individuals covered by private health insurance? (Use critical thinking to answer this question.)
   e. Which three concerns would face individuals who do not have health insurance coverage? (Use critical thinking to answer this question.)

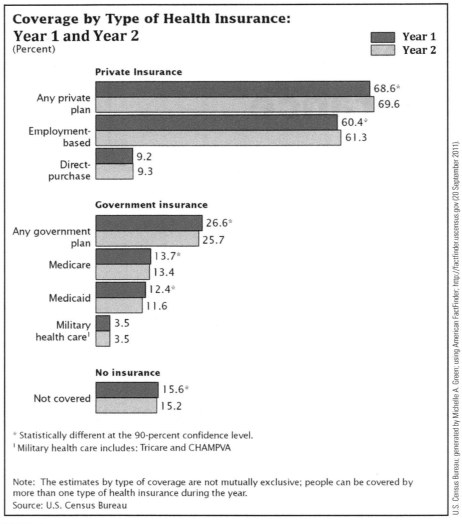

FIGURE 2-1 Coverage by type of health insurance: Year 1 and Year 2.

2. Refer to Figure 2-2 in this workbook chapter to answer the following questions:
   a. What does Figure 2-2 illustrate?
   b. Compare the percentage of men and women with health care coverage between
      Year 1 and Year 4. What conclusion can you draw from comparing these two populations?
   c. Which population group had the smallest percentage of individuals with continuous health insurance
      coverage?
   d. What trend applies to every population group identified in Figure 2-2?

3. **Case Study:** Dr. Jason Brook is an orthopedist in a small, rural town in New York State. His practice consists of a high percentage of patients who have either Medicaid or Medicare with Medicaid as a secondary payer. Dr. Brook will meet with colleagues and representatives of the state government to discuss the impact a proposed cut in Medicaid funding will have on providers who practice in rural areas of New York, including the impact on patient access to health care. Dr. Brook has asked you, his health insurance specialist, to assist by preparing a document that illustrates the office's patient population. Use the data in Table 2-1 to create a pie chart in Microsoft Excel (Table 2-2), illustrating the breakdown of health insurance coverage in the practice. (Dr. Brook has also instructed you to use vibrant colors and to create a three-dimensional effect.)

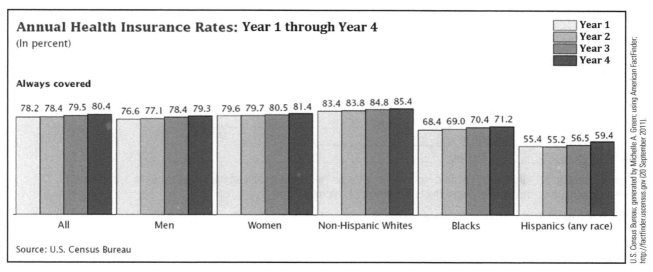

FIGURE 2-2 Annual health insurance rates: Year 1 through Year 4 (always covered).

TABLE 2-1 Dr. Brook's Patient Population According to Health Insurance Coverage

Type of Health Insurance Coverage	Percentage of Patients Covered
HMO	45%
Medicaid	18%
Medicare	23%
Military	4%
Self-pay	10%

TABLE 2-2 Instructions for Creating a Pie Chart Using Microsoft Excel

1.	Open Microsoft Excel.
2.	If a blank worksheet does not automatically display, left click on the Office Button (located in the upper left corner of Excel) to open a blank document.
3.	Key "Type of Health Insurance Coverage" in cell A1. Press the Enter key on your keyboard.
4.	Key "Percentage of Patients Covered" in cell B1. Press the Enter key on your keyboard.
5.	Key the types of health insurance coverage plans from column one in Table 2-1 in cells A2 through A6, respectively. Press the Enter key on your keyboard as you enter each type of plan.
6.	Key the data from column two in Table 2-1 in cells B2 through B6, respectively. Press the Enter key on your keyboard as you enter the data for each type of plan.
	a. Highlight cells B2 through B6, and left click on the Center icon in the Alignment toolbar.
	b. Highlight cells B2 through B6 (again), right click, left click on Format Cells . . . , and left click on Percentage.
	c. Increase the column width to properly display data. Place your cursor between columns A and B until the double arrow icon displays, and double click to increase the width of column A. Repeat to increase the width of column B by placing your cursor between columns B and C.

(continues)

TABLE 2-2 *(continued)*

	A	B
1	Type of Health Insurance Coverage	Percentage of Patients Covered
2	HMO	45%
3	Medicaid	18%
4	Medicare	23%
5	Military	4%
6	Self-pay	10%

7. Highlight cells A1 through B6, click Insert (located toolbar), left click on Pie, and left click on the exploded pie in 3-D. (The pie chart will appear on the spreadsheet, below the data entered in columns A and B.)

8. Save your document, using the naming convention of Lastname_Firstname_PieChart.xls (e.g., Green_Michelle_PieChart.xls).

9. Depending on your instructor's preference, print the spreadsheet and submit to your instructor or e-mail the *.xls file as an attachment to your instructor.

ASSIGNMENT 2.2 – MAJOR DEVELOPMENTS IN HEALTH INSURANCE (RESEARCH PAPER)

Objectives

At the conclusion of this assignment, the student should be able to:

1. Use information literacy skills to research topics.

2. Perform a literature search to evaluate resources appropriate for a research paper.

3. Prepare an annotated bibliography.

4. Cite literature sources to avoid plagiarism.

5. Write a research paper that explains major developments in health insurance for a specific period of time.

6. Demonstrate relationships between major developments in health insurance and their impact on health care access, delivery, quality, reimbursement, and technology.

Overview

Performing a literature search to select and evaluate information resources is the first step in writing a research paper. An annotated bibliography (Figure 2-3) is a great opportunity for students to learn how to conduct literature searches. It contains citations (reference sources, such as books or journal articles) and a brief description of each cited item that summarizes the accuracy, quality, and relevance of the source. Writing a research paper is an excellent way for students to demonstrate their understanding of concepts that require interpretation and critical thinking skills (e.g., impact of health insurance regarding current health care issues).

Plagiarism is the act of stealing someone else's words or phrases and presenting them as your own. This means that when content is cut and pasted from an article into a research paper, the literature source must be cited. Your college may require you to review and sign a plagiarism policy; a sample policy is shown in Figure 2-4.

Annotated Bibliography

1. Select a health care topic that interests you (e.g., health insurance programs for children in poverty).

2. Go to your academic library to locate citations (e.g., journal articles) about your topic. (Refer to Table 1-1, in Chapter 1 of this workbook, for a list of professional journals.)

This informative, practical article by the project director of the Payment Error Prevention Support Peer Review Organization (PEPSPRO) in Texas discusses the issue of diagnosis-related group (DRG) billing as a major contributor to inaccurate Medicare payments and describes the negative consequences of undercoding and upcoding for the hospital. Recommendations are made and tools provided for completing a comprehensive assessment of records, staff qualifications, training, and use of coding resources; coding policies; and safeguards against upcoding. The author also discusses the various aspects of following up on a completed assessment, including implementing new policies, providing appropriate training, and monitoring compliance.

Fletcher, R. "The importance of addressing inaccurate diagnosis related group assignment as a risk area." *Journal of Health Care Compliance* 4(5): 40–46.

The author reports on the trend of hospitals using Internet-based automated compliance checking in place of more traditional billing methods to fulfill the requirements of the Medicare Correct Coding Initiative (CCI). Using Holy Cross Hospital in Ft. Lauderdale, Florida, as a case example, the author fully details the many benefits of using the automated system, including the reduction of billing errors, ease of use, evaluation of coding risk areas, and preventing noncompliance and the resulting penalty fees.

Moynihan, James J. "Automated Compliance Checker Helps Ensure Billing Accuracy." *Healthcare Financial Management* vol. 54, no. 7, July 2000, p. 78.

FIGURE 2-3 Sample annotated bibliography with two works cited.

How to Avoid Plagiarism

The act of plagiarizing is a very serious offense; it occurs when you claim to have authored material that was actually authored by someone else. Plagiarism can happen accidentally—for instance, a student inserted a section of content from a third-party source into the report for reference but then neglected to remove that section prior to submission. Or an individual can purposefully plagiarize another source and claim those words as their own while hoping that that trick goes unnoticed.

There are ways to avoid this downfall, though!

Always remember to credit your source. If you want to use a quote, then abide by citing it, as shown in the following example. Keep in mind that there are different citations used for different courses/work. Always check with your instructor on the proper citation style that should be followed.

> Michelle Green summarizes the job interview experience as "during a job interview, you are evaluated on how well suited you are for the available position. Therefore, when preparing for a job interview, be sure that you have a good understanding of the organization, job responsibilities and duties, corresponding skills required, and how your experience relates to the position". (Green, 2021)

You would cite this source on your reference page/list:

> **Green, M. A. (2022).** *Workbook to accompany understanding health insurance: a guide to billing and reimbursement: 2021* **(16th ed.). Cengage.**

FIGURE 2-4 Sample plagiarism policy to be signed by students.

(continues)

FIGURE 2-4 *(continued)*

Paraphrasing is an option as well. You can reference another's words by giving them credit and not stealing the specific, original wording that was used. For example:

> Job interviews are a serious opportunity to showcase yourself to a potential employer. Time should be taken to ensure proper organizational knowledge as well as familiarizing yourself with the potential job tasks and accountabilities.

Simply credit Green appropriately in your reference page and you do not have to worry that you will be accused of stealing those words as your own. It is always a good sign to have appropriate references in your reports anyway.

Ensure that you allow yourself adequate time to prepare your report/paper so you can reflect on what you have learned from your sources but also put your knowledge into your own words, while citing/ referencing appropriately along the way. Be confident that you can present your thoughts in your own unique and intelligent manner!

By signing below, I indicate that I have read and understood the above anti-plagiarism policy.

_____   _____

Student name   Date

3. Review the citations to determine whether they contain useful information and ideas about your topic, and select two to read thoroughly.
4. Prepare the annotated bibliography in the American Psychological Association (APA) style or the Modern Language Association (MLA) style, depending on your instructor's preference (refer to Figure 2-3).

 NOTE:

The APA has established a style that is used in all its published books and journals, and many authorities in social and behavioral sciences have adopted this style as their standard. The MLA style is recommended for the preparation of scholarly manuscripts and student research papers. Be sure to ask your instructor which style you should use.

INTERNET LINK

Go to **https://www.citethisforme.com** to use its citation tool for the APA or MLA format.

5. Summarize the article, incorporating at least four of the items below:
   - Description of the content or focus of the article
   - Consideration of whether the article content is useful
   - Limitations of the article (e.g., outdated)
   - Audience for which the article is intended
   - Evaluation of any research methods used in the article
   - Author's background

- Any conclusions the author(s) made about the topic
- Your reaction to the article

6. Check and double-check spelling, grammar, and punctuation. Have at least one other person review your paper (e.g., college writing lab, English teacher, family member or friend who has excellent writing skills, and so on).

Plagiarism Policy

1. Review the plagiarism policy in Figure 2-4.
2. Sign and date the policy.
3. Remove the policy from the workbook and submit to your instructor.

Research Paper

Instructions

1. Select a period of time (e.g., 1995–2010) during which to conduct research on the major developments in health insurance, along with their impact on health care quality, access, technology, reimbursement, and so on.

2. Select a minimum of five references (other than the *UHI* textbook) to include in your paper:
   - Two references should be articles (consider using the two sources cited in your annotated bibliography).
   - Two references should be books.
   - One reference can be an Internet website.
   - A sixth reference can be the *UHI* textbook.

 NOTE:

You will need to conduct a literature search of at least 15–20 references before selecting just five to use as references in your paper.

3. Write an introductory paragraph that indicates the period of time selected and lists major developments in health insurance for that period. The last sentence of this paragraph should include a list of health care issues affected by those developments.

4. For each subsequent paragraph, explain how major developments in health insurance affected each health care issue (e.g., access, delivery, and so on). Write a separate paragraph for each issue.

5. Write a concluding paragraph that summarizes all of the points made in your paper, and indicate which health care issue was affected most significantly by developments in health insurance and why.

6. Write a bibliography in APA style. (Check with your instructor to see if footnotes are required.)

7. Check and double-check spelling, grammar, and punctuation. Be sure to double-space your paper and follow the format required by your instructor. Have at least one other person review your reference paper (e.g., college writing lab, English teacher, family member or friend who has excellent writing skills, and so on).

ASSIGNMENT 2.3 – CALCULATING REIMBURSEMENT

Objectives

At the conclusion of this assignment, the student should be able to:

1. Determine the amount for a physician's fee, patient's copayment, and/or patient's coinsurance.

2. Calculate the amount a patient reimburses a provider, payer reimburses a provider, and provider "writes off" a patient's account.

Overview

A *copayment (copay)* is a provision in an insurance policy that requires the policyholder or patient to pay a specified dollar amount to a health care provider (e.g., physician) for each visit or medical service received (e.g., $20 copayment paid by patient for evaluation and management services provided during an office visit). Coinsurance is the percentage of costs a patient shares with the health plan (e.g., plan pays 80 percent of costs and patient pays 20 percent or patient pays 20 percent for surgery performed in the office). The reimbursement amount due to the provider for provision of services includes the amount reimbursed by the payer after the copayment or coinsurance amount is paid by the patient. Any amount remaining is "written off" by the provider. For this activity, the physician is a participating provider (PAR), which means the provider has contracted with the third-party payer and will provide a discount to the patient.

Instructions

Calculate the amounts paid by the payer and the patient and the amount the provider must "write off."

1. The patient is seen by his family physician for follow-up treatment of recently diagnosed asthmatic bronchitis. The physician's fee is $75. The patient's copayment is $20, and the patient is not required to pay any additional amount to the provider. The payer reimburses the physician $28.

   a. Enter the amount the patient pays the provider: _____

   b. Enter the amount the payer reimburses the provider: _____

   c. Enter the amount the provider "writes off" the account: _____

2. The patient undergoes chemical ablation of one facial lesion in the physician's office. The physician's fee is $240. The patient's copayment is $18, and the patient is not required to pay any additional amount to the provider. The payer reimburses the physician $105.

   a. Enter the amount the patient pays the provider: _____

   b. Enter the amount the payer reimburses the provider: _____

   c. Enter the amount the provider "writes off" the account: _____

3. The patient undergoes arthroscopic surgery at an ambulatory surgical center. The surgeon's fee is $890. The patient's coinsurance is 20 percent of the $700 fee schedule, and the patient is not required to pay any additional amount to the provider. The payer reimburses the surgeon 80 percent of the $700 fee schedule.

   a. Enter the amount the patient pays the provider: _____

   b. Enter the amount the payer reimburses the provider: _____

   c. Enter the amount the provider "writes off" the account: _____

4. The patient was referred to an orthopedic specialist for evaluation of chronic ankle pain. The physician's fee is $150. The patient's coinsurance is 30 percent of the $100 fee schedule, and the patient is not required to pay any additional amount to the provider. The payer reimburses the physician 70 percent of the $100 fee schedule for this service.

   a. Enter the amount the patient pays the provider: _____

   b. Enter the amount the payer reimburses the provider: _____

   c. Enter the amount the provider "writes off" the account: _____

5. The patient received preventive medicine services. The physician's fee is $150. The patient's copayment is $10 of the $75 fee schedule, and the patient is not required to pay any additional amount to the provider. The payer reimburses the physician 80 percent of the $75 fee schedule.

   a. Enter the amount the patient pays the provider: _____

   b. Enter the amount the payer reimburses the provider: _____

   c. Enter the amount the provider "writes off" the account: _____

ASSIGNMENT 2.4 – HEALTH INSURANCE MARKETPLACE

Objectives

At the conclusion of this assignment, the student should be able to:

1. Describe provisions of the Patient Protection and Affordable Care Act (PPACA), including its abbreviated name (Affordable Care Act) and nickname (Obamacare).

2. Utilize the Health Insurance Marketplace website to locate information about how to get coverage, change or update a health plan, learn more about government programs, and determine coverage eligibility.

3. Explain that the Health Insurance Marketplace does not replace other health insurance programs, nor is it a national health insurance program.

Overview

The *Patient Protection and Affordable Care Act (PPACA)* was signed into federal law by President Obama on March 23, 2010, and resulted in creation of a health insurance marketplace (or health insurance exchange) effective October 1, 2013. The PPACA is abbreviated as the Affordable Care Act (ACA), and it was nicknamed Obamacare because it was signed into federal law by President Obama. The Health Insurance Marketplace does not replace other health insurance programs (e.g., individual and group commercial health insurance, Medicaid, Medicare, TRICARE). The Marketplace allows Americans to purchase health coverage that fits their budget and meets their needs. It is a resource where individuals, families, and small businesses can:

- Learn about their health coverage options

- Compare health insurance plans based on costs, benefits, and other important features

- Choose a plan

- Enroll in coverage

    The Marketplace includes information about programs to help people with low to moderate income and resources pay for health coverage. Information includes ways to save on the monthly premiums and out-of-pocket costs of coverage available through the Marketplace and information about other programs, including Medicaid and the Children's Health Insurance Program (CHIP). The Marketplace encourages competition among private health plans, and it is accessible through websites, call centers, and in-person assistance. In some states it is run by the state, and in others it is run by the federal government. Most individuals who do not currently have health insurance through their place of work or otherwise are eligible to use the Health Insurance Marketplace to compare and choose a plan. To be eligible for health coverage through the marketplace, individuals must be a U.S. citizen or national (or be lawfully present), live in the United States, and *not* be incarcerated.

Instructions

Go to the Health Insurance Marketplace at **www.healthcare.gov**, and scroll over the Get Answers heading to click on links that provide information about how to get coverage, change or update a health plan, learn more about government programs (e.g., Medicaid, CHIP, Medicare), and determine coverage eligibility. *Remember!* The Health Insurance Marketplace is not a health insurance plan or program; it is a website that facilitates enrollment in health insurance plans offered by private companies and the government.

ASSIGNMENT 2.5 – QUALITY PAYMENT PROGRAM—MERIT-BASED INCENTIVE PAYMENT SYSTEM

Objectives

At the conclusion of this assignment, the student should be able to:

1. Describe component of the quality payment program.

2. Differentiate between advanced alternate payment models and the merit-based incentive payment program.

3. Interpret merit-based incentive payment program data.

Overview

The *Medicare Access and CHIP Reauthorization Act of 2015 (MACRA)* implemented the quality payment program (QPP), which includes:

- Advanced Alternative Payment Models (Advanced APMs)

- Merit-based Incentive Payment System (MIPS)

An *Alternative Payment Model (APM)* is a payment approach that allows for added incentive payments to provide high-quality and cost-efficient care. The QPP's *Advanced alternative payment models (Advanced APMs)* are a subset of APMs and include new ways for CMS to reimburse health care providers for care provided to Medicare beneficiaries (e.g., accountable care organizations, patient-centered medical homes, and bundled payment models).

The *merit-based incentive payment system (MIPS)* allows providers to earn a performance-based payment adjustment that considers quality, resource use, clinical practice improvement, and meaningful use of certified electronic health record technology. (Clinicians can also participate in *MIPS APMs*, a hybrid of MIPS and Advanced APMs; there are different reporting requirements and scoring.) MIPS contains the following four performance categories that are scored and weighted, and the result is a MIPS final score that impacts clinician Medicare payments: quality, cost, improvement activities, and promoting interoperability (PI). (Bonus points can also be earned.)

Instructions

1. The practice printed a data report entitled "MIPS Dashboard—Promoting Interoperability (PI)" (Table 2-3) from the electronic health record. The clinician has asked you to review the data report to identify measures that do not meet the practice's targeted performance rate of 90 percent.

   a. Review the MIPS Dashboard report, and list the seven measures that do not meet the target performance rate of 90 percent.

   _____

   _____

   _____

   _____

   _____

TABLE 2-3 Sample MIPS Dashboard—Promoting Interoperability (PI)

Measures	MIPS Dashboard—Promoting Interoperability (PI)	
	Measure Performance Rate	Raw Data Reported by Clinician
Base Measures		
Security risk analysis	REQUIRED	☒ Complete
E-prescribing with controlled substances	94.10%	5519/5865
Patient electronic access	49.22%	475/965
Health information exchange	0%	0/218
Performance Measures		
Patient electronic access	49.07%	475/968
View, download, transmit	7.95%	77/968
Patient-specific education	97.31%	942/968
Secure messaging	0.62%	6/968
Health information exchange	0%	0/218
Medication reconciliation	89.63%	147/164
Immunization registry reporting	N/A	☒ Complete
Bonus Measures		
Syndromic surveillance reporting	N/A	☒ Complete
Specialized registry reporting	N/A	☒ Complete

_____

_____

_____

   b. What action should the clinician take to implement MIPS PI measures that did not meet the target performance of 90 percent?

_____

_____

2. The Centers for Medicaid and Medicare Services (CMS) mailed MIPS Cost Measures reports (Table 2-4) to the practice. The clinician has asked you to review the cost measures reports to determine whether the practice's targeted performance is compliant with targeted percentile ranks. The MSPB clinician measure targeted percentile rank is 90. The TPCC clinician measure targeted percentile rank is 15.

   a. Review the MIPS Cost Measures reports, including the narrative in the last row.

   b. Did the MSPB cost measure percentile rank meets its practice target?_____

   c. Did the TPCC cost measure percentile rank meet its practice target? _____

   d. What is the significance of meeting (or not meeting) the practice target for the TPCC cost measure percentile rank? (Base your answer on content located in the last paragraph of Table 2-4.)

_____

_____

_____

TABLE 2-4 Sample Cost Measures Reports (Permission to Reuse in Accordance with www.cms.gov Website Content Reuse Policy.)

MIPS Cost Measures Reports
Medicare Spending Per Beneficiary (MSPB) Clinician Measure Report

Arthur McKay, M.D., New York

National Provider Identifier (NPI): 1234567890

Last four digits of your Taxpayer Identification Number (TIN): 1234

Measurement Period: January 1, YYYY–December 31, YYYY

Your TIN's MSPB Clinician Field Test Report Measure Score:

	MSPB Clinician Measure
Your TIN's Score	$16,000
National Median	$18,696
Percentile Rank	95

The *Medicare Spending Per Beneficiary (MSPB)* measure assesses the average amount spent for Medicare services performed by providers/groups per episode of care, which is the period immediately prior to, during, and following a patient's inpatient hospital stay.

Total Per Capita Cost (TPCC) Clinician Measure Report

Arthur McKay, M.D., New York

Last four digits of your Taxpayer Identification Number (TIN): 1234

Measurement Period: October 1, YYYY–September 30, YYYY

Your TIN's TPCC Clinician Field Test Report Measure Score:

	TPCC Clinician Measure
Your TIN's Score	$891.95
National Median	$755.38
Percentile Rank	17

The *Total Per Capita Cost (TPCC)* measure is a payment-standardized, annualized, risk-adjusted, and specialty-adjusted measure that evaluates the overall efficiency of care provided to beneficiaries attributed to solo practitioners and groups, as identified by their Medicare Taxpayer Identification Number (TIN). A lower measure score indicates that your episode cost is lower than (or similar to the) expected for the particular patients and episodes included in the calculation, and a higher measure score indicates that your episode cost is higher than expected. The national distribution of TPCC measure scores range from $0–$100 through $1,600–$1,700. The national distribution of TPCC percentile ranks range from 0.0 to 32.

Courtesy of the Centers for Medicare and Medicaid Services, www.cms.gov.

ASSIGNMENT 2.6 – MULTIPLE CHOICE REVIEW

1. Evidence of the first health insurance policy to provide private health care coverage for injuries that did not result in death appeared in which year?
   a. 1842
   b. 1850
   c. 1915
   d. 1920

2. Which has as its goal access to health coverage for every individual, regardless of the system implemented to achieve that goal?
   a. government health programs
   b. single-payer plan
   c. socialized medicine
   d. universal health insurance

3. The terms electronic health record (EHR) and electronic medical record (EMR) are often used interchangeably, but the _____ is a more global concept that includes the collection of patient information documented by a number of providers at different facilities regarding one patient.
   a. computer-based patient record
   b. electronic health record
   c. electronic medical record
   d. personal health record

4. *Current Procedural Terminology (CPT)* was developed by which organization in 1966?
   a. American Hospital Association
   b. American Medical Association
   c. Social Security Administration
   d. World Health Organization

5. Total practice management software (TPMS) is used to generate the EMR, automating which of the following medical practice functions?
   a. medical necessity
   b. patient registration
   c. personal health record
   d. health care clearinghouse

6. If a veteran is rated as 100 percent permanently and totally disabled as a result of a service-connected condition, which program will provide benefits to the veteran's dependents?
   a. CHAMPUS
   b. CHAMPVA
   c. COBRA
   d. TRICARE

7. Which coding system was created in 1984?
   a. CPT
   b. DSM
   c. HCPCS
   d. ICD-10-CM

8. A new fee schedule for Medicare services was implemented as part of OBRA in 1989 and 1990, replacing the regional "usual and reasonable" payment basis with a fixed fee schedule called
   a. DRGs.
   b. RBRVS.
   c. RUGs.
   d. SNFPPS.

9. Quality standards for all laboratory testing to ensure the accuracy, reliability, and timeliness of patient test results regardless of where the tests are performed were established specifically by _____ legislation.
   a. CLIA
   b. COBRA
   c. DRG
   d. TEFRA

10. CMS developed the National Correct Coding Initiative (NCCI) to
    a. decrease the amount of money paid out by the Medicare program.
    b. eliminate improper coding and promote national correct coding methodologies.
    c. encourage coders to further their education to qualify for advancement.
    d. reduce the number of codes in the CPT and HCPCS coding systems.

11. The skilled nursing facility prospective payment system (SNFPPS) generates _____ payments for each skilled nursing facility admission.
    a. capitation
    b. cost-based
    c. fee-for-service
    d. *per diem*

12. In 2000, which type of health plan was introduced as a way to encourage individuals to locate the best health care at the lowest price possible, with the goal of holding down health care costs?
    a. consumer-driven
    b. major medical
    c. private
    d. retrospective

13. By whom is the employer identification number (EIN) assigned?
    a. Centers for Medicare and Medicaid Services
    b. Department of Health and Human Services
    c. Internal Revenue Service
    d. Social Security Administration

14. The systematic method of documentation that consists of four components (database, problem list, initial plan, and progress notes) is called the
    a. integrated record.
    b. problem-oriented record.
    c. SOAP notes.
    d. source-oriented record.

15. The primary purpose of the record is to provide for _____, which involves documenting patient care services so that others who treat the patient have a source of information to assist with additional care and treatment.
    a. continuity of care
    b. personal health recordkeeping
    c. record linkage
    d. surveillance and reporting

16. Which would be considered a Medicare *meaningful EHR user* if it can demonstrate that certified EHR technology is connected in a manner that provides for the electronic exchange of health information to improve the quality of health care?
    a. clinic
    b. hospital
    c. physician
    d. nursing facility

17. Which is the focus of promoting intraoperability (PI) programs?
    a. improving patient access to health information and reducing the time and cost required of providers to comply with the programs' requirements
    b. managing medical practice functions, including patient registration, appointment scheduling, insurance claims processing, and payment processing
    c. repealing the sustainable growth rate formula and meaningful use payment adjustments (and its separate quality reporting incentives)
    d. verifying measures that modernize the nation's infrastructure, including the Health Information Technology for Economic and Clinical Health

18. In a teaching hospital, general documentation guidelines allow _____ to document physician services in the patient's medical record.
    a. both residents and teaching physicians
    b. neither residents nor teaching physicians
    c. residents only
    d. teaching physicians only

19. The Patient Protection and Affordable Care Act (PPCA) amended the time period for filing Medicare fee-for-service claims to _____ calendar year(s) after the date of service as the maximum time period for submission of all Medicare FFS claims to one calendar year after the date of service.
    a. one
    b. two
    c. three
    d. four

20. The Health Care and Education Reconciliation Act (HCERA) amended PACA to implement health care reform initiatives, which _____ tax credits for individuals so they could purchase health care insurance.
    a. decreased
    b. denied
    c. increased
    d. reduced

Managed Health Care

## CHAPTER 3

INTRODUCTION

This chapter familiarizes students with types of managed care plans, legislation that has affected the managed care industry, and ways in which consumers and professionals can obtain information about the quality of health insurance plans.

ASSIGNMENT 3.1 – NATIONAL COMMITTEE FOR QUALITY ASSURANCE (NCQA) HEALTH PLAN REPORT CARD

Objectives

At the conclusion of this assignment, the student should be able to:

1. State the purpose of the NCQA health plan report card.

2. Generate and interpret an NCQA health plan report card.

Overview

The NCQA health plan report card can be customized to prepare a report card created from hundreds of NCQA-Accredited health plans. Physician and hospital quality (PHQ) standards are used to evaluate how organizations measure physicians to ensure that measurement methods are fair and rely not only on cost, but also on accepted measures of quality. For hospitals, the standards evaluate if organizations provide members with performance information on hospitals from reliable government and other sources to inform decision making.

PHQ evaluation measures physician and hospital performance, and an organization can be reviewed according to either or both standards. PHQ standards are based on standardization and sound methodology, allowing results to be compared across organizations; transparency, giving physicians and hospitals the opportunity to provide input on measurement programs and how measurement results will be used; collaboration, pooling data on standardized measures to produce results with greater statistical reliability; and, action on quality and cost, avoiding the use of cost measurement results alone.

Instructions

1. Create a customized report card about health plans in your state by going to **https://reportcards.ncqa.org** and clicking on the Health Plans link.

2. Enter your state in the Search box.

3. Click on one of the plans.

4. Review the results, and identify whether the health plan is accredited.

5. View additional information about organizations, such as insurance type, product type, and so on.

6. Prepare a one-page, double-spaced, word-processed document that summarizes the results of each report card generated. Be sure to compare the accreditation outcomes of the plans selected.

7. Double-check spelling, grammar, and punctuation. Have at least one other person review your document (e.g., college writing lab, English teacher, family member or friend who has excellent writing skills).

ASSIGNMENT 3.2 – MANAGED HEALTH CARE FEDERAL LEGISLATION

Objectives

At the conclusion of this assignment, the student should be able to:

1. List managed health care federal legislation and year of implementation.

2. Identify legislation that most significantly influenced the growth of managed care, and state why this legislation was significant.

Instructions

1. Review Table 3-1, "Significant managed care federal legislation," in Chapter 3 of the textbook, and select legislation that most significantly influenced the growth of managed care. (You can select more than one piece of legislation for this purpose.)

 NOTE:

Base your selection of significant legislation on classroom discussion as well as the textbook description of each piece of legislation. You are welcome to select more than one piece of legislation.

2. Conduct a literature search to locate at least 10 articles about the legislation you selected. Print (or make a copy of) each article.

 NOTE:

If you selected more than one piece of legislation, be sure you conduct literature searches on each. You will probably locate more than 10 articles.

3. Carefully review each article to identify reasons the legislation you selected most significantly influenced the growth of managed care. (Using a highlighter pen to mark pertinent material in the articles may be helpful. Be sure you mark up a *copy* of the article, not the original article.)

4. Prepare a two- to three-page, double-spaced, word-processed document that summarizes your findings. Be sure to organize the document as follows:

a. First paragraph—legislation you selected as most significantly influencing the growth of managed care
b. Second and subsequent paragraphs—reasons that support your choice of that legislation as being the most influential regarding the growth of managed care (based on content in articles)
c. Last paragraph—conclusion about the growth of managed care as the result of the legislation you selected as being most influential
d. Bibliography (of 10 articles located as the result of performing the literature search)

5. Check and double-check spelling, grammar, and punctuation. Have at least one other person review your paper (e.g., college writing lab, English teacher, family member or friend who has excellent writing skills, and so on).

ASSIGNMENT 3.3 – THE JOINT COMMISSION

Objectives

At the conclusion of this assignment, the student should be able to:

1. State the types of facilities accredited by The Joint Commission.

2. List the types of certifications granted by The Joint Commission.

3. Define and discuss a sentinel event.

4. Discuss The Joint Commission's performance measurement initiatives.

Overview

The Joint Commission is an independent, not-for-profit organization that provides accreditation to a variety of health care facilities. Given the variety of health care facilities and the ability of all of these facilities to utilize the expertise of a medical coding or medical billing expert, it is important that you are aware of The Joint Commission's role in the U.S. health care system.

Instructions

1. Go to the website for The Joint Commission at **www.jointcommission.org** and explore the site to find out information about this organization.

2. Prepare a one- to two-page, double-spaced, word-processed document summarizing information on The Joint Commission that was accessed from the website. Be sure to include the following information in your summary:
   a. Identify types of health care facilities that The Joint Commission accredits.
   b. Identify types of certifications that The Joint Commission awards.
   c. Define and discuss a sentinel event.
   d. Discuss The Joint Commission's performance measurement initiatives.

3. Double-check spelling, grammar, and punctuation. Have at least one person review your document (e.g., college writing lab, English teacher, family member or friend who has excellent writing skills).

 NOTE:

Navigate The Joint Commission website to research information needed for your summary. This will help you learn how to locate information using the Internet as a research tool and how to use websites, which often require using tool bars and pull-down menus.

ASSIGNMENT 3.4 – FAIRVIEW HEALTH SERVICES INTEGRATED DELIVERY SYSTEM

Objectives

At the conclusion of this assignment, the student should be able to:

1. Discuss privacy policy related to payment for the Fairview Health Services integrated delivery system.

2. Discuss other aspects of this integrated delivery system (wellness, disease programs, etc.).

Overview

Fairview Health Services is an integrated delivery system (IDS) that provides a variety of medical services to a diverse population of patients. The IDS also has many wellness and health programs focused on disease prevention.

Instructions

1. Go to the website for Fairview Health Services at **fairview.org** and explore the site to find out information about this organization.

2. Prepare a one- to two-page, double-spaced, word-processed document that summarizes information on HealthEast that was accessed from the website. Be sure to include the following information in your summary:
   a. Discuss the IDS's privacy policy for payment purposes.
   b. Identify types of disease-focused programs offered by this IDS.
   c. Explain the IDS's patient safety focus.
   d. Discuss the IDS's wellness program.

3. Check and double-check spelling, grammar, and punctuation. Have at least one person review your document (e.g., college writing lab, English teacher, family member or friend who has excellent writing skills, and so on).

 NOTE:

Navigate the Fairview Health Services integrated delivery system website to research information needed for your summary. This will help you learn how to locate information using the Internet as a research tool and how to use websites, which often require using tool bars and pull-down menus.

ASSIGNMENT 3.5 – CREATING A MANAGED CARE CONTRACT QUICK REFERENCE SHEET

Objectives

At the conclusion of this assignment, the student should be able to:

1. Explain the purpose of managed care plans, and list six managed care models.

2. State the purpose of a *managed care quick reference sheet*, and interpret managed care contract provisions to prepare the quick reference sheet.

Overview

Managed care plans provide benefits to subscribers (or enrollees) who are required to receive services from network providers (physicians or health care facilities under contract to the managed care plan). Network providers sign contracts (Figure 3-1) with the managed care organization, and subscribers are generally required to coordinate health care services through their primary care physician (PCP). Managed care is categorized according to six models:

1. Exclusive provider organization (EPO)

2. Integrated delivery system (IDS)

3. Health maintenance organization (HMO)

a. direct contract model
b. group model
c. individual practice association (IPA)
d. network model
e. staff model

4. Point-of-service plan (POS)

5. Preferred provider organization (PPO)

6. Triple option plan

Physician offices create a *managed care plan quick reference sheet* as a resource for identifying health care services that require preauthorization and expediting claims completion and submission. The information located on a managed care plan quick reference sheet is based on significant provisions contained in each managed care health plan contract, and the original contract should be referenced for details about such provisions.

PROHEALTH MANAGED CARE PLAN CONTRACT

THIS CONTRACT is entered into by and between <u>ProHealth Managed Care Company, Inc.,</u> a managed care corporation, (NETWORK) and <u>Alfred Moore, M.D.</u> (PHYSICIAN).

WHEREAS, the NETWORK is creating a provider network that consists of physicians, institutional facilities, and providers of ancillary health; and

WHEREAS, the PHYSICIAN wishes to be a PARTICIPATING PHYSICIAN in the NETWORK.

NOW, THEREFORE, in consideration of the mutual promises contained herein, the parties agree as follows:

- The NETWORK desires to engage PHYSICIAN to deliver or arrange for the delivery of medical services to the ENROLLEES of its plans.

- The PHYSICIAN is capable of meeting the credentialing criteria of NETWORK.

- This AGREEMENT is effective <u>September 1, YYYY</u> and shall continue for a term of five (5) years from that date after signatures are obtained from PHYSICIAN and NETWORK representatives.

- The NETWORK and PHYSICIAN agree to comply with terms and conditions of this Scope of Work and its ATTACHMENTS, which are by this reference made a part of this Agreement:

  ○ Attachment 1 – Organization and Administration of the Managed Care Plan
  ○ Attachment 2 – Financial Information
  ○ Attachment 3 – Management Information System
  ○ Attachment 4 – Utilization Review and Quality Management Plan
  ○ Attachment 6 – Provider Network
  ○ Attachment 7 – Provider Relations
  ○ Attachment 8 – Provider Compensation Arrangements
  ○ Attachment 9 – Access and Availability
  ○ **Attachment 10 – Scope of Services**
  ○ Attachment 11 – Case Management
  ○ Attachment 12 – Coordination of Care

  NOTE: *Attachment 10 – Scope of Services* is boldfaced in the above list because it is located at the end of this sample managed care agreement. Students will use *Attachment 10 – Scope of Services* to create a *managed care plan quick reference sheet* of conditions that must be met for provision of health care services to managed care enrollees (e.g., copayment amount, coinsurance amounts, deductible amounts, covered services for which no preauthorization is required, covered services for which preauthorization must be obtained by the physician, and so on).

FIGURE 3-1 ProHealth managed care plan contract.

(continues)

FIGURE 3-1 *(continued)*

I.	DEFINITIONS

I.   DEFINITIONS

1.1   BENEFIT PLAN includes those health care services that are included as health care benefits pursuant to provisions of ENROLLEES' benefit plan and reimbursed by PAYER.

1.2   COVERED SERVICES include medical and other health care services that are covered by NETWORK that are deemed medically necessary by NETWORK.

1.3   EMERGENCY means the sudden and unexpected onset of a condition or symptoms requiring medical or surgical care to screen and/or treat the ENROLLEE, authorization for which is obtained upon onset or immediately after onset (or as soon thereafter as care can be made available) and is of such immediate nature that ENROLLEE'S life or health might be jeopardized if not treated as soon as possible.

1.4   FEE SCHEDULE means the maximum amount Network will allow for a specific service.

1.5   MEDICAL NECESSITY or MEDICALLY NECESSARY means those services or supplies which, under the terms and conditions of this AGREEMENT, are determined to be appropriate and necessary for the symptoms, diagnosis or treatment of the medical conditions of the ENROLLEE; provided for the diagnosis or direct care and treatment of the medical condition of the ENROLLEE; within standards of medical practice within the community; and not primarily for the convenience of the ENROLLEE, the ENROLLEE'S physician or another provider.

1.6   ENROLLEE means any person eligible to receive COVERED SERVICES whose BENEFIT PLAN has access to the NETWORK.

1.7   PARTICIPATING PHYSICIAN (PAR) means a physician who has entered into an AGREEMENT with NETWORK to provide COVERED SERVICES to ENROLLEES.

1.8   PAYER means an organization that has contracted with NETWORK for the purpose of processing CLAIMS submitted by PHYSICIAN. NETWORK warrants that its contracts with PAYERS require PAYERS to comply with all PAYER requirements and responsibilities described in this AGREEMENT, and that such contracts also require PAYERS to acknowledge that they will not be allowed to participate in the negotiated rates and other terms of this AGREEMENT if they fail to comply with such requirements.

1.9   PRIMARY CARE PHYSICIAN means a PAR who is designated by the network as a provider of primary care services, and who is primarily responsible for managing and coordination of the overall health care needs of the ENROLLEE.

1.10   PHYSICIAN MANUAL means the manual that has been prepared by NETWORK and sets forth all policies and procedures governing PHYSICIAN participation in NETWORK.

1.11   SPECIALTY CARE PHYSICIAN means a PARTICIPATING PHYSICIAN who is designated by the NETWORK as a provider of specialty services *other than primary care services*.

1.12   UTILIZATION REVIEW AND QUALITY ASSURANCE PLAN (UR/QA PLAN) means programs(s) adopted by the NETWORK and carried out by PARTICIPATING PHYSICIANS with NETWORK, which authorizes and monitors the utilization of PHYSICIANS offered to ENROLLEES.

1.13   CLAIM means a CMS-1500 submitted by PHYSICIAN to NETWORK for physician services provided to an ENROLLEE.

1.14   CLEAN CLAIM means a CLAIM for payment for covered services that can be processed without obtaining additional information from PHYSICIAN or another third party. It does not include a CLAIM under review for medical necessity.

1.15   NON-COVERED SERVICES means accommodations, products, services, and supplies that NETWORK is not required to provide to ENROLLEES pursuant to a contract, including but not limited to that which is not authorized by NETWORK as part of the UR/QA PLAN.

(continues)

FIGURE 3-1 *(continued)*

II.	**PHYSICIAN RESPONSIBILITIES**

2.1   PHYSICIAN agrees to provide to ENROLLEES those COVERED SERVICES to the same extent and availability, and with the same degree of care, as PHYSICIAN normally provides such services to the general community.

2.2   PHYSICIAN shall maintain reasonable office hours in a location convenient to ENROLLEES, and agrees to be accessible to ENROLLEES either personally or by arranging for coverage by another PARTICIPATING PHYSICIAN or by another qualified physician approved by NETWORK. PHYSICIAN shall assist NETWORK in ensuring that the covering physician complies with the UR/QA PLAN established by NETWORK and PAYER, and that PHYSICIAN complies with compensation terms of this AGREEMENT.

2.3   If PHYSICIAN arranges with either a PARTICIPATION PHYSICIAN or a non-participating physician to cover ENROLLEES in PHYSICIAN'S absence, it will be the PHYSICIAN'S responsibility to ascertain that the covering physician will accept compensation from NETWORK as full payment for COVERED SERVICES in accordance with the applicable NETWORK compensation schedule; not bill the ENROLLEE directly *except for any applicable copayment, coinsurance, or deductibles;* obtain approval as designated by NETWORK prior to all non-emergency hospitalizations and non-emergency referrals of ENROLLEES; and comply with all NETWORK procedures, programs, protocols, and rules.

2.4   PHYSICIAN shall maintain adequate medical records for ENROLLEES and shall retain and preserve such records for the full period of time required by state and federal law. PHYSICIAN and NETWORK shall maintain the confidentiality of ENROLLEES' medical records in accordance with all applicable laws and regulations. Subject to such requirements, the PHYSICIAN will make the ENROLLEES' medical records readily available to any PARTICIPATING PHYSICIAN or other health care professional who needs the records in order to treat the ENROLLEE, and upon reasonable request, shall make the records available for review by NETWORK, PAYER, or their designee for UR/QA PLAN purposes or for other reasonable and necessary purposes.

2.5   NETWORK or its designee shall have the right to inspect and audit any of the PHYSICIAN'S accounting, administrative, and medical records operations. Any review will be limited to ENROLLEES and COVERED SERVICES. PAYER shall contact PHYSICIAN at least thirty (30) days in advance of any review to schedule a mutually agreeable time for the review. NETWORK may not request or have any access to PHYSICIAN'S non-public financial data, information, or records, which PHYSICIAN determines to be confidential.

2.6   PHYSICIAN represents that information provided in NETWORK application is correct.

2.7   PHYSICIAN warrants that PHYSICIAN is licensed to practice medicine or osteopathy in the State of New York; has met all qualifications and standards for appointment to the medical staff of at least one participating health care facility; will have and maintain, where appropriate, a current and unrestricted narcotics number issued by the Drug Enforcement Administration (DEA); and has specialized training in the area in which PHYSICIAN practices.

2.8   PHYSICIAN shall report any reportable occurrences including, but not limited to, any action, investigation, or proceeding initiated or taken by any professional society or organization, by any facility, by any medical group or practice, by any licensure or certification agency, by any reimbursement entity or managed care organization, or by any similar entity or organization, to revoke, suspend, restrict, or otherwise adversely affect his privileges,

(continues)

FIGURE 3-1 *(continued)*

license, certification, or professional standing or membership. The PHYSICIAN agrees to notify the NETWORK immediately of any suspension, reduction, or termination of liability insurance, or of any lawsuit filed against PHYSICIAN alleging malpractice or negligence and requesting damages in excess of $5,000.00.

2.9   PHYSICIAN shall provide and maintain professional liability insurance, in amounts of $250,000 per claim and $750,000 annual aggregate during this AGREEMENT.

2.10   PHYSICIAN agrees that NETWORK shall not be responsible for any claims, actions, liability, or damages arising out of the acts or omissions of PHYSICIAN or the acts or omissions of any non-participating physician who covers ENROLLEES for the PHYSICIAN.

2.11   PHYSICIAN agrees to cooperate with marketing programs established or approved by NETWORK, and agrees to allow the NETWORK and PAYERS to list the PHYSICIAN'S name, specialty, address, telephone number, willingness to accept additional ENROLLEES, and other relevant information in PARTICIPATING PROVIDER directories and similar informational materials.

2.12   NETWORK shall distribute identification cards identifying NETWORK to all ENROLLEES, and each card shall include a toll-free number that PHYSICIAN may use during normal business hours to verify eligibility of coverage, obtain general coverage information, and obtain authorizations.

III.   UTILIZATION REVIEW AND QUALITY MANAGEMENT PLAN (UR/QM PLAN)

3.1   NETWORK shall determine criteria and goals for establishing and monitoring the MEDICAL NECESSITY, appropriateness, and quality of services provided by PARTICIPATING PROVIDERS.

3.2   PHYSICIAN agrees to cooperate with all NETWORK rules, protocols, procedures, and programs in establishing its UR/QM PLAN, including benefit management, denials of admissions or continued stay, and other programs created to manage the cost and utilization of medical services.

3.3   PHYSICIAN agrees to refer ENROLLEES to other PARTICIPATING PROVIDERS when PHYSICIAN is unable to provide the required services and when consistent with sound medical judgment.

3.4   PHYSICIAN agrees that failure to cooperate with NETWORK procedures, programs, protocols, and rules may result in penalties as set forth by the NETWORK included in the PHYSICIAN office manual.

3.5   PHYSICIAN agrees to cooperate with any applicable NETWORK grievance procedure and decisions.

3.6   PHYSICIAN shall comply with all determinations rendered by the UR/QM PLAN.

3.7   NETWORK shall provide PHYSICIAN with an authorization code, which indicates approval upon which PHYSICIAN may conclusively rely for the delivery of authorized services to the ENROLLEE.

3.8   Nothing in this AGREEMENT shall be construed to interfere with or affect in any way the exercise of the independent medical judgment of PHYSICIAN or PHYSICIAN'S employees in rendering health care services to ENROLLEES. The PHYSICIAN or PHYSICIAN'S employees shall be permitted to communicate with ENROLLEES concerning all matters necessary or appropriate for the delivery of health care services, treatment alternatives regardless of the provisions or limitations of coverage, and the reimbursement arrangements under which the PHYSICIAN is compensated.

(continues)

FIGURE 3-1 *(continued)*

IV.	**COMPENSATION**	
	4.1	For COVERED SERVICES provided to ENROLLEES, PHYSICIAN shall be compensated in accordance with Exhibit A.
	4.2	PHYSICIAN agrees to look solely to NETWORK for payment for COVERED SERVICES.
	4.3	PHYSICIAN has the right to bill ENROLLEES for all non-covered services.
	4.4	NETWORK may offset overpayments against future payments to PHYSICIAN.
	4.5	NETWORK will notify PHYSICIAN within thirty (30) calendar days of receipt of claim, of any claim pended for review or audit.
	4.6	PHYSICIAN acknowledges that the coverage provided and authorization(s) required for maximum benefits, for particular COVERED SERVICES may vary under different health benefit plans. Under certain health benefit plans, no coverage is available if PREAUTHORIZATION has not been obtained for the COVERED SERVICE.
	4.7	CLAIMS submitted by PHYSICIAN to NETWORK must be submitted no later than ninety (90) days after the date of service. NETWORK shall not be obligated to pay any such CLAIMS submitted after the ninety (90) day period.
	4.8	PHYSICIAN agrees to cooperate with NETWORK coordination of benefits (COB) requirements and in the recovery of claims from other insurers and third-party payers.
V.	**TERM AND TERMINATION**	
	5.1	This AGREEMENT shall be effective as of <u>September 1, YYYY</u> and shall continue for a term of five (5) years from that date. Unless otherwise terminated as set forth below, the AGREEMENT shall automatically be renewed for subsequent one-year terms. Renegotiations of AGREEMENT shall only occur ninety (90) days prior to the end of the term of the AGREEMENT.
	5.2	Either party may terminate this Agreement, with or without cause, at any time, upon one hundred and eighty (180) days' prior written notice to the other party.
	5.3	Either party shall have the right to terminate this AGREEMENT upon thirty (30) days' prior written notice to the other party if the party to whom such notice is given is in breach of any material provision of this AGREEMENT. Such notice shall set forth the facts underlying the alleged breach. If the breach is cured within the notice period, then the AGREEMENT shall continue in effect for its remaining term, subject to any other provision of this AGREEMENT.
	5.4	NETWORK may terminate this AGREEMENT immediately upon (i) the revocation, suspension, or restriction of PHYSICIAN'S license to practice medicine; (ii) the revocation, suspension, or restriction of PHYSICIAN'S license, certification, registration, permit, or approval required for the lawful and reasonable conduct of his practice and the provision of COVERED SERVICES to ENROLLEES; (iii) PHYSICIAN'S failure to maintain general and professional liability insurance as required under this AGREEMENT; (iv) revocation, suspension, or restriction of PHYSICIAN'S medical staff appointment or the necessary clinical privileges required to provide COVERED SERVICES at a participating hospital or any other hospital; (v) NETWORK'S determination that any ENROLLEE would be endangered or impaired by the continuation of this AGREEMENT.
	5.5	In the event of any material changes in laws affecting the structure of the NETWORK, or affecting the provision or reimbursement of health care services similar to those provided hereunder, the parties agree to negotiate in good faith to amend this AGREEMENT to conform to applicable law. In the event that such changes adversely affect either party,

(continues)

FIGURE 3-1 *(continued)*

> such party may terminate this AGREEMENT upon sixty (60) days' written notice if the parties are unable to renegotiate the AGREEMENT on mutually agreeable terms within such 60-day period.
>
> 5.6 In the event of termination of this AGREEMENT, the NETWORK and PHYSICIAN shall use their best efforts to arrange for an orderly transition of patient care, consistent with appropriate medical standards, for ENROLLEES who have been or are at the time under the care of the PHYSICIAN, to the care of another physician selected by ENROLLEE or PAYER, but for no longer than (1) one year. Such services shall be provided according to this AGREEMENT.
>
> **VI. MISCELLANEOUS**
>
> 6.1 All NETWORK business, medical, and other records, and all information generated by or relating to NETWORK or its management information systems shall be and remain the sole property of NETWORK. PHYSICIAN agrees to keep such information strictly confidential.
>
> 6.2 The parties are independent contractors, and neither is or shall represent itself as the employer, employee, partner, agent, principal, or joint venture of the other. The PHYSICIAN understands and agrees that in the provision of medical care services, the PHYSICIAN acts as an independent entity and that the physician-patient relationship shall in no way be affected.
>
> 6.3 Any notice or communication required, permitted, or desired to be given hereunder shall be deemed effectively given or mailed, addressed on the signature page.
>
> 6.4 The waiver by either party of a breach or violation of any provision of this AGREEMENT shall not operate as or be construed to be a waiver of any subsequent breach hereof.
>
> 6.5 This AGREEMENT shall be governed by and construed in accordance with the laws of the State of New York.
>
> 6.6 This AGREEMENT may be amended by NETWORK upon thirty (30) days' written notice of such proposed amendment. Failure of PHYSICIAN to provide written objection to such amendment within the thirty (30) day period shall constitute PHYSICIAN'S approval of such amendment.
>
> 6.7 The invalidity or unenforceability of any term or condition hereof shall in no way affect the validity or enforceability of any other term or provision.
>
> 6.8 PHYSICIAN may not assign this AGREEMENT without NETWORK'S prior written consent.
>
> 6.9 NETWORK and PHYSICIAN agree to submit to binding arbitration any dispute or claim arising out of the interpretation of or performance under this AGREEMENT which cannot be settled by informal means.
>
> ### ATTACHMENT 10 — SCOPE OF SERVICES
>
> - COPAYMENT – $20 per encounter
> - COINSURANCE – 20% for office surgery
> - DEDUCTIBLE – $500 for out-of-network physician services
> - COVERED SERVICES FOR WHICH PREAUTHORIZATION IS *NOT* REQUIRED –

(continues)

FIGURE 3-1 *(continued)*

a. *Initial Health Assessment (IHA)* that includes a history and physical examination and an individual health education behavioral assessment, which enables the PHYSICIAN to comprehensively assess each ENROLLEE'S current acute, chronic, and preventive health needs.

- *For adults,* IHA services include blood pressure, height, weight, total serum cholesterol lab testing for men and women over age 40, clinical breast examination for women over age 40, baseline mammogram for women over age 40, annual mammograms for women over age 50, screening for Chlamydia for men and women over age 21, screening for TB risk factors including a Mantoux skin test for all ENROLLEES determined to be at risk, health education behavioral risk assessment, immunizations, and health education.

- *For ENROLLEES under twenty-one (21) years of age,* IHA services include blood pressure, height, weight, screening for TB risk factors including a Mantoux skin test for all ENROLLEES determined to be at risk, health education behavioral risk assessment, immunizations, and health education.

b. *Medically necessary covered services* include those that are reasonable and necessary to protect life, prevent significant illness or significant disability, or to alleviate severe pain through the diagnosis or treatment of disease, illness, or injury.

- *For all ENROLLEES,* the provision of all medically necessary diagnostic, treatment, and follow-up services as a result of findings or risk factors identified in the initial health assessment (or during visits for routine, urgent, or emergent health care situations), and health education. Also included is tuberculosis screening, diagnosis, treatment, and follow-up.

- *For pregnant women,* the provision of prenatal care; risk assessment during initial assessment encounter, each trimester thereafter, and at the postpartum encounter; referral to appropriate specialists (e.g., perinatologist) for women who are at high risk of a poor pregnancy outcome; and health education

c. *Services for ENROLLEES who are under twenty-one (21) years of age* include the following preventive services: immunizations, blood lead screening, screening for Chlamydia, and Early and Periodic Screening, Diagnosis and Treatment (EPSDT) supplemental services.

d. *Emergency care for all ENROLLEES* includes emergency department professional services, facility charges for encounters, diagnostic testing, medical transportation (e.g., ambulance), and medications.

- *PREAUTHORIZATION MUST BE OBTAINED* FOR THE FOLLOWING COVERED SERVICES –
  a. Post-stabilization of emergency patient.

  - For example, patient is discharged from hospital emergency department to home and, within 48 hours, schedules office appointment with primary care provider as follow-up to emergency services.

  b. Non-urgent care of patient following emergency room encounter.

  - For example, patient is discharged from hospital emergency department to home and schedules office appointment with primary care provider for routine care of chronic condition(s), preventative services (e.g., annual physical examination), and/or care of non-urgent condition(s) (e.g., sinus pain).

  c. Treatment regimen already established.

  - For example, patient undergoing treatment regimen (e.g., allergy testing and treatment) with a specialist physician requests that the regimen continue with primary care physician, discontinuing the regimen with the specialist physician.

(continues)

FIGURE 3-1 *(continued)*

> d. Specialty physician services (e.g., oncologist, psychiatrist).
> e. Out-of-network physician services, which are not otherwise exempt from preauthorization.
> f. Hospice inpatient care.
> g. Major organ transplants.
> h. *EXPEDITED AUTHORIZATION* FOR COVERED SERVICES MAY BE OBTAINED when the PHYSICIAN determines that following the contracted preauthorization timeframe could seriously jeopardize the ENROLLEE'S life or health or ability to attain, maintain, or regain maximum function.
>
> • NON-COVERED SERVICES FOR WHICH THE PHYSICIAN CAN BILL THE PATIENT DIRECTLY include office encounters for cosmetic procedures *including encounters for complications due to the performance of such procedures.*

Instructions

1. Review Figure 3-1 (sample managed care plan contract), locate Attachment 10 — Scope of Services, and review its provisions.

2. Using the *Sample Managed Care Plan Quick Reference Sheet* (below), complete row three by entering details about the scope of services provisions (referring to content in rows one and two as examples).

Sample Managed Care Plan Quick Reference Sheet						
Contract	Copay	Coinsurance	Deductible	Covered Services	Preauthorization Required	Noncovered Services
Aetna	$25	20%[1]	$750	Prenatal care Preventive services Emergency care	Cesarean section Specialty physician services	Cosmetic procedures Dental care
BCBS	$30	20%[1]	$250	Prenatal care Preventive services Emergency care	Specialty physician services	Cosmetic procedures Vision care
ProHealth						
[1]Coinsurance amount applies to office surgery only.						

ASSIGNMENT 3.6 – MULTIPLE CHOICE REVIEW

1. Employees and dependents who join a managed care plan are called
   a. case managers.
   b. enrollees.
   c. providers.
   d. health plans.

2. Which act of legislation permitted large employers to self-insure employee health care benefits?
   a. ERISA
   b. HEDIS
   c. OBRA
   d. TEFRA

3. If a physician provides services that cost less than the managed care capitation amount, the physician will
   a. lose money.
   b. lose the managed care contract.
   c. make a profit.
   d. reduce the patient load.

4. The primary care provider is responsible for
   a. ensuring that enrollees pay their premiums.
   b. providing care according to the enrollee's preferences.
   c. supervising and coordinating health care services for enrollees.
   d. the quality of care provided by consultants.

5. Which is the method of controlling health care costs and quality of care by reviewing the appropriateness and necessity of care provided to patients?
   a. administrative oversight
   b. case management
   c. quality assurance
   d. utilization management

6. Accreditation is a _____ process that a health care facility can undergo to show that standards are being met.
   a. required
   b. licensure
   c. voluntary
   d. mandatory

7. Which type of health plan funds health care expenses by insurance coverage and allows the individual to select one of each type of provider to create a customized network?
   a. capitated plan
   b. customized sub-capitation plan
   c. health care reimbursement account
   d. health savings security account

8. Which type of consumer-directed health plan carries the stipulation that any funds unused will be lost?
   a. managed care organization
   b. health care reimbursement account
   c. health reimbursement arrangement
   d. health savings security account

9. Which is assessed by the National Committee for Quality Assurance?
   a. ambulatory care facilities
   b. hospitals
   c. long-term care facilities
   d. managed care plans

10. A case manager is responsible for
    a. educating enrollees about their health plan benefits.
    b. developing patient care plans for health services provided to enrollees.
    c. providing health care services to enrollees.
    d. submitting claims on behalf of enrollees.

11. Currently, more than 70 _____ Americans are enrolled in some type of managed care program in response to regulatory initiatives affecting health care cost and quality.
    a. thousand
    b. million
    c. billion
    d. trillion

12. Accreditation organizations develop _____ that are reviewed during a survey process that is conducted both offsite and onsite.
    a. laws
    b. legislation
    c. regulations
    d. standards

13. Which was created to provide standards to assess managed care systems in terms of indicators such as membership, utilization of services, quality, and access?
    a. ERISA
    b. HEDIS
    c. HIPAA
    d. TEFRA

14. Which act of legislation provided states with the flexibility to establish HMOs for Medicare and Medicaid programs?
    a. BBA
    b. COBRA
    c. OBRA
    d. TEFRA

15. Which would likely be subject to a managed care plan quality review?
    a. amount of money spent on construction upgrades
    b. cost of new equipment for a member facility
    c. number of patient payments made by credit card
    d. results of patient satisfaction surveys

16. The Quality Improvement System for Managed Care (QISMC) was established by
    a. The Joint Commission.
    b. Medicaid.
    c. Medicare.
    d. the National Committee for Quality Assurance.

17. Arranging for a patient's transfer to a rehabilitation facility is an example of
    a. concurrent review.
    b. discharge planning.
    c. preadmission review.
    d. preauthorization.

18. Administrative services performed on behalf of a self-insured managed care company can be outsourced to a(n)
    a. accrediting agency.
    b. external quality review organization.
    c. third-party administrator (TPA).
    d. utilization management company.

19. Managed care originally focused on cost _____ by restricting health care access through utilization management and availability of limited benefits.
    a. growths
    b. increases
    c. proliferations
    d. reductions

20. Managed care organizations impact a practice's administrative procedures by requiring
    a. a tracking system for authorization of specialty care after the patient has been seen by the specialist and treatment was provided.
    b. case managers that are employed by the medical practice to monitor patients who fail to keep a preauthorized appointment.
    c. special patient interviews to ensure preauthorization and to explain out-of-network requirements if the patient is self-referring.
    d. up-to-date lists for referrals to managed care organizations that contract with medical practices to provide patient care.

Revenue Cycle Management

INTRODUCTION

This chapter familiarizes students with the encounter form, remittance advice (RA), and explanation of benefits (EOB) form used in the payment of health insurance claims. Students will learn the contents of an encounter form, as well as how to interpret data contained on a remittance advice and an explanation of benefits.

ASSIGNMENT 4.1 – COMPLETING INSURANCE VERIFICATION FORMS

Objectives

At the conclusion of this assignment, the student should be able to:

1. Explain the purpose of an insurance verification form.

2. Accurately complete insurance verification form.

Overview

Accounts receivable management assists providers in the collection of appropriate reimbursement for services rendered, and includes the function entitled *insurance verification and eligibility,* which involves confirming patient insurance plan and eligibility information with the third-party payer to determine the patient's financial responsibility for services rendered.

Example of a Set of Forms:

ONLINE INSURANCE ELIGIBILITY VERIFICATION		
Rogers, Melissa, A	05-05-68	☒ Female ☐ Male
Patient's Last Name, First Name, Middle Initial	Patient's DOB	Gender
Mary Smith, CMA	06-20-YY	Beth Watkins, M.D.
Insurance Specialist or Office Manager's Name	Date Verified	Provider's Name
Bell Atlantic HMO	n/a	987654321-01
Health Insurance Plan Name	Group No.	Health Insurance Policy Number
04-29-1989	Eligible	n/a
Health Insurance Plan Effective Date	Status	Health Insurance Plan Termination Date

Plan Type (circle one):	PPO (HMO) POS	Group	MC	Capitated	WC
$ NONE	$ NONE	$10		☐ Yes ☒ No	
Deducible Amount	Amount not Satisfied	Copayment Amount		Pre-existing Clause	

Percentage of Reimbursement: **NONE %**
Coinsurance

What is plan coverage?	Medical, Dental, Vision, Prescriptions
What are the plan requirements?	Referral required for specialist services (1-800-333-5555)

DOCTORS GROUP · MAIN STREET · ALFRED NY 12345
NPI: 8529637410   **PATIENT REGISTRATION FORM**

PATIENT INFORMATION

Last Name	First Name	Middle Name
Rogers	Melissa	Ann

Street	City	State / Zip Code
5 High Street	Alfred	NY 14802

Patient's Date of Birth	Social Security Number	Home Phone Number
05/05/1968	123-45-6789	(101) 555-1234

Student Status	Employment Status	Marital Status
☐ Full-time ☐ Part-time	☒ Full-time ☐ Part-time ☐ Unemployed	☒ Single ☐ Married ☐ Separated ☐ Divorced ☐ Widowed

Gender	Visit is related to on-the-job injury	Prior treatment received for injury
☐ Male ☒ Female	☒ No ☐ Yes Date: _____	☒ No ☐ Yes Doctor: _____ WC No. _____

Employer Phone Number	Referred by:
(101) 555-8521	

Emergency Contact	Address	Telephone Number
Cindy Reynolds	235 Church Street, Elmira NY 14901	(101) 732-1234

Name/Address of Employer	Occupation
Bon Ton Department Store, PO Box 183, Rochester NY 14201	Director of Human Resources

Visit is related to automobile accident	Name and Credentials of Treating Provider	NPI
☒ No ☐ Yes Date: _____	Beth Watkins, MD	7419638520

GUARANTOR'S BILLING INFORMATION

Last Name	First Name	Middle Name
Rogers	Melissa	Ann

Street	City	State / Zip Code
5 High Street	Alfred	NY 14802

Relationship to Patient	Social Security Number	Home Phone Number
Self	123-45-6789	(101) 555-1234

Name of Employer	Address of Employer	Employer Phone Number
Bon Ton Department Store	PO Box 183, Rochester NY 14201	(101) 555-8521

INSURANCE INFORMATION

PRIMARY INSURED INFORMATION		SECONDARY INSURED INFORMATION	
Last Name	First Name / Middle Initial	Last Name	First Name / Middle Initial
Rogers	Melissa A.		
Address	City / State / Zip Code	Address	City / State / Zip Code
5 High Street	Alfred NY 14802		
Relationship to Insured	Gender	Relationship to Insured	Gender
☒ Self ☐ Spouse ☐ Child ☐ Other	☐ Male ☒ Female	☐ Self ☐ Spouse ☐ Child ☐ Other	☐ Male ☐ Female
Insured's Date of Birth	Home Phone Number	Insured's Date of Birth	Home Phone Number
05/05/1968	(101) 555-1234		
Name and Address of Insurance Company		Name and Address of Insurance Company	
Bell Atlantic, 100 Provider Row, Anywhere NY 12345-9597			
Insurance Identification Number	Group Number / Effective Date	Insurance Identification Number	Group Number / Effective Date
987654321-01	04-29-1989		
Name of Employer Sponsoring Plan		Name of Employer Sponsoring Plan	
Bon Ton Department Store			

 Bell Atlantic HMO
(800) 333-5555

Medical ■ Dental ■ Vision ■ Prescriptions
EFFECTIVE DATE OF COVERAGE: 04-29-1989

POLICYHOLDER: ROGERS, MELISSA, A
IDENTIFICATION NUMBER: 987654321-01
OFFICE COPAYMENT: $10
RX BIN: 61410
FOR REFERRAL TO SPECIALISTS, CALL (800) 333-5555.

Instructions

1. Review content in the patient registration form below, and complete the insurance verification form.

DOCTORS GROUP · MAIN STREET · ALFRED NY 12345 NPI: 8529637410		PATIENT REGISTRATION FORM

PATIENT INFORMATION

Last Name	First Name	Middle Name
Zapp	Dawn	Laura

Street	City	State / Zip Code
663 Hilltop Drive	Anywhere	NY 12345

Patient's Date of Birth	Social Security Number	Home Phone Number
02/12/1967	444-55-6666	(101) 333-4445

Student Status	Employment Status	Marital Status
❏ Full-time ❏ Part-time	☒ Full-time ❏ Part-time ❏ Unemployed	☒ Single ❏ Married ❏ Separated ❏ Divorced ❏ Widowed

Gender	Visit is related to on-the-job injury	Prior treatment received for injury
❏ Male ☒ Female	☒ No ❏ Yes Date: _____	☒ No ❏ Yes Doctor: _____ WC No. _____

Employer Phone Number	Referred by:
(101) 313-9854	

Emergency Contact	Address	Telephone Number
Bill Miller	3301 Sunny Drive, NY 12346	(101) 937-0070

Name/Address of Employer	Occupation
Superfresh Foods, PO Box 111, Main NY 12458	Cashier

Visit is related to automobile accident	Name and Credentials of Treating Provider	NPI
☒ No ❏ Yes Date: _____	Donald Givings, MD	1234567890

GUARANTOR'S BILLING INFORMATION

Last Name	First Name	Middle Name
Zapp	Dawn	Laura

Street	City	State / Zip Code
663 Hilltop Drive	Anywhere	NY 12345

Relationship to Patient	Social Security Number	Home Phone Number
Self	444-55-6666	(101) 333-4445

Name of Employer	Address of Employer	Employer Phone Number
Superfresh Foods	PO Box 111, Main NY 12458	(101) 313-9854

INSURANCE INFORMATION

PRIMARY INSURED INFORMATION		SECONDARY INSURED INFORMATION	
Last Name	First Name / Middle Initial	Last Name	First Name / Middle Initial
Zapp	Dawn L.		
Address	City / State / Zip Code	Address	City / State / Zip Code
663 Hilltop Drive	Anywhere NY 12345		
Relationship to Insured	Gender	Relationship to Insured	Gender
☒ Self ❏ Spouse ❏ Child ❏ Other	❏ Male ☒ Female	❏ Self ❏ Spouse ❏ Child ❏ Other	❏ Male ❏ Female
Insured's Date of Birth	Home Phone Number	Insured's Date of Birth	Home Phone Number
02/12/1967	(101) 333-4445		
Name and Address of Insurance Company		Name and Address of Insurance Company	
NorthWest Health, 500 Carr Street, Anywhere NY 12345-9597			
Insurance Identification Number / Group Number / Effective Date		Insurance Identification Number / Group Number / Effective Date	
444556666-01 430 10-20-2004			
Name of Employer Sponsoring Plan		Name of Employer Sponsoring Plan	
Superfresh Foods			

NORTHWEST HEALTH PPO
(877) 555-6598

Medical ▪ Prescriptions

EFFECTIVE DATE OF COVERAGE: 10-20-2004

POLICYHOLDER: ZAPP, DAWN, L

IDENTIFICATION NUMBER: 444556666-01

OFFICE COPAYMENT: $25

COINSURANCE: 80/20

DEDUCTIBLE: $200

RX BIN: A304/RX GRP: 430

PRESCRIPTION COPAYMENT: BRAND: $25   GENERIC: $10

INSURANCE ELIGIBILITY VERIFICATION

❑ Female   ❑ Male

_____   _____   _____
Patient's Last Name, First Name, Middle Initial   Patient's DOB   Gender

_____   _____   _____
Insurance Specialist or Office Manager's Name   Date Verified   Provider Name

_____   _____   _____
Health Insurance Plan Name   Group No.   Health Insurance Policy Number

_____   _____   _____
Health Insurance Plan Effective Date   Status   Health Insurance Plan Termination Date

Plan Type (circle one):   **PPO**   **HMO**   **POS**   **Group**   **MC**   **Capitated**   **WC**

$ _____ $ _____ $ _____   ❑ Yes   ❑ No
Deducible Amount   Amoun not Satisfied   Copayment Amount   Pre-existing Clause

Percentage of Reimbursement: _____ %
Coinsurance

What is plan coverage?   _____

What are the plan requirements?   _____

2. Review content in the patient registration form below, and complete the insurance verification form.

DOCTORS GROUP · MAIN STREET · ALFRED NY 12345 **NPI: 8529637410**		**PATIENT REGISTRATION FORM**

PATIENT INFORMATION

Last Name Branch	First Name James	Middle Name	
Street 401 Cartvalley Court	City Anywhere	State / Zip Code NY 12345	
Patient's Date of Birth 05/03/1986	Social Security Number 345-67-9910	Home Phone Number (101) 333-5555	
Student Status ☐ Full-time ☐ Part-time	Employment Status ☒ Full-time ☐ Part-time ☐ Unemployed	Marital Status ☐ Single ☒ Married ☐ Separated ☐ Divorced ☐ Widowed	
Gender ☒ Male ☐ Female	Visit is related to on-the-job injury ☒ No ☐ Yes Date: _____	Prior treatment received for injury ☒ No ☐ Yes Doctor: _____ WC No. _____	
Employer Phone Number (101) 499-7117	Referred by:		
Emergency Contact Bethany Branch	Address 401 Cartvalley Court, Anywhere NY 12345	Telephone Number (101) 333-5555	
Name/Address of Employer Gateway US, 2021 Blue Ave, Nowhere NY 12354	Occupation Sales		
Visit is related to automobile accident ☒ No ☐ Yes Date: _____	Name and Credentials of Treating Provider Lisa M. Mason, M.D.	NPI 4567897890	

GUARANTOR'S BILLING INFORMATION

Last Name Branch	First Name James	Middle Name
Street 2021 Blue Ave	City Nowhere	State / Zip Code NY 12354
Relationship to Patient Self	Social Security Number 345-67-9910	Home Phone Number (101) 333-5555
Name of Employer Gateway US	Address of Employer 2021 Blue Ave, Nowhere NY 12354	Employer Phone Number (101) 499-7117

INSURANCE INFORMATION

PRIMARY INSURED INFORMATION		SECONDARY INSURED INFORMATION	
Last Name Branch	First Name / Middle Initial James	Last Name	First Name / Middle Initial
Address 2021 Blue Ave	City / State / Zip Code Nowhere NY 12354	Address	City / State / Zip Code
Relationship to Insured ☒ Self ☐ Spouse ☐ Child ☐ Other	Gender ☒ Male ☐ Female	Relationship to Insured ☐ Self ☐ Spouse ☐ Child ☐ Other	Gender ☐ Male ☐ Female
Insured's Date of Birth 05/03/1986	Home Phone Number (111) 333-5555	Insured's Date of Birth	Home Phone Number
Name and Address of Insurance Company Metropolitan, PO Box 232, Nowhere NY 12354		Name and Address of Insurance Company	

Insurance Identification Number 2122245-01	Group Number M411	Effective Date 09-08-2010	Insurance Identification Number	Group Number	Effective Date
Name of Employer Sponsoring Plan Gateway US			Name of Employer Sponsoring Plan		

METROPOLITAN
(800) 319-6531

HMO PLAN
Medical ▪ Dental ▪ Rx

INSURED: BRANCH, JAMES   **ISSUE DATE:** 09/08/2010
ID Number: 2122245-01   **Group No.** M411
OFFICE COPAYMENT: $20   **EMG:** $250
Rx COPAYMENT: **BRAND:** $25   **GENERIC:** $15

NURSE ADVISOR AVAILABLE 24 HOURS

```
┌─────────────────────────────────────────────────────────────────────────┐
│                  INSURANCE ELIGIBILITY VERIFICATION                       │
│                                           ❑ Female    ❑ Male             │
│  _____    _____    _____   │
│  Patient's Last Name, First Name, Middle Initial   Patient's DOB    Gender │
│                                                                           │
│  _____    _____    _____   │
│  Insurance Specialist or Office Manager's Name   Date Verified   Provider Name │
│                                                                           │
│  _____    _____    _____   │
│  Health Insurance Plan Name         Group No.    Health Insurance Policy Number │
│                                                                           │
│  _____    _____    _____   │
│  Health Insurance Plan Effective Date   Status   Health Insurance Plan Termination Date │
│                                                                           │
│  Plan Type (circle one):    PPO    HMO    POS    Group    MC    Capitated    WC │
│  $_____    $_____    $_____    ❑ Yes  ❑ No │
│     Deducible Amount      Amount not Satisfied   Copayment Amount   Pre-existing Clause │
│                                                                           │
│        Percentage of Reimbursement:          _____ %                     │
│                                               Coinsurance                  │
│                                                                           │
│  What is plan coverage?    _____    │
│                                                                           │
│  What are the plan requirements?  _____  │
└─────────────────────────────────────────────────────────────────────────┘
```

ASSIGNMENT 4.2 – PAYMENT OF CLAIMS: ENCOUNTER FORM

Objectives

At the conclusion of this assignment, the student should be able to:

1. Explain the purpose of an encounter form.
2. Interpret the information contained on an encounter form.

Overview

An *encounter form* is the source document used to generate the insurance claim. In addition to patient identification information and the date of service, it contains abbreviated diagnosis and brief procedure/service descriptions and corresponding codes (e.g., ICD, CPT, HCPCS). The provider circles the appropriate codes on the encounter form, and the insurance specialist enters the office charge, amount paid by the patient, and total due.

Instructions

Review the encounter form in Figure 4-1 to familiarize yourself with its organization and contents. Then, analyze the contents of the encounter form to answer the following questions:

1. Which CPT codes listed on the encounter form are reported for new patient office visits? (Refer to your CPT coding manual to answer this question.)
2. The provider administered an influenza virus vaccine to a patient. What is the title of the section of the encounter form that the provider would reference to select a service code?
3. The provider performed an EKG with interpretation during the office visit. Identify the CPT code located on the encounter form that would be reported for this service.
4. During processing of the encounter form (to generate the claim), the insurance specialist notices that the provider entered a check mark in front of the procedure, "Blood, occult (feces)," and a check mark in front of the diagnosis, "Hypertension." Because *medical necessity* requires the diagnosis selected to justify the procedure performed, what should the insurance specialist do next?
5. The patient paid his $20 copayment during registration for today's encounter. What is the title of the section of the encounter form where the amount received is entered?

ENCOUNTER FORM

Tel: (101) 555-1111	Kim Donaldson, M.D.	EIN: 11-9876543
Fax: (101) 555-2222	INTERNAL MEDICINE	NPI: 1234567890
	101 Main Street, Suite A	
	Alfred, NY 14802	

OFFICE VISITS	NEW	EST	OFFICE PROCEDURES		INJECTIONS	
☐ Level I		99211	☐ EKG with interpretation	93000	☐ Influenza virus vaccine	_____
☐ Level II	99202	99212	☐ Spirometry	94010	☐ Admin of Influenza vaccine	G0008
☐ Level III	99203	99213	**LABORATORY TESTS**		☐ Pneumococcal vaccine	90732
☐ Level IV	99204	99214	☐ Blood, occult (feces)	82270	☐ Admin of pneumococcal vaccine	G0009
☐ Level V	99205	99215	☐ Skin test, Tb, intradermal (PPD)	86580	☐ Hepatitis B vaccine	90746
					☐ Admin of Hepatitis B vaccine	G0010
					☐ Tetanus and diptheria toxoids vaccine	90714
					☐ Immunization administration	90471

DIAGNOSIS

☐ Abnormal heart sounds	R00.__	☐ Chronic ischemic heart disease	I25.9	☐ Hypertension	I10
☐ Abdominal pain	R10.8__	☐ Chronic obstructive lung disease	J44.9	☐ Hormone replacement	Z79.890
☐ Abnormal feces	R19.5	☐ Congestive heart failure	I50.9	☐ Hyperlipidemia	E78.5
☐ Allergic rhinitis	J30.9	☐ Cough	R05	☐ Hyperthyroidism	E05.9__
☐ Anemia, pernicious	D51.0	☐ Depressive disorder	F32.9	☐ Influenza	J11.1
☐ Anxiety	F41.9	☐ Diabetes mellitus, type 2	E11.____	☐ Loss of weight	R63.4
☐ Asthma	J45.909	☐ Diarrhea	R19.7	☐ Nausea	R11.0
☐ Atrophy, cerebral	G31.9	☐ Dizziness	R42	☐ Nausea with vomiting	R11.2
☐ B-12 deficiency	D51.9	☐ Emphysema	J43.__	☐ Pneumonia	J18.__
☐ Back pain	M54.9	☐ Fatigue	R53.83	☐ Sore throat	J02.9
☐ Bronchitis	J40	☐ Fever	R50.9	☐ Vaccine, hepatitis B	Z23
☐ Cardiovascular disease	I25.1__	☐ Gastritis	K29.50	☐ Vaccine, influenza	Z23
☐ Cervicalgia	M54.2	☐ Heartburn	R12	☐ Vaccine, pneumococcus	Z23
☐ Chest pain	R07.9	☐ Hematuria	R31.9	☐ Vaccine, tetanus toxoid	Z23
☐	_____	☐	_____	☐	_____

PATIENT IDENTIFICATION

PATIENT NAME:	
PATIENT NUMBER:	
DATE OF BIRTH:	

ENCOUNTER DATE

| DATE OF SERVICE: | / / |

RETURN VISIT DATE

| DATE OF RETURN VISIT: | / / |

FINANCIAL TRANSACTION DATA

INVOICE NO.	
ACCOUNT NO.	
TOTAL FOR SERVICE:	$
AMOUNT RECEIVED:	$
PAID BY:	☐ Cash ☐ Check ☐ Credit Card
CASHIER'S INITIALS:	

Permission to reuse granted by Bibbero Systems, Inc.

FIGURE 4-1 Encounter form.

ASSIGNMENT 4.3 – PAYMENT OF CLAIMS: REMITTANCE ADVICE

Objectives

At the conclusion of this assignment, the student should be able to:

1. Explain the purpose of a remittance advice.

2. Interpret data contained in a remittance advice.

Overview

Once the claims adjudication process has been finalized, the claim is either denied or approved for payment. The provider receives a remittance advice (RA), which contains information used to process payments and adjustments to patient accounts. Payers often include multiple patients on the same remittance advice, which means that the insurance specialist must carefully review the document to properly process payments and adjustments. The remittance advice is also reviewed to make sure that there are no processing errors, which would result in the office resubmitting a corrected claim (e.g., coding errors).

Instructions

Review the remittance advice forms in Figures 4-2 through 4-7 to familiarize yourself with its organization and legend (explanation of abbreviated terms). Then, analyze the contents of each to answer each question.

 NOTE:

Use the remittance advice in Figure 4-2 to answer questions 1 through 5.

1. What is the check number and amount paid to the provider as recorded on the remittance advice? (HINT: This information is recorded in two different places on the remittance advice.)   _____

2. What was patient John Cofee's coinsurance amount for his visit on 0406YYYY?   _____

3. Patient James Eicher was not charged a coinsurance amount for his 0415YYYY visit. What is a possible explanation for this?   _____

4. What is patient Jenny Baker's account number?   _____

5. What is the allowed amount for procedure code 99213?   _____

 NOTE:

Use the remittance advice in Figure 4-3 to answer questions 6 through 10.

6. What is patient John Humphrey's health insurance claim number?   _____

7. How many patients in Figure 4-3 authorized assignment of benefits to Dr. Wilkins?   _____

8. What is patient Grayson Kihlberg's coinsurance amount for CPT code 99204?   _____

9. What was Craig Zane's coinsurance amount for code 73600?   _____

10. What was the amount billed for patient Angel Brennan's visit?   _____

```
ABC INSURANCE COMPANY
100 MAIN STREET
ALFRED, NY 14802
1-800-555-1234                                                              REMITTANCE ADVICE

DAVID MILLER, M.D.                                                          PROVIDER #:   123456
101 NORTH STREET                              PAGE #: 1 OF 1                 DATE:         05/05/YY
ALFRED, NY 14802                                                            CHECK#:       235698
```

	SERV DATES	POS	PROC	BILLED	ALLOWED	COINS		REIM
BAKER, JENNY	HICN 235962541		ACNT BAKE1234567-01			ASG	Y	MOA MA01
236592ABC	0405YY 0405YY	11	99213	75.00	60.00	15.00		45.00
PT RESP: 15.00		CLAIM TOTAL: 75.00						
								NET: 45.00
COFEE, JOHN	HICN 569856217		ACNT COFE2326254-01			ASG	Y	MOA MA01
326526ABC	0406YY 0406YY	11	99214	100.00	80.00	20.00		60.00
PT RESP: 20.00		CLAIM TOTAL: 100.00						
								NET: 60.00
DAVIS, JEANNE	HICN 562659452		ACNT DAVI2369214-01			ASG	Y	MOA MA01
123652ABC	0410YY 0410YY	11	99212	50.00	40.00	10.00		30.00
PT RESP: 10.00		CLAIM TOTAL: 50.00						
								NET: 30.00
EICHER, JAMES	HICN 626594594		ACNT EICH2365214-01			ASG	Y	MOA MA01
126954ABC	0415YY 0415YY	11	99385	125.00	125.00	0.00		125.00
PT RESP: 0.00		CLAIM TOTAL: 125.00						
$0 COPAY FOR PREVENTIVE SERVICES								NET: 125.00
FEINSTEIN, ED	HICN 365956214		ACNT FEIN1236521-01			ASG	Y	MOA MA01
695214ABC	0420YY 0420YY	11	17000	750.00	650.00	50.00		600.00
PT RESP: 50.00		CLAIM TOTAL: 750.00						
								NET: 600.00

TOTALS:					
# BILLED		BILLED	ALLOWED	COINSURANCE	NET	CHECK
CLAIMS		AMOUNT	AMOUNT	AMOUNT	AMOUNT	AMOUNT
5		1100.00	955.00	95.00	860.00	860.00

LEGEND
HICN (health insurance claim number)
SERV DATES (dates of service)
POS (place-of-service code)
PROC (CPT procedure/service code)
BILLED (amount provider billed payer)
ALLOWED (amount authorized by payer)
COINS (amount patient paid)
PROVIDER PAID (amount provider was reimbursed by payer)
NET (amount payer paid to provider)
PT RESP (amount patient paid)
ACNT (account number)
ASG Y (patient has authorized provider to accept assignment)
MOA MA01 (indicator that if denied, claim can be appealed)

FIGURE 4-2 Remittance advice (multiple claims).

```
XYZ INSURANCE COMPANY
500 SOUTH STREET
CHICAGO, ILLINOIS 60186
1-800-555-4321                                                    REMITTANCE ADVICE

CYNTHIA WILKINS M.D.                                              PROVIDER #:  654321
100 STATE STREET                                                  DATE:        05/31/YY
DENVER, COLORADO 80200                                            CHECK #:     871267
                    SERV DATES        POS         PROC    BILLED     ALLOWED    COINS    REIMB
```

	SERV DATES		POS	PROC	BILLED	ALLOWED	COINS	REIMB
ALDRIDGE, MORTON	HICN 370553029		ACNT ALDR4557516-01			ASG Y		
112233XYZ	05/05/YY	05/05/YY	11	10120	120.00	100.00	20.00	80.00
PT RESP: 20.00			CLAIM TOTAL: 120.00					NET: 80.00
BRENNAN, ANGEL	HICN 703459203		ACNT BREN5761282-01			ASG Y		
757557XYZ	05/05/YY	05/05/YY	11	99213	80.00	65.00	15.00	50.00
PT RESP: 15.00			CLAIM TOTAL: 80.00					NET: 50.00
HUMPHREY, JOHN	HICN 454545544		ACNT HUMP6721357-01			ASG Y		
673112XYZ	05/10/YY	05/10/YY	11	29130	50.00	35.00	15.00	20.00
PT RESP: 15.00			CLAIM TOTAL: 50.00					NET: 20.00
KIHLBERG, GRAYSON	HICN 716372688		ACNT KIHL1242495-02			ASG Y		
876543XYZ	05/12/YY	05/12/YY	11	99204	135.00	125.00	27.00	98.00
PT RESP: 27.00			CLAIM TOTAL: 125.00					NET: 98.00
ZANE, CRAIG	HICN 737682574		ACNT ZANE4963518-01			ASG Y		
302353XYZ	05/17/YY	05/17/YY	11	99213	80.00	65.00	15.00	50.00
				73600	55.00	45.00	0.00	45.00
PT RESP: 15.00			CLAIM TOTAL: 110.00					NET: 95.00

```
TOTALS:
# BILLED                    BILLED            ALLOWED          COINSURANCE          NET
CLAIMS:                     AMOUNT:           AMOUNT:          AMOUNT:              AMOUNT:

5                           520.00            435.00           92.00                343.00
```

LEGEND
HICN (health insurance claim number)
SERV DATES (dates of service)
POS (place-of-service code)
PROC (CPT procedure/service code)
BILLED (amount provider billed payer)
ALLOWED (amount authorized by payer)
COINS (amount patient paid)
PROVIDER PAID (amount provider was reimbursed by payer)
NET (amount payer paid to provider)
PT RESP (amount patient paid)
ACNT (account number)
ASG Y (patient has authorized provider to accept assignment)
MOA MA01 (indicator that if denied, claim can be appealed)

FIGURE 4-3 Remittance advice (multiple claims).

NOTE:

Use the remittance advice in Figure 4-4 to answer questions 11 through 15.

11. What was the date of service for patient Christopher Hess?   _____

12. What procedure code is listed for patient Mary Schwartz?   _____

13. How much did the provider bill the insurance company
    for the care of patient Andrew Gagner?   _____

14. Identify the place-of-service code for each patient.   _____

15. According to the remittance advice, how much was Dr. Kelley paid?   _____

NOTE:

Use the remittance advice in Figure 4-5 to answer questions 16 through 20.

16. What does the abbreviation "NET" represent, according to
    the legend at the bottom of the remittance advice?   _____

17. How much was the allowed amount for code 11442?   _____

18. What was the total coinsurance amount paid on the Figure 4-5 remittance advice?   _____

19. How much is patient Paulette Melfi's coinsurance
    amount for the visit on 05/01/YY?   _____

20. What is patient Susan Brisbane's account number?   _____

NOTE:

Use the remittance advice in Figure 4-6 to answer questions 21 through 25.

21. How much was Dr. Horne paid by the insurance company
    for patient Jason Brook's visit?   _____

22. What is Dr. Horne's provider number?   _____

23. What is the telephone number for White Health Care Systems?   _____

24. How much did the provider bill the insurance company
    for the care of patient Jason Brook?   _____

25. What does "POS" represent, according to the legend at the
    bottom of the remittance advice?   _____

NOTE:

Use the remittance advice in Figure 4-7 to answer questions 26 through 30.

26. What is Dr. Brown's title?   _____

27. What was the date of service for Kathleen Smith's visit?   _____

28. On what date was the remittance advice generated?   _____

29. How many patient visits were listed for 05/22/YY?   _____

30. How much was the allowed amount for code 30300?   _____

```
ACME INSURANCE COMPANY
911 RED LIGHT DRIVE
DALLAS, TEXAS 52222
1-800-555-5555                                              REMITTANCE ADVICE

ROSS KELLEY, M.D.                                           PROVIDER #:  5872
100 STATE STREET                                            DATE:        05/31/YY
BUFFALO, NEW YORK 14202                                     CHECK #:     37767
```

	SERV DATES		POS	PROC	BILLED	ALLOWED	COINS	REIMB
GAGNER, ANDREW	HICN 621884549	ACNT GAGN032974-01				ASG Y		
745221	05/07/YY	05/07/YY	11	99204	150.00	135.00	15.00	120.00
				74240	320.00	285.00	57.00	228.00
PT RESP: 72.00		CLAIM TOTAL: 470.00						NET: 348.00
HESS, CHRISTOPHER	HICN 258369147	ACNT HESS3129657-01				ASG Y		
246810	05/08/YY	05/08/YY	11	99213	80.00	65.00	20.00	45.00
PT RESP: 20.00		CLAIM TOTAL: 80.00						NET: 45.00
SCHWARTZ, MARY	HICN 147953128	ACNT SCHW4963813-01				ASG Y		
999924	05/10/YY	05/10/YY	11	46600	212.00	185.00	37.00	148.00
PT RESP: 37.00		CLAIM TOTAL: 212.00						NET: 148.00
STAVE, GABRIELLA	HICN 752319567	ACNT STAV462978-04				ASG Y		
225932	05/12/YY	05/12/YY	11	99212	90.00	80.00	10.00	70.00
PT RESP: 10.00		CLAIM TOTAL: 90.00						NET: 70.00
THOMAS, MICHAEL	HICN 121770222	ACNT THOM699224-02				ASG Y		
930512	05/17/YY	05/17/YY	11	83013	110.00	95.00	30.00	65.00
PT RESP: 30.00		CLAIM TOTAL: 110.00						NET: 65.00

```
TOTALS:
# BILLED                    BILLED              ALLOWED            COINS              NET
CLAIMS:                     AMOUNT:             AMOUNT:            AMOUNT:            AMOUNT:

5                           962.00              845.00             169.00             676.00
```

LEGEND
HICN (health insurance claim number)
SERV DATES (dates of service)
POS (place-of-service code)
PROC (CPT procedure/service code)
BILLED (amount provider billed payer)
ALLOWED (amount authorized by payer)
COINS (amount patient paid)
PROVIDER PAID (amount provider was reimbursed by payer)
NET (amount payer paid to provider)
PT RESP (amount patient paid)
ACNT (account number)
ASG Y (patient has authorized provider to accept assignment)
MOA MA01 (indicator that if denied, claim can be appealed)

FIGURE 4-4 Remittance advice (multiple claims).

UPAY INSURANCE COMPANY
1000 MAIN STREET
BOSTON, MASSACHUSETTS 02100
1-800-555-5432

GEORGE WILLIAMS, M.D.
25 SOUTH STREET
NORFOLK, VIRGINIA 23500

REMITTANCE ADVICE

PROVIDER #:   21137
DATE: 05/31/YY
CHECK #:   665821

	SERV DATES		PROC	Code(s)	BILLED	ALLOWED		COINS	REIMB
BRISBANE, SUSAN	HICN 125692479		ACNT BRIS396715-01			ASG	Y		
456212UPAY	05/01/YY	05/01/YY	11	11402	105.00	100.00		20.00	80.00
PT RESP: 20.00		CLAIM TOTAL: 105.00							NET: 80.00
MELFI, PAULETTE	HICN 746931251		ACNT MELF551374-02			ASG	Y		
221123UPAY	05/01/YY	05/01/YY	11	99211	40.00	25.00		0.00	25.00
PT RESP: 0.00		CLAIM TOTAL: 40.00							NET: 25.00
SWANSON, LYNN	HICN 446285791		ACNT SWAN333333-01			ASG	Y		
821547UPAY	05/06/YY	05/06/YY	11	11442	220.00	190.00		38.00	152.00
PT RESP: 38.00		CLAIM TOTAL: 220.00							NET: 152.00
WILSON, STACEY	HICN 020868543		ACNT WILS211232-01			ASG	Y		
323215UPAY	05/08/YY	05/08/YY	11	99203	140.00	125.00		15.00	110.00
PT RESP: 15.00		CLAIM TOTAL: 140.00							NET: 110.00
ZIGLER, PEGGY	HICN 702515313		ACNT ZIGL945625-03			ASG	Y		
565981UPAY	05/10/YY	05/10/YY	11	11720	75.00	70.00		10.00	60.00
PT RESP: 10.00		CLAIM TOTAL: 75.00							NET: 60.00

TOTALS:

# BILLED CLAIMS:	BILLED AMOUNT:	ALLOWED AMOUNT:	COINS AMOUNT:	NET AMOUNT:
5	580.00	510.00	83.00	427.00

LEGEND
HICN (health insurance claim number)
SERV DATES (dates of service)
POS (place-of-service code)
PROC (CPT procedure/service code)
BILLED (amount provider billed payer)
ALLOWED (amount authorized by payer)
COINS (amount patient paid)
PROVIDER PAID (amount provider was reimbursed by payer)
NET (amount payer paid to provider)
PT RESP (amount patient paid)
ACNT (account number)
ASG Y (patient has authorized provider to accept assignment)
MOA MA01 (indicator that if denied, claim can be appealed)

FIGURE 4-5 Remittance advice (multiple claims).

WHITE HEALTH CARE SYSTEMS
500 SEASIDE LANE
SAN FRANCISCO, CALIFORNIA 94100
1-800-555-2468

REMITTANCE ADVICE

DAVID HORNE, M.D.
1 EYEBALL LANE
ORLANDO, FLORIDA 31000

PROVIDER #:   31055
DATE :   05/31/YY
CHECK #:   26854

	SERV DATES		POS	PROC	BILLED	ALLOWED	COINS	REIMB
BROOK, JASON	HICN 123456789	ACNT BROO444444-01			ASG Y			
WHCS242678	05/15/YY	05/15/YY	11	99203	112.00	95.00	20.00	75.00
PT RESP: 20.00		CLAIM TOTAL: 112.00						NET: 75.00
CAPTAIN, TERESA	HICN 875123466	ACNT CAPT5881125			ASG Y			
WHCS082543	05/16/YY	05/16/YY	11	65205	80.00	72.00	15.00	57.00
PT RESP: 15.00		CLAIM TOTAL: 80.00						NET: 57.00

TOTALS:

# BILLED CLAIMS:	BILLED AMOUNT:	ALLOWED AMOUNT:	COINS AMOUNT:	NET AMOUNT:
2	192.00	167.00	35.00	132.00

LEGEND
HICN (health insurance claim number)
SERV DATES (dates of service)
POS (place-of-service code)
PROC (CPT procedure/service code)
BILLED (amount provider billed payer)
ALLOWED (amount authorized by payer)
COINS (amount patient paid)
PROVIDER PAID (amount provider was reimbursed by payer)
NET (amount payer paid to provider)
PT RESP (amount patient paid)
ACNT (account number)
ASG Y (patient has authorized provider to accept assignment)
MOA MA01 (indicator that if denied, claim can be appealed)

FIGURE 4-6 Remittance advice (multiple claims).

SOUTHWEST ADMINISTRATORS
24 HOUR STREET
MIAMI, FLORIDA 33010
1-800-555-6789

MARK BROWN, D.O.
1500 ANGLER BOULEVARD
NORFOLK, VIRGINIA 23500

REMITTANCE ADVICE

PROVIDER # : 21137
DATE: 05/31/YY
CHECK #:   665821

	SERV DATES		POS	PROC	BILLED		ALLOWED	COINS		REIMB
BRISTER, SUZETTE	HICN 121113659		ACNT BRIS061667-04			ASG	Y	MOA		MA01
SA4452814	05/20/YY	05/20/YY	11	99214	135.00		120.00	0.00		120.00
PT RESP: 0.00		CLAIM TOTAL: 135.00								NET: 120.00
SMITH, KATHLEEN	HICN 112167258		ACNT SMIT081159-05			ASG	Y	MOA		MA01
SA216552	05/22/YY	05/22/YY	11	99212	90.00		75.00	5.00		70.00
PT RESP: 5.00		CLAIM TOTAL: 90.00								NET: 70.00
WHITE, AMOS	HICN 020347181		ACNT WHIT020347-03			ASG	Y	MOA		MA01
SA12300405	05/22/YY	05/22/YY	11	30300	75.00		65.00	15.00		50.00
PT RESP: 15.00		CLAIM TOTAL: 75.00								NET: 50.00

TOTALS:

# BILLED CLAIMS:	BILLED AMOUNT:	ALLOWED AMOUNT:	COINS AMOUNT:	NET AMOUNT:
3	300.00	260.00	20.00	240.00

LEGEND
HICN (health insurance claim number)
SERV DATES (dates of service)
POS (place-of-service code)
PROC (CPT procedure/service code)
BILLED (amount provider billed payer)
ALLOWED (amount authorized by payer)
COINS (amount patient paid)
PROVIDER PAID (amount provider was reimbursed by payer)
NET (amount payer paid to provider)
PT RESP (amount patient paid)
ACNT (account number)
ASG Y (patient has authorized provider to accept assignment)
MOA MA01 (indicator that if denied, claim can be appealed)

FIGURE 4-7 Remittance advice (multiple claims).

ASSIGNMENT 4.4 – PAYMENT OF CLAIMS: EXPLANATION OF BENEFITS

Objectives

At the conclusion of this assignment, the student should be able to:

1. Explain the purpose of an explanation of benefits.

2. Interpret data contained in an explanation of benefits.

Overview

Once the claims adjudication process has been finalized, the claim is either denied or approved for payment. The patient receives an explanation of benefits (EOB), which contains information about the claim with regard to what was paid by the insurance company and what amount (if any) is the patient's responsibility for payment. The patient should review the explanation of benefits to make sure that there are no errors. If the patient detects an error, the patient may contact the provider's office and speak with a health insurance specialist for assistance and resubmission of a corrected claim as necessary.

 NOTE:

If the physician is a nonparticipating provider (nonPAR), the office will not receive a remittance advice from Medicare. To assist patients in obtaining Medicare reimbursement so that they can pay the bills mailed to them by the physician's office, the insurance specialist will need to review the EOB that the patient received from Medicare. This exercise provides students with practice interpreting an EOB.

Instructions

Review the EOB forms in Figures 4-8 through 4-12 to familiarize yourself with its organization and contents. Then, analyze the contents of the EOB forms to answer each question.

NOTE:

Use the EOB in Figure 4-8 to answer questions 1 through 5.

1. How much was The Keystone Plan charged for Mary S. Patient's visit of 04/05/YY?   _____

2. How much has Mary S. Patient paid out of pocket year to date?   _____

3. What is Mary S. Patient's identification number?   _____

4. What was the allowed amount charged by Dr. Miller for Mary S. Patient's visit of 04/05/YY?   _____

5. What is Mary S. Patient's annual medical/surgical deductible, according to the explanation of benefits?   _____

THE KEYSTONE PLAN

P.O. BOX 900
ALFRED NY 14802-0900
(800) 555-9000

DATE:	04/05/YYYY
ID#	BLS123456789
ENROLLEE:	MARY S. PATIENT
HICN:	300500
BENEFIT PLAN:	STATE OF NEW YORK

MARY S. PATIENT
100 MAIN ST
ALFRED NY 14802

EXPLANATION OF BENEFITS

SERVICE DETAIL

PATIENT/RELAT CLAIM NUMBER	PROVIDER/ SERVICE	DATE OF SERVICE	AMOUNT CHARGED	NOT COVERED	AMOUNT ALLOWED	COPAY/ DEDUCTIBLE	%	PLAN BENEFITS	REMARK CODE
ENROLLEE	D MILLER								
5629587	OFFICE VISITS	04/05/YY	60.25		40.25	8.00	100	32.25*	D1

PLAN PAYS	32.25

*THIS IS A COPY OF INFORMATION SENT TO THE PROVIDER. THANK YOU FOR USING THE PARTICIPATING PROVIDER PROGRAM.

REMARK CODE(S) LISTED BELOW ARE REFERENCED IN THE *SERVICE DETAIL* SECTION UNDER THE HEADING *REMARK CODE*

(D1)   THANK YOU FOR USING A NETWORK PROVIDER. WE HAVE APPLIED THE NETWORK CONTRACTED FEE. THE MEMBER IS NOT
RESPONSIBLE FOR THE DIFFERENCE BETWEEN THE AMOUNT CHARGED AND THE AMOUNT ALLOWED BY THE CONTRACT.

BENEFIT PLAN PAYMENT SUMMARY INFORMATION	
D MILLER	$32.25

PATIENT NAME	MEDICAL/SURGICAL DEDUCTIBLE		MEDICAL/SURGICAL OUT OF POCKET		PHYSICAL MEDICINE DEDUCTIBLE	
	ANNUAL DEDUCT	YYYY YEAR TO-DATE	ANNUAL MAXIMUM	YYYY YEAR TO-DATE	ANNUAL DEDUCT	YYYY YEAR TO-DATE
ENROLLEE	$249.00	$0.00	$1804.00	$121.64	$250.00	$0.00

THIS CLAIM WAS PROCESSED IN ACCORDANCE WITH THE TERMS OF YOUR EMPLOYEE BENEFITS PLAN. IN THE EVENT THIS CLAIM HAS BEEN DENIED, IN WHOLE OR IN PART, A REQUEST
FOR REVIEW MAY BE DIRECTED TO THE KEYSTONE PLAN AT THE ALFRED ADDRESS OR PHONE NUMBER SHOWN ABOVE. THE REQUEST FOR REVIEW MUST BE SUBMITTED WITHIN 60 DAYS
AFTER THE CLAIM PAYMENT DATE, OR THE DATE OF THE NOTIFICATION OF DENIAL OF BENEFITS. WHEN REQUESTING A REVIEW, PLEASE STATE WHY YOU BELIEVE THE CLAIM
DETERMINATION OR PRE-CERTIFICATION IMPROPERLY REDUCED OR DENIED YOUR BENEFITS. ALSO, SUBMIT ANY DATA OR COMMENTS TO SUPPORT THE APPEAL.

THIS IS NOT A BILL.

FIGURE 4-8 Sample explanation of benefits (EOB) form.

United HealthCare

P.O. BOX 100
ALFRED NY 14802-0100
(800) 555-1000

JOHN PATIENT
100 MAIN ST
ALFRED NY 14802

DATE: 10/01/YYYY
ID #:   BLS123456789
ENROLLEE: JOHN PATIENT
HICN: 895632
BENEFIT PLAN: ALSTOM

EXPLANATION OF BENEFITS

SERVICE DETAIL

PATIENT/RELAT CLAIM NUMBER	PROVIDER/ SERVICE	DATE OF SERVICE	AMOUNT CHARGED	NOT COVERED	AMOUNT ALLOWED	COPAY/ DEDUCTIBLE	%	PLAN BENEFITS	REMARK CODE
ENROLLEE 6759235	D MILLER OFFICE VISIT	06/10/YY	75.00		40.00	18.00	100	22.00	D1
						PLAN PAYS		22.00	

THIS IS A COPY OF INFORMATION SENT TO THE PROVIDER. THANK YOU FOR USING THE PARTICIPATING PROVIDER PROGRAM.

REMARK CODE(S) LISTED BELOW ARE REFERENCED IN THE *SERVICE DETAIL* SECTION UNDER THE HEADING *REMARK CODE*
(D1)   THANK YOU FOR USING A NETWORK PROVIDER. WE HAVE APPLIED THE NETWORK CONTRACTED FEE. THE MEMBER IS NOT RESPONSIBLE FOR THE DIFFERENCE BETWEEN THE AMOUNT CHARGED AND THE AMOUNT ALLOWED BY THE CONTRACT.

BENEFIT PLAN PAYMENT SUMMARY INFORMATION	
D MILLER	$22.00

PATIENT NAME	MEDICAL/SURGICAL DEDUCTIBLE		MEDICAL/SURGICAL OUT OF POCKET		PHYSICAL MEDICINE DEDUCTIBLE	
	ANNUAL DEDUCT	YYYY YEAR TO-DATE	ANNUAL MAXIMUM	YYYY YEAR TO-DATE	ANNUAL DEDUCT	YYYY YEAR TO-DATE
ENROLLEE	$850.00	$0.00	$2500.00	$1699.50	$1250.00	$0.00

THIS CLAIM WAS PROCESSED IN ACCORDANCE WITH THE TERMS OF YOUR EMPLOYEE BENEFITS PLAN. IN THE EVENT THIS CLAIM HAS BEEN DENIED, IN WHOLE OR IN PART, A REQUEST FOR REVIEW MAY BE DIRECTED TO THE KEYSTONE PLAN AT THE ALFRED ADDRESS OR PHONE NUMBER SHOWN ABOVE. THE REQUEST FOR REVIEW MUST BE SUBMITTED WITHIN 60 DAYS AFTER THE CLAIM PAYMENT DATE, OR THE DATE OF THE NOTIFICATION OF DENIAL OF BENEFITS. WHEN REQUESTING A REVIEW, PLEASE STATE WHY YOU BELIEVE THE CLAIM DETERMINATION OR PRE-CERTIFICATION IMPROPERLY REDUCED OR DENIED YOUR BENEFITS. ALSO, SUBMIT ANY DATA OR COMMENTS TO SUPPORT THE APPEAL.

THIS IS NOT A BILL.

FIGURE 4-9 Explanation of benefits (EOB).

NOTE:

Use the EOB in Figure 4-9 to answer questions 6 through 10.

6. What was the copayment for this encounter?   _____

7. What is the payer's health insurance contract number (HICN)? _____

8. What amount did Dr. Miller charge for this encounter?   _____

9. What amount did the plan benefit allow for this encounter?   _____

10. What amount did Dr. Miller "write off" for this encounter?   _____

Aetna

P.O. BOX 500
ALFRED NY 14802-0500
(800) 555-5000

CINDY MATTESON
5 GREENE ST
ALFRED NY 14802

DATE:	10/01/YYYY
ID #:	BLS123456789
ENROLLEE:	CINDY MATTESON
HICN:	123XYZ
BENEFIT PLAN:	COMMERCIAL

EXPLANATION OF BENEFITS

SERVICE DETAIL

PATIENT/RELAT CLAIM NUMBER	PROVIDER/ SERVICE	DATE OF SERVICE	AMOUNT CHARGED	NOT COVERED	AMOUNT ALLOWED	COPAY/ DEDUCTIBLE	%	PLAN BENEFITS	REMARK CODE
ENROLLEE 5629587	A SMITH OFFICE VISIT	09/01/YY	875.00		367.00	18.00	100	349.00	D1
						PLAN PAYS		349.00	

*THIS IS A COPY OF INFORMATION SENT TO THE PROVIDER. THANK YOU FOR USING THE PARTICIPATING PROVIDER PROGRAM.

REMARK CODE(S) LISTED BELOW ARE REFERENCED IN THE *SERVICE DETAIL* SECTION UNDER THE HEADING *REMARK CODE*
(D1)   THANK YOU FOR USING A NETWORK PROVIDER. WE HAVE APPLIED THE NETWORK CONTRACTED FEE. THE MEMBER IS NOT RESPONSIBLE FOR THE DIFFERENCE BETWEEN THE AMOUNT CHARGED AND THE AMOUNT ALLOWED BY THE CONTRACT.

BENEFIT PLAN PAYMENT SUMMARY INFORMATION	
A SMITH	$349.00

PATIENT NAME	MEDICAL/SURGICAL DEDUCTIBLE		MEDICAL/SURGICAL OUT OF POCKET		PHYSICAL MEDICINE DEDUCTIBLE	
	ANNUAL DEDUCT	YYYY YEAR TO-DATE	ANNUAL MAXIMUM	YYYY YEAR TO-DATE	ANNUAL DEDUCT	YYYY YEAR TO-DATE
ENROLLEE	$850.00	$875.00	$2500.00	$1699.50	$1250.00	$0.00

THIS CLAIM WAS PROCESSED IN ACCORDANCE WITH THE TERMS OF YOUR EMPLOYEE BENEFITS PLAN. IN THE EVENT THIS CLAIM HAS BEEN DENIED, IN WHOLE OR IN PART, A REQUEST FOR REVIEW MAY BE DIRECTED TO THE KEYSTONE PLAN AT THE ALFRED ADDRESS OR PHONE NUMBER SHOWN ABOVE. THE REQUEST FOR REVIEW MUST BE SUBMITTED WITHIN 60 DAYS AFTER THE CLAIM PAYMENT DATE, OR THE DATE OF THE NOTIFICATION OF DENIAL OF BENEFITS. WHEN REQUESTING A REVIEW, PLEASE STATE WHY YOU BELIEVE THE CLAIM DETERMINATION OR PRE-CERTIFICATION IMPROPERLY REDUCED OR DENIED YOUR BENEFITS. ALSO, SUBMIT ANY DATA OR COMMENTS TO SUPPORT THE APPEAL.

THIS IS NOT A BILL.

FIGURE 4-10 Explanation of benefits (EOB).

NOTE:

Use the EOB in Figure 4-10 to answer questions 11 through 15.

11. What was the date of service for this encounter?   _____

12. What type is the benefit plan on this EOB?   _____

13. What amount did Dr. Smith charge for this encounter?   _____

14. What amount did the patient pay at the time of the encounter?   _____

15. What amount did the payer reimburse Dr. Smith for this encounter?   _____

CONN GENERAL

P.O. BOX 800
ALFRED NY 14802-0900
(800) 555-8000

DATE:	04/01/YY
ID #:	2100010121
ENROLLEE:	IMA GAYLE
HICN:	300400
BENEFIT PLAN:	STATE OF NEW YORK

IMA GAYLE
101 HAPPY DRIVE
ANYWHERE NY 12345-1234

EXPLANATION OF BENEFITS

SERVICE DETAIL

PATIENT/RELAT CLAIM NUMBER	PROVIDER/ SERVICE	DATE OF SERVICE	AMOUNT CHARGED	NOT COVERED	AMOUNT ALLOWED	COPAY/ DEDUCTIBLE	%	PLAN BENEFITS	REMARK CODE
ENROLLEE 0930194	S RAJA OFFICE VISIT	03/05/YY	85.00		60.00	12.00	100	48.00	D1
						PLAN PAYS		48.00	

THIS IS A COPY OF INFORMATION SENT TO THE PROVIDER. THANK YOU FOR USING THE PARTICIPATING PROVIDER PROGRAM.

REMARK CODE(S) LISTED BELOW ARE REFERENCED IN THE *SERVICE DETAIL* SECTION UNDER THE HEADING *REMARK CODE*
(D1)   THANK YOU FOR USING A NETWORK PROVIDER. WE HAVE APPLIED THE NETWORK CONTRACTED FEE. THE MEMBER IS NOT RESPONSIBLE FOR THE DIFFERENCE BETWEEN THE AMOUNT CHARGED AND THE AMOUNT ALLOWED BY THE CONTRACT.

BENEFIT PLAN PAYMENT SUMMARY INFORMATION	
S RAJA	$48.00

PATIENT NAME	MEDICAL/SURGICAL DEDUCTIBLE		MEDICAL/SURGICAL OUT OF POCKET		PHYSICAL MEDICINE DEDUCTIBLE	
	ANNUAL DEDUCT	YYYY YEAR TO-DATE	ANNUAL MAXIMUM	YYYY YEAR TO-DATE	ANNUAL DEDUCT	YYYY YEAR TO-DATE
ENROLLEE	$100.00	$0.00	$1500.00	$80.00	$250.00	$0.00

THIS CLAIM WAS PROCESSED IN ACCORDANCE WITH THE TERMS OF YOUR EMPLOYEE BENEFITS PLAN. IN THE EVENT THIS CLAIM HAS BEEN DENIED, IN WHOLE OR IN PART, A REQUEST FOR REVIEW MAY BE DIRECTED TO THE KEYSTONE PLAN AT THE ALFRED ADDRESS OR PHONE NUMBER SHOWN ABOVE. THE REQUEST FOR REVIEW MUST BE SUBMITTED WITHIN 60 DAYS AFTER THE CLAIM PAYMENT DATE, OR THE DATE OF THE NOTIFICATION OF DENIAL OF BENEFITS. WHEN REQUESTING A REVIEW, PLEASE STATE WHY YOU BELIEVE THE CLAIM DETERMINATION OR PRE-CERTIFICATION IMPROPERLY REDUCED OR DENIED YOUR BENEFITS. ALSO, SUBMIT ANY DATA OR COMMENTS TO SUPPORT THE APPEAL.

THIS IS NOT A BILL.

FIGURE 4-11 Explanation of benefits (EOB).

NOTE:

Use the EOB in Figure 4-11 to answer questions 16 through 20.

16. What is Ima Gayle's identification number? _____

17. What was the allowed amount charged by Dr. Raja for Ima Gayle's visit of 03/05/YY? _____

18. What is Ima Gayle's annual medical/surgical deductible, according to the EOB? _____

19. What was the date of service for this encounter? _____

20. How much has Ima Gayle paid year to date for the medical/ surgical out of pocket? _____

BELL ATLANTIC

P.O. BOX 600
ALFRED NY 14802-0900
(800) 555-6000

JOSE X RAUL
10 MAIN STREET
ANYWHERE NY 12345-1234

DATE: 07/19/YY
ID #:   222304040
ENROLLEE: JOSE X RAUL
HICN: J5987558
BENEFIT PLAN: STATE OF NEW YORK

EXPLANATION OF BENEFITS

SERVICE DETAIL

PATIENT CLAIM NUMBER	PROVIDER/ SERVICE	DATE OF SERVICE	AMOUNT CHARGED	NOT COVERED	AMOUNT ALLOWED	COPAY/ DEDUCTIBLE	%	PLAN BENEFITS	REMARK CODE
ENROLLEE 0101196	H CARDIAC OFFICE VISIT	06/20/YY	60.00		47.00	10.00	100	37.00	D1
	OFFICE VISIT	06/25/YY	60.00		47.00	10.00	100	37.00	D1
						PLAN PAYS		74.00	

THIS IS A COPY OF INFORMATION SENT TO THE PROVIDER. THANK YOU FOR USING THE PARTICIPATING PROVIDER PROGRAM.

REMARK CODE(S) LISTED BELOW ARE REFERENCED IN THE *SERVICE DETAIL* SECTION UNDER THE HEADING *REMARK CODE*
(D1)   THANK YOU FOR USING A NETWORK PROVIDER. WE HAVE APPLIED THE NETWORK CONTRACTED FEE. THE MEMBER IS NOT RESPONSIBLE FOR THE DIFFERENCE BETWEEN THE AMOUNT CHARGED AND THE AMOUNT ALLOWED BY THE CONTRACT.

BENEFIT PLAN PAYMENT SUMMARY INFORMATION
H CARDIAC $74.00

PATIENT NAME	MEDICAL/SURGICAL DEDUCTIBLE		MEDICAL/SURGICAL OUT OF POCKET		PHYSICAL MEDICINE DEDUCTIBLE	
	ANNUAL DEDUCT	YYYY YEAR TO-DATE	ANNUAL MAXIMUM	YYYY YEAR TO-DATE	ANNUAL DEDUCT	YYYY YEAR TO-DATE
ENROLLEE	$150.00	$25.00	$1000.00	$0.00	$150.00	$0.00

THIS CLAIM WAS PROCESSED IN ACCORDANCE WITH THE TERMS OF YOUR EMPLOYEE BENEFITS PLAN. IN THE EVENT THIS CLAIM HAS BEEN DENIED, IN WHOLE OR IN PART, A REQUEST FOR REVIEW MAY BE DIRECTED TO THE KEYSTONE PLAN AT THE ALFRED ADDRESS OR PHONE NUMBER SHOWN ABOVE. THE REQUEST FOR REVIEW MUST BE SUBMITTED WITHIN 60 DAYS AFTER THE CLAIM PAYMENT DATE, OR THE DATE OF THE NOTIFICATION OF DENIAL OF BENEFITS. WHEN REQUESTING A REVIEW, PLEASE STATE WHY YOU BELIEVE THE CLAIM DETERMINATION OR PRE-CERTIFICATION IMPROPERLY REDUCED OR DENIED YOUR BENEFITS. ALSO, SUBMIT ANY DATA OR COMMENTS TO SUPPORT THE APPEAL.

THIS IS NOT A BILL.

FIGURE 4-12 Explanation of benefits (EOB).

 NOTE:

Use the EOB in Figure 4-12 to answer questions 21 through 25.

21. What is Jose X. Raul's annual medical/surgical deductible, according to the EOB? _____

22. How much was Bell Atlantic charged for Jose X. Raul's visit of 06/25/YY? _____

23. What amount did the patient pay at the time of the encounter for visit of 06/20/YY? _____

24. What amount did Dr. Cardiac "write off" for both encounters? _____

25. What is the telephone number for Bell Atlantic? _____

ASSIGNMENT 4.5 – WRITING APPEAL LETTERS

Objectives

At the conclusion of this assignment, the student should be able to:

1. Review a remittance advice to determine claims submission errors that resulted in payment denials.

2. Prepare appeal letters that explain why a resubmitted claim should be reconsidered for third-party payer payment.

Overview

Denied claims are reviewed, and a determination is made about whether to submit an appeal letter for reconsideration of payment. Denied claims are often categorized as technical or clinical, and that results in the need for appropriate health care facility staff involvement in the appeals process. *Technically denied claims* usually include errors in payer name or address or codes, and health insurance and billing staff can generate such appeals. *Clinically denied claims* include not meeting medical necessity for procedures/services reported, not having obtained written preauthorization for procedures/services performed (but having obtained telephone preauthorization from the payer), and incorrect codes reported; coding and clinical staff need to be involved in generating these appeals.

An *appeal* is documented as a letter signed by the provider explaining why a claim should be reconsidered for payment. If appropriate, copies of patient record documentation are included with the appeal letter (for which the patient has signed a release-of-information authorization). A remittance advice (Figure 4-13) indicates payment denials for reasons other than processing errors, which may include (1) procedure or service not medically necessary, (2) preexisting condition not covered, (3) noncovered benefit, (4) termination of coverage, (5) failure to obtain preauthorization, (6) out-of-network provider used, or (7) lower level of care could have been provided.

When starting the appeal process, make sure the provider's documentation in the patient record is accurate, clear, and complete. A copy of pertinent portions of the patient record may need to be included with the appeal letter. When preparing appeal letters (Figures 4-14 and 4-15), include the following information:

- Patient demographic information

- Third-party payer information

- Date of service or procedure

- Place of service or procedure

- Remittance advice denial code and reason

- Proof of medical necessity of the service or procedure

Sending the appeal letter via certified mail ensures that the office has a record of its receipt by the third-party payer.

Instructions

1. Review the remittance advice (Figure 4-13), and circle the *payment denial reason codes*.

2. Determine whether each *payment denial reason code* would result in writing a(n):

   - Appeal letter to the third-party payer (Figure 4-14)

   - Collection letter to the patient (Figure 4-15)

3. Refer to the sample letters in Figures 4-14 and 4-15, and prepare appeal letter(s) and/or collection letter(s) for each *payment denial reason code*. (Do not prepare provider letters of medical necessity.)

```
US HEALTH                                              DATE: 05/25/YYYY
100 MAIN STREET          Remittance Advice                  (800) 555-1234
ALFRED NY 14802                                         FAX: (800) 555-4321
```

ERIN A HELPER MD   PROVIDER#: 98979697
101 MEDIC DRIVE   ┌─── **PAGE#: 1 OF 1** ───┐   CHECK#:   1121314
ANYWHERE NY 12345   └──────────────────────────┘

PATIENT: DOVER, AILEEN   **ACCOUNT#:** DOVER123456-01
                                        HICN: 1231199091

Service Date	POS	CPT	Billed	Allowed	Copay/Coins	ASG	Paid	Adjustment	Reason Code(s)
0416YYYY	11	99212	45.00	34.00	0.00	Y	34.00	11.00	001
Totals:			45.00	34.00	0.00		34.00	11.00	NET: 34.00

PATIENT: SHOWER, ANITA   **ACCOUNT#:** SHOWER778899-01
                                        HICN: 1234587702

Service Date	POS	CPT	Billed	Allowed	Copay/Coins	ASG	Paid	Adjustment	Reason Code(s)
0409YYYY	11	99211	40.00	35.00	10.00	Y	25.00	5.00	001
0409YYYY	11	81003	12.00	0.00	0.00	Y	0.00	12.00	005
Totals:			52.00	35.00	10.00		25.00	17.00	NET: 25.00

PATIENT: LOTT, NOAH   **ACCOUNT#:** LOTT556633-01
                                        HICN: 5758594631

Service Date	POS	CPT	Billed	Allowed	Copay/Coins	ASG	Paid	Adjustment	Reason Code(s)
0407YYYY	11	99213	60.00	0.00	0.00	Y	0.00	0.00	002, 003
Totals:			60.00	0.00	0.00		0.00	0.00	NET: 0.00

PATIENT: PAYNE, OPHELIA   **ACCOUNT#:** PAYNE223344-01
                                        HICN: 4263355970

Service Date	POS	CPT	Billed	Allowed	Copay/Coins	ASG	Paid	Adjustment	Reason Code(s)
0429YYYY	11	74270	118.00	0.00	0.00	Y	0.00	0.00	005
Totals:			118.00	0.00	0.00		0.00	0.00	NET: 0.00

LEGEND

ASG	Accept assignment
	Y = Provider accepts assignment
	N = Provider does not accept assignment
Copay/Coins	Copayment or coinsurance amount paid by patient
CPT	Current Procedural Terminology (CPT code number)
POS	Place of Service
	11 = Provider's office

Reason Codes

001 Patient receives discount—care received from in-network provider
002 Denied—invalid HICN number
003 Denied—termination of coverage
004 Denied—procedure or service not covered
005 Denied—service not medically necessary
006 Covered service—no charge

FIGURE 4-13 Remittance advice.

ERIN A. HELPER M.D.
101 MEDIC DRIVE, ANYWHERE NY 12345
(800) 555-1234 (OFFICE)   (800) 555-4321 (FAX)

May 5, YYYY

Name of Patient: **Mary Jane Shumway**
HICN: **987456321**

To Whom It May Concern:

Per our review of the remittance advice dated **May 1, YYYY**, please accept this letter as an appeal of the **BlueCross BlueShield** decision to deny payment for services provided on **April 18, YYYY** due to reason code **005 (service not medically necessary)**.

Attached for your review is the **provider's letter of medical necessity, which includes a description of services rendered and reasons for services**. **Also attached is a copy of the patient's record for services provided on April 18, YYYY**. Please review the attached information and reprocess the outstanding claim immediately.

If you have any questions, please contact me at (800) 555-1234. Thank you for your prompt attention to this matter.

Sincerely,

Sandy Schilling

Sandy Schilling, CPC
Medical Billing Specialist

FIGURE 4-14 Sample appeal letter to third-party payer.

ERIN A. HELPER M.D.
101 MEDIC DRIVE, ANYWHERE NY 12345
(800) 555-1234 (OFFICE)   (800) 555-4321 (FAX)

May 5, YYYY

Jane Samson
5 Main St
Somewhere NY 12367

Dear Ms. Samson,

The CMS-1500 insurance claim that our office submitted on your behalf to **BlueCross BlueShield** for services provided during your visit on **April 1, YYYY** was denied and returned due to an **invalid insurance ID number**, which means the insurance company will not send reimbursement to our office.

Please call our office to provide a **valid insurance ID number**. Should the ID number you provide match that which was submitted on the CMS-1500 insurance claim, **BlueCross BlueShield** will deny a resubmitted claim. Thus, per the advance beneficiary notice that you signed prior to our providing services to you on **April 15, YYYY**, you will receive an invoice in the amount of **$150.00** that must be paid promptly.

If you have any questions, please contact me at (800) 555-1234. Thank you for your prompt attention to this matter.

Sincerely,

Sandy Schilling

Sandy Schilling, CPC
Medical Billing Specialist

FIGURE 4-15 Sample collection letter to patient.

ASSIGNMENT 4.6 – CALCULATING PATIENT COINSURANCE, DEDUCTIBLE, AND PROVIDER REIMBURSEMENT AMOUNTS

Objectives

At the conclusion of this assignment, the student should be able to:

1. Define coinsurance and deductible terms.

2. Calculate coinsurance, deductible, and provider reimbursement amounts.

Overview

Coinsurance is the percentage the patient pays for covered services after the deductible has been met and the copayment has been paid. For example, with an 80/20 plan, the insurance company pays 80 percent and the patient pays 20 percent. A *copayment* (or *copay*) is the fixed amount the patient pays each time health care services are provided. A *deductible* is the total amount of covered medical expenses a policyholder must pay each year out of pocket before the insurance company is obligated to pay any benefits. The *provider reimbursement amount* includes applicable coinsurance, copayment, and deductible amounts paid by the patient plus reimbursement amounts paid by third-party payers.

Instructions

Calculate patient coinsurance, deductible, and physician reimbursement amounts.

1. On February 23, Anita Hanke was referred to Dr. Graff by the primary physician Dr. Mayfield for abdominal pain. Dr. Graff performed an ultrasound. The patient's third-party payer determined the reasonable charge for the procedure to be $260.
   a. The patient must pay _____, which is the 20 percent coinsurance due at the time of the office visit.
   b. The physician will receive a check in the amount of _____, which is the 80 percent that will be reimbursed by the insurance company.

2. Iona Ford was referred to the hospital for lab work ordered by the primary physician. The insurance determined the reasonable charge to be $425.
   a. The patient will be billed _____, which is the 20 percent coinsurance.
   b. The physician will receive a check in the amount of _____, which is the 80 percent that will be reimbursed by the insurance company.

3. Rita Booke is a new patient at Alfred Physical Therapy. The third-party payer determined the reasonable charge to be $100 after the annual deductible of $250 has been met. Rita has only paid $100 toward the deductible this year. The patient is responsible for paying 20 percent for the coinsurance. The physician will receive 80 percent for accepting assignment. Rita will need to pay _____ at today's visit.

4. The patient underwent surgery on December 31, and the third-party payer determined the reasonable charge to be $1,000. The patient paid the 20 percent coinsurance at the time of the surgery. The physician received a check for $1,000 from the payer.
   a. The overpayment was _____.
   b. The _____ will reimburse the payer for that overpayment.

5. Sandy Banks underwent surgery on November 1, and the third-party payer determined the reasonable charge to be $700. The patient has a $500 deductible that has already been met. The patient paid the 20 percent coinsurance plus the $500 deductible at the time of the surgery. The physician received a check for $560 from the third-party payer.
   a. The overpayment was _____.
   b. The _____ must reimburse the patient.

ASSIGNMENT 4.7 – CHARGEMASTER MAINTENANCE

Objectives

At the conclusion of this assignment, the student should be able to:

1. Describe the purpose of a chargemaster.
2. Explain the significance of chargemaster maintenance.
3. Review and update a chargemaster to ensure accuracy of use.

Overview

A *chargemaster* (or charge description master [CDM]) is a document that contains a computer-generated master list of devices, procedures, services, and supplies with charges for each. Chargemaster data are entered in the facility's patient accounting system, and charges are automatically posted to the patient's bill (UB-04). The bill is then submitted to the payer to generate payment for inpatient, ancillary, and other services (e.g., emergency department, laboratory, radiology, and so on). The chargemaster allows the facility to accurately and efficiently bill the payer for services rendered, and it usually contains the following:

- Department code (refers to the specific ancillary department where the service is performed)
- Service code (internal identification of specific service rendered)
- Service description (narrative description of the service, procedure, or supply)
- Revenue code (UB-04 revenue code that is assigned to each procedure, service, or product)
- Charge amount (dollar amount facility charges for each procedure, service, or supply)
- Relative value units (RVUs) (numeric value assigned to a procedure; based on difficulty and time consumed)

Chargemaster (sample portion)						
Goodmedicine Hospital, Anywhere US 12345			Radiology Department			Revised 04/05/YYYY
Department Code	Service Code	Service Description	Revenue Code	CPT Code	Charge Amount	Relative Value Units
01-822	8550001	Chest x-ray, single view	0324	71045	74.50	0.70
01-822	8550002	Chest x-ray, two views	0324	71046	82.50	0.95
01-822	8550025	Computed tomography, lumbar spine; with contrast material	0350	72132	899.0	8.73
01-822	8550026	Computed tomography, lumbar spine; without contrast material followed by contrast material(s) and further sections	0350	72133	999.50	11.10

Chargemaster maintenance is the process of updating and revising key elements of the chargemaster (or charge description master [CDM]) to ensure accurate reimbursement. Because a chargemaster allows a health care facility to capture charges as procedures are performed and services are provided, inaccurate and outdated chargemasters can result in claims rejection, fines and penalties (for submitting false information on a claim), and overpayment or underpayment. A **chargemaster team** jointly shares the responsibility of updating and revising the chargemaster to ensure its accuracy, and it consists of representatives of a variety of departments, such as coding compliance financial services (e.g., billing department), health information management, information services, other departments (e.g., laboratory, pharmacy, radiology, and so on), and physicians. Chargemaster maintenance requires expertise in billing regulations, clinical procedures, coding guidelines, and patient record documentation. While the entire chargemaster is reviewed periodically (e.g., annually to incorporate coding updates), the chargemaster team could be gathered any time a new procedure or service is offered by the facility so that appropriate data can be added to the chargemaster.

Instructions

Complete each blank chargemaster change request form in response to the following case scenario.

CASE STUDY: Upon review of the radiology department's chargemaster, Tina Boyd, Radiology Department Manager, noticed that the charge amount for service code 8550001 should be changed to $124.50 and that new service code 8550027 is needed for service description *computed tomography, abdomen; without contrast material*, revenue code 0350, CPT code 74150, charge amount $1450.00, and relative value units 13.05. Tina completed two chargemaster change request forms and submitted them to the chargemaster for consideration.

Chargemaster Change Request #1					Goodmedicine Hospital, Anywhere US 12345		
Date of Request:							
Name of Department:							
Department Code:							
Submitted By:							
Reason for Request:	☐ Addition		☐ Deletion		☐ Revision		☐ Other: _____
Justification for Request:							
		Enter requested changes below					
Department Code	Service Code	Service Description	Revenue Code	CPT Code	Charge Amount		Relative Value Units

Chargemaster Change Request #2					Goodmedicine Hospital, Anywhere US 12345		
Date of Request:							
Name of Department:							
Department Code:							
Submitted By:							
Reason for Request:	☐ Addition		☐ Deletion		☐ Revision		☐ Other: _____
Justification for Request:							
		Enter requested changes below					
Department Code	Service Code	Service Description	Revenue Code	CPT Code	Charge Amount		Relative Value Units

ASSIGNMENT 4.8 – MONITORING THE REVENUE CYCLE

Objectives

At the conclusion of this assignment, the student should be able to:

1. Explain the significance of the revenue cycle management process.

2. Assess the revenue cycle using established metrics.

Overview

Revenue cycle management is the process by which health care facilities and providers ensure their financial viability by increasing revenue, improving cash flow, and enhancing the patient's experience. *Revenue cycle monitoring* involves assessing the revenue cycle to ensure financial viability stability using the following **metrics**, which are standards of measurement:

- *Cash flow*, which is the total amount of money transferred into and out of a business; measure of liquidity, which is the amount of capital available for investment and expenditures.

- *Days in accounts receivable (A/R)*, which is the number of days outstanding money is owed the organization and a measure of how long it usually takes for a service/procedure to be paid by all financially responsible parties, such as third-party payers, government health programs, and patients. The formula for calculating *Days in A/R* = [Receivables − (Credit balance)] ÷ [Gross charges ÷ 365 days].

- *Percentage of accounts receivable older than 30, 60, 90, and 120 days*, which is a measure of the organization's ability to get procedures/services paid in a timely manner.

- *Net collection rate*, which is the percentage of allowed reimbursement received; it is a measure of the organization's effectiveness in collecting reimbursement. The formula for calculating the *Net Collection Rate* = [(Payments − Refunds) ÷ (Charges − Write-offs)] × 100. Net collection rates should be more than 90 percent.

- *Denial rate*, which is the percentage of claims denied by payers and a measure of the organization's effectiveness in submitting *clean claims* (claims paid in full upon initial submission). The formula for calculating the *Denial Rate* = (Total dollar amount of denied claims ÷ Total dollar amount of claims submitted) × 100. Denial rates should be less than 5 percent.

Revenue cycle auditing is an assessment process that is conducted as a follow-up to revenue cycle monitoring so that areas of poor performance can be identified and corrected. Auditing processes include:

- *Compliance monitoring*, which is monitoring of the level of compliance with established managed care contracts, provider performance per managed care contractual requirement, and compliance risk.

- *Denials management*, which involves the analysis of claims denials to prevent future denials. As a result, rejected claims are resubmitted with appropriate documentation.

- *Tracking resubmitted claims and appeals for denied claims*, which involves tracking resubmitted and appealed claims to ensure payment by payers.

- *Posting lost charges and late charges*, which is conducted after late claims are submitted and reimbursement is received.

Instructions

Review each revenue cycle monitoring case study, apply the formula to calculate each metric, and determine which revenue cycle auditing assessment processes should be conducted.

1. *Cash flow.* The office manager reconciled the medical practice's financial accounts and determined that last year, $1,495,000 of third-party payer and patient self-pay reimbursements was deposited. Expenditures for last year totaled $1,095,000.
   a. The *cash flow* is _____.
   b. What is the significance of the calculated *cash flow*, which resulted in *liquidity* for the medical practice?
   _____
   _____

2. *Days in accounts receivable.* Last year, the medical practice's gross charges for procedures/services totaled $1,189,000. The current accounts receivables (A/R) is $495,000, and the credit balance (from the previous year) is $49,500.
   a. The *days in A/R* is _____.
   b. According to national standards, *days in A/R* should average 35 or less; therefore, this medical practice should _____
   _____.

3. *Percentage of accounts receivable older than 30, 60, 90, and 120 days.* The medical center's A/R > 120 (3.5%) compares favorably to the national average (12% or less). However, the A/R 0–30 (46.5%) and A/R 31–60 (38.5%) total 85% (46.5% + 38.5%), which is on the high end of the national average (60–85%). To reduce the A/R percentages, the medical office conducts *revenue cycle auditing*, which reveals that more than half of initial claims are submitted to third-party payers 60 days after the patient's encounter. What corrective measures could the medical office implement to resolve this problem? _____
   _____
   _____

Anywhere Medical Center					
Annual Report of Percentage of Accounts Receivable Older than 30, 60, 90, and 120 Days					
0–30	31–60	61–90	91–120	> 120	Total A/R
$66,500	$55,000	$9,000	$7,500	$5,000	$143,000
46.5%	38.5%	6.3%	5.2%	3.5%	100%
According to national standards, A/R > 120 should be less than 12%. This organization's A/R > 120 is 3.5%, which is excellent.					

4. *Net collection rate.* The hospital's payments received is $7,945,000. Refunds paid to payers and patients total $300,000. Total charges for inpatient and outpatient services are $10,500,000, and total write-offs are $1,525,000.
   a. The net *collection rate* is _____,
   b. What is the significance of the calculated *net collection rate for* the hospital? _____
   _____

5. *Denial rate.* The health care organization's total dollar amount of denied claims for the month of January was $33,000, and the total dollar amount of claims submitted is $765,000.
   a. The *denial rate* is _____,
   b. What is the significance of the calculated *denial rate* for this organization? _____
   _____

ASSIGNMENT 4.9 – MULTIPLE CHOICE REVIEW

1. Which is an example of supporting documentation?
   a. completed CMS-1500 claim
   b. explanation of benefits
   c. operative report
   d. remittance advice

2. Supporting documentation that is attached to the CMS-1500 is either copied from the patient's chart or developed (e.g., letter delineating unlisted service provided). The latter is referred to (in the CPT coding manual) as a(n)
   a. attachment.
   b. detailed report.
   c. enclosed note.
   d. special report.

3. Which claim status is assigned by the payer to allow the provider to correct errors or omissions on the claim and resubmit for payment consideration?
   a. clean
   b. denied
   c. pending
   d. voided

4. The patient underwent office surgery on October 10, and the third-party payer determined the reasonable charge to be $1,000. The patient paid the 20 percent coinsurance at the time of the office surgery. The physician and patient each received a check for $500, and the patient signed the check over to the physician. The overpayment was _____, and the _____ must reimburse the insurance company. (Remember! Coinsurance is the percentage of costs a patient shares with the health plan.)
   a. $200, patient
   b. $200, physician
   c. $500, patient
   d. $500, physician

5. The intent of mandating the Health Insurance Portability and Accountability Act (HIPAA) national standards for electronic transactions was to
   a. decrease the costs associated with Medicare and Medicaid programs.
   b. improve the continuity and the quality of care provided to patients.
   c. improve the efficiency and effectiveness of the health care system.
   d. increase the number of individuals enrolled in government health plans.

6. Electronic claims are
   a. always submitted by health insurance professionals who are certified by the AAPC.
   b. checked for accuracy by billing software programs or a health care clearinghouse.
   c. not complicated by such requirements as claims attachments or other documents.
   d. submitted directly to payers for the processing of reimbursement to patients.

7. Which CPT modifier will require supporting documentation for payment?
   a. -22 (unusual procedural services)
   b. -26 (professional component)
   c. -50 (bilateral procedure)
   d. -57 (decision for surgery)

8. Patients can be billed for
   a. extended procedures.
   b. noncovered procedures.
   c. reduced services.
   d. unauthorized services.

9. If the claim was denied because the service is not covered by the payer, the claim is
   a. appealed by the provider's office.
   b. filed with a clearinghouse instead.
   c. not paid by the third-party payer.
   d. submitted to a third-party administrator.

10. The person in whose name the insurance policy is issued is the
    a. patient.
    b. plan.
    c. policyholder.
    d. provider.

11. The cycle of an insurance claim is initiated when the
    a. health insurance specialist completes the CMS-1500 claim.
    b. patient pays the balance due after the provider has been reimbursed.
    c. payer sends the provider an electronic remittance advice.
    d. provider sends supporting documentation for unusual services.

12. Which is considered the financial source document?
    a. history and physical exam
    b. patient registration
    c. statement of charges
    d. superbill or encounter form

13. Another name for the patient account record is the patient
    a. day sheet.
    b. encounter form.
    c. explanation of benefits.
    d. ledger.

14. A chronological summary of all transactions posted to individual patient accounts on a specific day is recorded on a(n)
    a. day sheet.
    b. encounter form.
    c. patient ledger.
    d. remittance advice.

15. What special handling is required if a patient requests a copy of the remittance advice (remit) that contains information about multiple patients?
    a. Patients are not permitted to view or receive copies of the remittance advice.
    b. Identifying information about all patients except the requesting patient is removed.
    c. The patient must sign a confidentiality statement prior to receiving a copy of the remit.
    d. The provider must document the request for a copy of the remit in the patient's record.

16. Which federal law protects consumers against harassing or threatening phone calls from collectors?
    a. Fair Credit and Charge Card Disclosure Act
    b. Fair Credit Billing Act
    c. Fair Credit Reporting Act
    d. Fair Debt Collection Practices Act

17. To determine whether a claim is delinquent, review the status of all outstanding claims from each payer and payments due from patients by generating an accounts receivable _____ report.
    a. aging
    b. collection
    c. receivables
    d. past-due

18. The provision in group health insurance policies that specifies in what sequence coverage will be provided when more than one policy covers the claim is
    a. accepting assignment.
    b. assignment of benefits.
    c. claims adjudication.
    d. coordination of benefits.

19. A clearinghouse that coordinates with other entities to provide additional services during the processing of claims is a
    a. claims processor.
    b. network commission.
    c. third-party administrator.
    d. value-added network.

20. To determine if a patient is receiving concurrent care for the same condition by more than one provider, the payer will check the claim against the
    a. common data file.
    b. electronic flat file.
    c. insurance claims registry.
    d. patient's billing history.

21. Diagnosis and procedure codes that are entered incorrectly during billing and claims processing result in _____ by the third-party payer.
    a. appeals processing
    b. balancing patient payments
    c. collections notices sent
    d. denied and rejected claims

22. CMS-1500 or UB-04 claims that are resubmitted to third-party payers usually result in payment delays and claims denials. The resubmission of claims is a result of
    a. analyzing self-pay balances billed to patients, including deductibles, copayments, and noncovered charges.
    b. entering late or lost charges or making corrections to previously processed CMS-1500 or UB-04 claims.
    c. posting payment from third-party payers that was a result of rejected claims due to incorrect data submitted.
    d. receiving third-party payer reimbursement in an electronic format and reconciling payments with claims.

23. The process of posting electronic remittances based on third-party payer reimbursement involves
    a. analyzing electronic reimbursement received from payers to identify variations in expected payments.
    b. capturing charge data by using an automated system that links to the hospital's chargemaster.
    c. posting payment from third-party payers that was a result of rejected claims due to incorrect data submitted.
    d. receiving reimbursement from third-party payers in an electronic format and submitted collections notices.

24. The analysis of reimbursement received from third-party payers identifies variations in expected payments or contracted rates and may result in submission of _____ to third-party payers.
    a. appeal letters
    b. collection notices
    c. initial claims
    d. self-payments

25. Deductibles, copayments, and noncovered charges are considered
    a. amounts that a provider must waive.
    b. disbursements from insurance companies.
    c. payments to be processed by payers.
    d. self-pay balances billed to the patient.

Legal Aspects of Health Insurance and Reimbursement

INTRODUCTION

This chapter emphasizes the importance of maintaining the confidentiality of protected health information (or patient information). In addition, students will review case studies to determine if health care fraud or abuse was present.

ASSIGNMENT 5.1 – HIPAA: STUDENT CONFIDENTIALITY STATEMENT

Objectives

At the conclusion of this assignment, the student should be able to:

1. Explain the importance of maintaining the confidentiality of patient information.
2. State the significance of signing a student confidentiality statement prior to beginning a professional practice experience (or internship).

Overview

Health insurance specialist students who complete professional practice experiences (or internships) as part of their course of study will have access to protected health information (PHI) at the provider's office. It is essential that students maintain the confidentiality of PHI at all times. This assignment allows the student to review and sign a student confidentiality statement.

Instructions

1. Carefully review the student confidentiality statement in Figure 5-1.
2. Sign and date the statement, and have a witness sign and date the form.
3. Submit the completed form to your instructor.

ASSIGNMENT 5.2 – HIPAA: PREVENTING HEALTH CARE FRAUD AND ABUSE

Objectives

At the conclusion of this assignment, the student should be able to:

1. Define health care fraud and abuse.
2. Differentiate between forms of health care fraud and abuse.

PROTECTED HEALTH INFORMATION (PHI) CONFIDENTIALITY STATEMENT

In consideration of my status as a student at _____ and/or association with health care facilities and provider offices that offer internship opportunities, I agree that I will not at any time access or use protected health information, or reveal or disclose to any persons within or outside the health care facility or provider office, any protected health information except as may be required in the course of my duties and responsibilities and in accordance with applicable legislation, and corporate and departmental policies governing proper release of information.

I understand that my obligations outlined above will continue after my association with the school and/or facility ends. I further understand that my obligations concerning the protection of the confidentiality of health information relate to all protected health information whether I acquired the information through my association with the school and/or facility.

I also understand that unauthorized use or disclosure of such information will result in a disciplinary action up to and including involuntary expulsion from the school, the imposition of fines pursuant to relevant state and federal legislation, and a report to my professional regulatory body.

_____   _____
Date Signed   Signature of Student

                                     _____
                                     Student's Printed Name

_____   _____
Date Signed   Signature of Witness

Permission to reuse granted by Alfred State College.

FIGURE 5-1 Student confidentiality statement.

Overview

The Health Insurance Portability and Accountability Act (HIPAA) defines *fraud* as "an intentional deception or misrepresentation that someone makes, knowing it is false, that could result in an unauthorized payment." *Abuse* "involves actions that are inconsistent with accepted, sound medical, business or fiscal practices."

Instructions

Review Chapter 5 content in your textbook to familiarize yourself with examples of fraud and abuse. Then analyze each of the following situations to indicate which is fraud (F) or abuse (A).

_____ 1. An insurance company did not follow applicable rules when setting rates it charged for health care benefits under its Federal Employees Health Benefits Program (FEHBP) contracts, and failed to give the health care program the same discounted rates it gave similarly situated commercial customers. It also failed to coordinate FEHBP benefits with

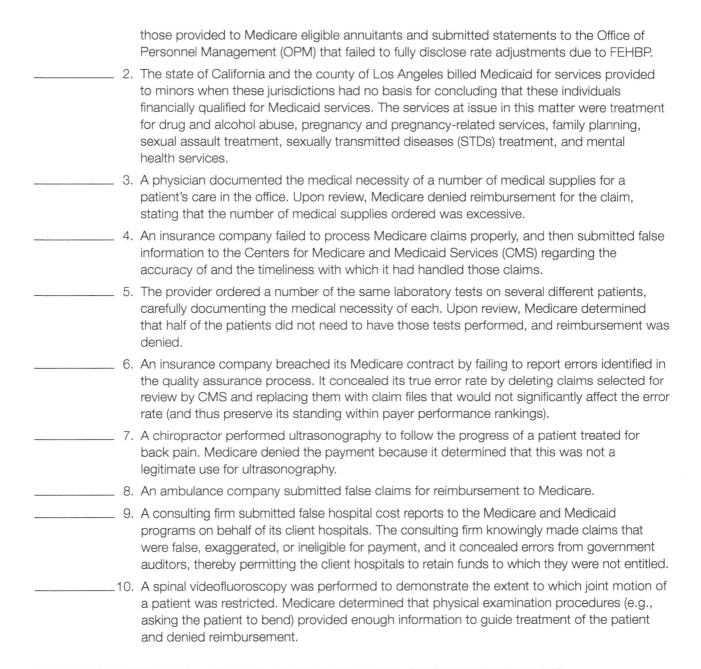

those provided to Medicare eligible annuitants and submitted statements to the Office of Personnel Management (OPM) that failed to fully disclose rate adjustments due to FEHBP.

_____ 2. The state of California and the county of Los Angeles billed Medicaid for services provided to minors when these jurisdictions had no basis for concluding that these individuals financially qualified for Medicaid services. The services at issue in this matter were treatment for drug and alcohol abuse, pregnancy and pregnancy-related services, family planning, sexual assault treatment, sexually transmitted diseases (STDs) treatment, and mental health services.

_____ 3. A physician documented the medical necessity of a number of medical supplies for a patient's care in the office. Upon review, Medicare denied reimbursement for the claim, stating that the number of medical supplies ordered was excessive.

_____ 4. An insurance company failed to process Medicare claims properly, and then submitted false information to the Centers for Medicare and Medicaid Services (CMS) regarding the accuracy of and the timeliness with which it had handled those claims.

_____ 5. The provider ordered a number of the same laboratory tests on several different patients, carefully documenting the medical necessity of each. Upon review, Medicare determined that half of the patients did not need to have those tests performed, and reimbursement was denied.

_____ 6. An insurance company breached its Medicare contract by failing to report errors identified in the quality assurance process. It concealed its true error rate by deleting claims selected for review by CMS and replacing them with claim files that would not significantly affect the error rate (and thus preserve its standing within payer performance rankings).

_____ 7. A chiropractor performed ultrasonography to follow the progress of a patient treated for back pain. Medicare denied the payment because it determined that this was not a legitimate use for ultrasonography.

_____ 8. An ambulance company submitted false claims for reimbursement to Medicare.

_____ 9. A consulting firm submitted false hospital cost reports to the Medicare and Medicaid programs on behalf of its client hospitals. The consulting firm knowingly made claims that were false, exaggerated, or ineligible for payment, and it concealed errors from government auditors, thereby permitting the client hospitals to retain funds to which they were not entitled.

_____ 10. A spinal videofluoroscopy was performed to demonstrate the extent to which joint motion of a patient was restricted. Medicare determined that physical examination procedures (e.g., asking the patient to bend) provided enough information to guide treatment of the patient and denied reimbursement.

ASSIGNMENT 5.3 – HIPAA: PRIVACY AND SECURITY RULES

Objectives

At the conclusion of this assignment, the student should be able to:

1. Explain the HIPAA privacy and security rules.

2. Differentiate between privacy and security provisions of HIPAA.

Overview

The *privacy rule* establishes standards for how protected health information should be controlled, and it establishes the uses (e.g., continuity of care) and disclosures (e.g., third-party reimbursement) authorized or required, as well as the rights patients have with respect to their health information (e.g., patient access). The *security rule* defines administrative, physical, and technical safeguards to protect the availability, confidentiality, and integrity of electronic PHI. HIPAA provisions require covered entities to implement basic safeguards to protect electronic PHI from unauthorized access, alteration, deletion, and transmission.

Instructions

Analyze each of the statements below to determine whether each is associated with the HIPAA privacy rule (P) or the security rule (S).

_____ 1. Defines authorized users of patient information to control access.

_____ 2. Implements a tracking procedure to sign out records to authorized personnel.

_____ 3. Establishes fines and penalties for misuse of protected health information.

_____ 4. Limits record storage access to authorized users.

_____ 5. Gives patients greater access to their own medical records and more control over how their personal health information is used.

_____ 6. Creates national standards to protect individuals' medical records and other personal health information.

_____ 7. Requires that record storage areas be locked at all times.

_____ 8. Addresses obligations that physicians, hospitals, and other health care providers have to obtain a patient's written consent and an authorization before using or disclosing PHI to carry out treatment, payment, or health care operations (TPO).

_____ 9. Exempts psychotherapy notes from a patient's right to access their own records.

_____10. Requires the original medical record to remain in the facility at all times.

ASSIGNMENT 5.4 – HIPAA: COVERED ENTITIES

Objectives

At the conclusion of this assignment, the student should be able to:

1. Define *covered entities* associated with HIPAA legislation.
2. Discuss the function of the Office for Civil Rights (OCR).

Overview

HIPAA has various components known as titles; one of these governs the privacy of protected health information (PHI). The Department of Health and Human Services provides consumers with information via the Internet on privacy rights and laws. This information is provided in the form of fact sheets and publications.

Instructions

Go to **www.hhs.gov,** click on the Laws & Regulations link, click on the HIPAA Privacy Rule link, and click on each link below The HIPAA Privacy Rule heading to locate answers to the following questions.

1. What three types of covered entities are specified in the HIPAA privacy rule? _____

_____

2. How many regions does the OCR divide the United States into to assign regional offices?

_____

3. In what region are the states of Maryland and Virginia? _____

_____

4. In what city is the regional office of the OCR located for region VI? _____

_____

5. In addition to using the website, what other method(s) can an individual use to find out more information about privacy rights? _____

 NOTE:

Navigate the insurance information website to research information needed for your summary. This will help you learn how to locate information using the Internet as a research tool and using websites, which often requires using tool bars and pull-down menus.

ASSIGNMENT 5.5 – HIPAA: TELEPHONE CALLS REQUESTING RELEASE OF PATIENT INFORMATION

Objectives

At the conclusion of this assignment, the student should be able to:

1. Explain the protocol for responding to telephone requests for release of patient information.

2. Appropriately respond to verbal requests for patient information.

Overview

Health care professionals receive numerous telephone requests for patient information. This assignment will familiarize students with the appropriate response to a verbal request for patient information.

Instructions

1. Carefully read the telephone simulations in Figure 5-2.

2. Respond to the following questions about each telephone simulation.

Simulation #1

1. How would you rate the RHIT's greeting?

_____

2. Did the RHIT respond appropriately to the patient's request?

_____

3. Do you agree with the RHIT's reason for not releasing records immediately to the new physician? Why or why not?

_____

4. What is the significance of the RHIT using the patient's name during the conversation?

_____

5. What would you have said differently from what was said in the scenario?

_____

SIMULATION #1: The caller is a patient who requests that the health records from a recent hospitalization be forwarded to a new physician in Billings, Montana. The patient, Janice McDonald, has relocated to a suburb of Billings, Montana.

The telephone in the health information department rings three times and the registered health information technician (RHIT) answers the phone.

RHIT [professional tone of voice]: "Good afternoon (morning). Health Information Department. May I help you?"

JANICE [questioning tone of voice]: "Hi! Ummm, this is Janice McDonald. I've moved to Montana and want to get my latest inpatient records sent to my new doctor. Can you do that?"

RHIT [friendly tone of voice]: "Sure, Ms. McDonald. I'll just need to send you a release of information authorization form. You'll need to complete it, sign it, and date it. Then, return it in the envelope provided."

JANICE [confused tone of voice]: "Oh. I'm seeing the new doctor next week. Do you think that you can just send the records to the doctor?"

RHIT [polite tone of voice]: "I'm sorry, Ms. McDonald. Your health records are confidential and we cannot release copies without your written authorization."

JANICE [resigned tone of voice]: "Oh, okay. I guess that will have to do."

RHIT [reassuring tone of voice]: "Ms. McDonald, the department is really just trying to maintain privacy of your records. If you like, I can fax the authorization form to you. Then, you could overnight express it to the department. We can't accept a fax of the completed form because we need your original signature. That's hospital policy."

JANICE [pleased tone of voice]: "Oh! That would be great. I'll call my new doctor and get his fax number and give you a call back with it. Okay?"

RHIT [friendly tone of voice]: "That would be just fine, Ms. McDonald."

The conversation is ended. The RHIT hangs up the phone.

FIGURE 5-2 Telephone simulations.

(continues)

FIGURE 5-2 *(continued)*

SIMULATION #2: Joe Turner from the State Farm Insurance Company is an angry insurance agent who calls to inform the physician's office that the company mailed a proper authorization three weeks ago for release of records on a recently discharged patient.

The telephone rings six times before the medical assistant (MA) answers the phone.

MA [quick professional tone of voice]: "Good afternoon (morning). Doctor's office."

TURNER [brusque tone of voice]: "Hello. I'm calling to find out why the records I requested three weeks ago have not been sent to me yet. Oh. This is Joe Turner from State Farm Insurance Company."

MA [courteous tone of voice—recognizes an impatient person]: "Could you tell me the name of the patient, please?"

TURNER [brusque tone of voice]: "Mary Jones. The birth date is 10/02/55. Mary Jones was discharged on September 1 of this year. I need copies of the doctor's notes in order to get the claim paid. Mary Jones has called me several times this past couple of weeks. I guess the office keeps mailing bills, and we are disgusted about this situation!"

MA [courteous tone of voice]: "Mr. Turner, would you like to hold while I check this or could I call you back?"

TURNER [brusque tone of voice]: "No way am I going to let you off the hook. I'll hold!"

MA [courteous tone of voice—but showing signs of wear]: "No problem Mr. Turner. I'll be with you in a couple of minutes."

One minute passes and the MA takes Mr. Turner off hold.

MA [pleasant tone of voice]: "Mr. Turner, I checked our correspondence log and found that copies of Mary Jones's records were forwarded to your attention last week. You should have them."

TURNER [impatient tone of voice]: "Well, I don't! Oh . . . I guess they were placed on my desk while I wasn't looking. Here they are. Sorry about that. Goodbye."

Mr. Turner hangs up.

(continues)

FIGURE 5-2   *(continued)*

SIMULATION #3: Barbara Allen is a new health information technology graduate hired by the medical center's health information management department. This is Barbara's first day on the job.

The telephone rings twice and is answered by the department secretary. The call is forwarded to Barbara Allen, correspondence technician.

BARBARA: "Correspondence Section. May I help you?"

DOCTOR: "Hello, this is Dr. Ahbibe from Breyne's Clinic in Columbia, New Mexico. We have a patient here by the name of Garrick Tanner who was admitted for status epilepticus. We need a past history for this patient and all pertinent documents sent to us immediately. The seizure activity is progressing in frequency and the patient is unable to provide information about drug allergies."

BARBARA: "Would you hold while I pull the patient's record?"

DOCTOR: "Certainly."

Several minutes pass as Barbara searches by checking the Master Patient Index (MPI) and retrieving the record. Upon inspection of the record, Barbara realizes that this is a "sealed file" because of a pending lawsuit. Barbara also notes that Garrick Tanner has an extensive history of cocaine abuse that has been the main cause of his seizures. Barbara closes the record, confused as to how this situation should be handled.

SIMULATION #4: Susie Sits is answering the telephone for the correspondence technician who is on break. Susie usually works in the discharge analysis section of the health information department.

The telephone rings twice, and Susie picks up.

SUSIE: "Good morning, Health Information Management Department. Susie Sits speaking."

DOCTOR: "This is Dr. Jones's office calling from Phoenix, Arizona. Could you please give me the final diagnosis for Alfred Peoples, who was recently discharged from your facility?"

SUSIE: "Well, just hold a minute and I will get everything you need."

The doctor is on hold for three minutes while Susie pulls the health record.

SUSIE: "Hello, I think I have everything you need. Mr. Peoples was a patient in our alcohol rehab unit last month."

Simulation #2

6. How would you rate the MA's phone response?

_____

7. Did the MA respond appropriately to the request?

_____

8. What would you have said differently from what was said in the scenario?

_____

Simulation #3

9. Critique Barbara's greeting.

_____

10. Determine how you would handle this situation if you were Barbara. What would you have done differently, if anything, from the onset?

_____

11. Given the situation, what would you do next?

_____

Simulation #4

12. What information can be released over the telephone?

_____

13. What information should Susie have requested from the caller?

_____

14. What release of information protocol did Susie violate?

_____

ASSIGNMENT 5.6 – HOSPITAL INPATIENT QUALITY REPORTING PROGRAM

Objectives

At the conclusion of this assignment, the student should be able to:

1. Explain the purpose of the hospital inpatient quality reporting program.
2. State the intent of the Hospital Compare website.
3. Use the Hospital Compare website.

Overview

The *Hospital Inpatient Quality Reporting (Hospital IQR) program* was developed to equip consumers with quality of care information so they can make more informed decisions about health care options. The Hospital IQR program requires hospitals to submit specific quality measures data about health conditions common among Medicare beneficiaries and that typically result in hospitalization. (Eligible hospitals that do not participate in the Hospital IQR program receive an annual market basket update with a 2.0 percentage point reduction.)

The CMS and the Hospital Quality Alliance (HQA) created the Hospital Compare website in cooperation with the HQA. The CMS is an agency of the Department of Health and Human Resources (DHHS), and the HQA is a public-private collaboration established to promote reporting on hospital quality of care. The HQA consists of organizations that represent consumers, hospitals, doctors and nurses, employers, accrediting organizations, and federal agencies.

Hospital Compare displays rates for the following:

- *Process of Care* measures, which indicate whether or not hospitals provide some of the care that is recommended for patients being treated for a heart attack, heart failure, pneumonia, asthma (children only), or patients having surgery. Hospitals submit data from patient records about treatments their patients receive for these conditions.

- *Outcome of Care* measures, which indicate what happened after patients with certain conditions received hospital care. Measures include death rate (whether patients died within 30 days of hospitalization) and readmission rate (whether patients were hospitalized again within 30 days).

- *Use of Medical Imaging,* which provides information about how hospitals use medical imaging tests for outpatients based on the (1) protecting patients' safety, such as keeping patients' exposure to radiation and other risks as low as possible; (2) following up properly when screening tests such as mammograms show a possible problem; and (3) avoiding the risk, stress, and cost of doing imaging tests that patients may not need.

- *Survey of Patients' Hospital Experiences,* which is the Hospital Consumer Assessment of Healthcare Providers and Systems (HCAHPS) national, standardized survey of hospital patients. HCAHPS (pronounced "*H-caps*") was created to publicly report the patient's perspective of hospital care. The survey is administered to a random sample of recently discharged patients and asks questions about important aspects of their hospital experience (e.g., communication with doctors, communication with nurses, responsiveness of hospital staff, pain management, communication about medicines, discharge information, cleanliness of the hospital environment, and quietness of the hospital environment).

- *Medicare Payment and Volume,* which displays selected MS-DRG information for each hospital from a predetermined range of dates (e.g., October 2007 through September 2008). Patients who have similar clinical characteristics and similar costs are assigned to an MS-DRG (Medicare severity diagnosis-related group). The MS-DRG is associated with a fixed payment amount based on the average cost of patients in the group. Patients are assigned to an MS-DRG based on diagnosis, surgical procedures, age, and other information. Medicare uses this information that is provided by hospitals on their bills to decide how much they should be paid.

Instructions

1. Go to the **www.medicare.gov** website, scroll down and click on the "Find care" link.

2. Enter the ZIP Code or City, State of a location (e.g., hometown, city you will move to after graduation, and so on), and click Search.

3. Click to select at least two facilities, and click on the Compare link.

4. Click on at least two of the data tabs (e.g., Overall ratings, Patient survey rating), and carefully review the results displayed to determine whether one hospital's results are significantly better (or worse) than the other.

5. As directed by your instructor, prepare a narrative summary of the results of your findings (e.g., word-processed document, discussion board posting).

The purpose of the narrative summary is to explain the significant differences between the facilities regarding the data tabs selected.

EXAMPLE: Sixty percent of patients who received care at Hospital A reported that they would definitely recommend the hospital, whereas almost 75 percent of patients who received care at Hospital B reported that they would definitely recommend the hospital. Also, indicate areas of concern that should be addressed by the facility. For example, at Hospital A, 50 percent of outpatients with low back pain underwent magnetic resonance imaging (MRI) prior to other recommended treatments such as physical therapy; this indicates that Hospital A may be performing unnecessary MRIs, and a quality management study of outpatient MRIs for low back pain should be performed.

ASSIGNMENT 5.7 – MULTIPLE CHOICE REVIEW

1. A provider was ordered by a judge to bring a patient's medical record to a court hearing. Which document was served on the provider?
   a. deposition
   b. interrogatory
   c. subpoena *duces tecum*
   d. subpoena

2. The type of law passed by legislative bodies is known as _____ law.
   a. common
   b. criminal
   c. regulatory
   d. statutory

3. Which civil case document contains a list of questions that must be answered in writing?
   a. deposition
   b. interrogatory
   c. precedent
   d. regulation

4. Which federal law has regulated the conduct of any contractor submitting claims for payment to the federal government since 1863?
   a. False Claims Act
   b. Federal Claims Collection Act
   c. Privacy Act
   d. Social Security Act

5. The Federal Claims Collection Act requires Medicare administrative contractors to
   a. attempt to recover any reimbursement funds sent as overpayment to providers and beneficiaries.
   b. enforce civil monetary penalties upon those who submit false or fraudulent claims to the government.
   c. protect the privacy of individuals identified in information systems maintained by government hospitals.
   d. provide free or reduced-charge medical services to persons unable to pay, in return for federal funds.

6. The Hospital IQR program equips consumers with _____ information so they can make more informed decisions about health care options.
   a. audit performance
   b. health care cost
   c. medically unlikely edit
   d. quality of care

7. The Physicians at Teaching Hospitals (PATH) legislation was passed to
   a. increase reimbursement amounts paid to teaching hospitals and other types of health care facilities.
   b. increase the number of physicians and other health care providers available to teach medical students.
   c. limit the types of patients that are seen by medical school residents in PATH health care settings.
   d. monitor Medicare rule compliance for payment of Part B services and proper coding and billing practices.

8. Which combats fraud and abuse in health insurance and health care delivery by alerting users to conduct a comprehensive review of a practitioner's, provider's, or supplier's past actions?
   a. Clinical Data Abstracting Center
   b. *Federal Register*
   c. Health Care Integrity and Protection Data Bank
   d. Peer Review Improvement Act

9. One of the provisions of HIPAA Title I designed to improve portability and continuity of health care coverage is
   a. excluding enrollment of employees with a history of poor health.
   b. increasing exclusions for preexisting conditions.
   c. prohibiting a change from group to individual coverage.
   d. providing credit for prior health coverage.

10. Which act protects whistleblowers—individuals who make specified disclosures relating to funds covered by the act?
    a. ARRA
    b. HIPAA
    c. MMA
    d. TEFRA

11. In addition to civil, criminal, and administrative penalties, those who commit health care fraud can also be tried for
    a. breach of contract.   c. mail and wire fraud.
    b. criminal negligence.   d. medical malpractice.

12. The first step a physician practice can take to identify areas of risk in the practice that are vulnerable to fraud and abuse is to
    a. conduct appropriate training and education sessions for employees.
    b. designate a compliance officer to monitor and enforce standards.
    c. enforce disciplinary standards through well-publicized guidelines.
    d. perform periodic audits to internally monitor billing processes.

13. An example of an overpayment is
    a. duplicate processing of a claim.
    b. incorrect application of EOB.
    c. payment based on reasonable charge.
    d. an unprocessed voided claim.

14. Unless the case involves fraud, administrative contractors are prohibited from seeking overpayment recovery when the
    a. amount paid in excess was less than or equal to $100.
    b. office manager sends a letter to request an exception.
    c. overpayment is not reopened within 48 months after payment.
    d. provider did not know the reasonable charge for the service.

15. The CMS is authorized to enter into contracts with entities to perform cost report auditing, medical review, and anti-fraud activities by the _____ program.
    a. CERT   c. Hospital VBR
    b. Error prevention   d. Medicare integrity

16. Which government agency is responsible for investigating a Medicare provider who is suspected of committing fraud?
    a. Centers for Medicare and Medicaid Services
    b. Office of Inspector General
    c. Social Security Administration
    d. U.S. Attorney General

17. The agency that assigns the National Standard Employer Identification Number (EIN) is the
    a. Centers for Medicare and Medicaid Services.
    b. HHS Office of Inspector General.
    c. Internal Revenue Service.
    d. Social Security Administration.

18. PSCs were replaced by the Zone Program Integrity Contractor in
    a. 2009.   c. 2011.
    b. 2010.   d. 2012.

19. Assigning passwords to users who are authorized to access patient records is a form of
    a. confidentiality.   c. privilege.
    b. privacy.   d. security.

20. What special handling is required to release medical information for a patient who is HIV-positive?
    a. A special notation should be made on the standard release of information.
    b. The insurance company must speak with the patient directly about the HIV diagnosis.
    c. The patient should sign an additional authorization statement for release of information.
    d. The provider must not release HIV-related information unless subpoenaed.

ICD-10-CM Coding

INTRODUCTION

This chapter familiarizes students with coding diseases and conditions using ICD-10-CM. Students will code diagnostic statements and case studies by applying ICD-10-CM coding conventions, principles, and rules.

 NOTE:

> Content about ICD-10-PCS, including coding exercises, is available in the online Student Resources. Accompanying answer keys are available in the online Instructor Resources. Sign up or sign in at www.cengage.com to search for and access this product and its online resources.

ASSIGNMENT 6.1 – INTERPRETING GENERAL EQUIVALENCE MAPPING

Objectives

At the conclusion of this assignment, the student should be able to:

1. Explain the purpose of general equivalence mappings.
2. Locate ICD-10-CM codes for their ICD-9-CM equivalents using general equivalence mappings.

Overview

NCHS and CMS annually publish *general equivalence mappings (GEMs)*, which are translation dictionaries or crosswalks of codes that can be used to roughly identify ICD-10-CM (and ICD-10-PCS) codes for their ICD-9-CM equivalent codes (and vice versa). GEMs facilitate the location of corresponding diagnosis (and procedure) codes between the two code sets.

Instructions

1. Reenter each ICD-9-CM code from column 1 (of the following table) *without a decimal* in column 2.
2. Refer to Table 6-1 to locate each ICD-9-CM diagnosis code (without decimals), and enter the GEM ICD-10-CM diagnosis code (without decimals) in column 3 (of the following table).
3. Then, enter the equivalent ICD-10-CM code *with* decimals in column 4 (of the following table).

	Column 1 ICD-9-CM Code	Column 2 GEM ICD-9-CM Code	Column 3 GEM ICD-10-CM Diagnosis Code	Column 4 ICD-10-CM Diagnosis Code
1.	003.24			
2.	001.9			
3.	002.3			
4.	001.0			
5.	003.22			

TABLE 6-1 Portion of GEM for ICD-9-CM to ICD-10-CM Diagnoses Codes

General Equivalence Mapping for Diagnoses	
ICD-9-CM Diagnosis Code	ICD-10-CM Diagnosis Code
0010	A000
0019	A009
0021	A011
0023	A013
0030	A20
00320	A0220
00322	A0222
00324	A0224
0010	A000
0019	A009

ASSIGNMENT 6.2 – OVERVIEW OF ICD-10-CM: COMPARING ICD-10-CM TO ICD-9-CM

Objectives

At the conclusion of this assignment, the student should be able to:

1. Explain how ICD-10-CM was expanded (as compared with ICD-9-CM).
2. Locate ICD-9-CM and ICD-10-CM codes to demonstrate greater specificity in ICD-10-CM.

Overview

ICD-10-CM far exceeds ICD-9-CM in the number of codes provided, having been expanded to (1) include health-related conditions, (2) provide much greater specificity at the sixth digit level, and (3) add a seventh digit extension (for some codes). Assigning the sixth and seventh characters when available for ICD-10-CM codes is mandatory because they report information documented in the patient record.

Instructions

Refer to Table 6-2, and enter the ICD-9-CM and ICD-10-CM code for each condition stated below. *Initial encounter* applies to each condition for ICD-10-CM coding purposes. Be prepared to explain the results.

TABLE 6-2 Comparing ICD-9-CM and ICD-10-CM Codes

ICD-9-CM Tabular List of Diseases	ICD-10-CM Tabular List of Diseases and Injuries

996.1 Mechanical complication of other vascular device, implant, or graft
 	
Mechanical complications involving:
    aortic (bifurcation) graft (replacement)
    arteriovenous:
        dialysis catheter ⎫
        fistula   ⎬ surgically created
        shunt   ⎭
    balloon (counterpulsation) device, intra-aortic
    carotid artery bypass graft
    femoral-popliteal bypass graft
    umbrella device, vena cava
 	
EXCLUDES   atherosclerosis of biological graft (440.30-440.32)
 	
        embolism (occlusion NOS) (thrombus) of (biological) (synthetic) graft (996.74)
 	
    peritoneal dialysis catheter (996.56)
	T82.3 Mechanical complication of other vascular grafts
	
	The appropriate 7th character is to be added to each code for category T82.
	
	    A initial encounter
	    D subsequent encounter
	    S sequel
	
	T82.31 Breakdown (mechanical) of other vascular grafts
	
	    T82.310 Breakdown (mechanical) of aortic (bifurcation) graft (replacement)
	
	    T82.311 Breakdown (mechanical) of carotid arterial graft (bypass)
	
	    T82.312 Breakdown (mechanical) of femoral arterial graft (bypass)
	
	    T82.318 Breakdown (mechanical) of other vascular grafts
	
	    T82.319 Breakdown (mechanical) of unspecified vascular grafts

ICD-9-CM Code   ICD-10-CM Code

_____   _____ 1. Mechanical breakdown of aortic graft (replacement)

_____   _____ 2. Mechanical breakdown of carotid arterial graft (bypass)

_____   _____ 3. Mechanical breakdown of femoral arterial graft (bypass)

_____   _____ 4. Mechanical breakdown of other vascular grafts

_____   _____ 5. Mechanical breakdown of unspecified vascular grafts

ASSIGNMENT 6.3 – ICD-10-CM CODING CONVENTIONS

Objectives

At the conclusion of this assignment, the student should be able to:

1. Interpret ICD-10-CM coding conventions.

2. Assign ICD-10-CM codes after applying coding conventions.

Overview

ICD-10-CM *coding conventions* are general rules that are incorporated into the index and tabular list instructional notes. The conventions include format, abbreviations, punctuation and symbols, includes and excludes notes, inclusion terms, other and unspecified codes, etiology and manifestation rules, and, with, *see,* and *see also*.

Instructions

Assign ICD-10-CM codes after interpreting coding conventions. Verify codes in the ICD-10-CM tabular list.

Format and Structure

_____ 1. Kaposi's sarcoma, left lung

_____ 2. Chronic blood loss anemia

_____ 3. Acute narrow angle glaucoma, right eye

_____ 4. Subarachnoid hematoma (newborn)

_____ 5. Acute cortical necrosis, left kidney

NEC and NOS Abbreviations

_____ 6 Bacterial enteritis

_____ 7. Anemia

_____ 8. Nonsyphilitic neurogenic spondylopathy

_____ 9. Chronic granulomatous hepatitis

_____ 10. Dry eye syndrome of right lacrimal gland

Punctuation

_____ 11. Abasia

_____ 12. Amyloidosis, heart

_____ 13. Detachment of retina with retinal break, right eye

_____ 14. Taboparesis

_____ 15. Thyrotoxic heart disease with thyroid storm

Includes, Excludes1, Excludes2, and Inclusion Terms

_____ 16. Portal vein thrombosis and phlebitis of portal vein

_____ 17. Secondary lymphedema

_____ 18. Acute sore throat due to streptococcus

_____ 19. Acute subglottic laryngitis

_____ 20. Oligodontia

Other, Other Specified, and Unspecified

_____ 21. Polyalgia

_____ 22. Bile duct adhesions

_____ 23. Gout

_____ 24. Hypertrophic tongue

_____ 25. Venofibrosis

And, Due to, With

_____ 26. Abscess of mediastinum

_____ 27. Vitiligo due to pinta

_____ 28. Fever with chills

_____ 29. Furuncle of trunk

_____ 30. Pneumonia due to pulmonary actinomycosis

Cross References: Code Also, *See, See Also, See* Category, *See* Condition

_____ 31. Castleman disease, human herpesvirus 8 infection

_____ 32. Chronic valvulitis

_____ 33. Duplication of teeth

_____ 34. Acute osteitis of jaw

_____ 35. Injury of right thumb, crushing (initial encounter)

_____ 36. Fistula of right external ear canal

_____ 37. Aortic valve aneurysm

_____ 38. Corrosive burn of right hand (initial encounter)

_____ 39. Gastric atrophia

_____ 40. Type C cephalitis

ASSIGNMENT 6.4 – ICD-10-CM INDEX TO DISEASES AND INJURIES

Objectives

At the conclusion of this assignment, the student should be able to:

1. Identify the condition in a diagnostic statement that is used to locate the main term in the ICD-10-CM Index to Diseases and Injuries.

2. Locate main terms in the ICD-10-CM Index to Diseases and Injuries.

3. Use the Neoplasm Table to locate anatomic sites, cellular classifications (malignant, benign, uncertain behavior, unspecified nature), and malignant neoplasm divisions (primary, secondary, carcinoma *in situ*).

4. Use the Table of Drugs and Chemicals to locate medicinal, chemical, and biological substances that result in poisonings and adverse effects.

5. Use the Index of External Causes of Injuries to classify how an injury or health condition occurred, and the intent (e.g., accidental), place where the event occurred, activity of the patient at the time of an event, and person's status (e.g., military).

Instructions

Use the appropriate section of the ICD-10-CM Index to Diseases and Injuries to assign codes to each condition stated below, verifying each code in the ICD-10-CM Tabular List of Diseases and Injuries.

Identifying Main Terms and Assigning Codes

Instructions: Underline the main term in each condition, and use the ICD-10-CM Index to Diseases and Injuries to assign codes. Verify codes in the ICD-10-CM tabular list.

_____ 1. Herpes zoster

_____ 2. Parkinson's disease

_____ 3. Maxillary sinusitis

_____ 4. Pneumonia with influenza

_____ 5. Hiatal hernia

_____ 6. Skene's gland abscess

_____ 7. Skin eruption due to chemical product

_____ 8. Infectional erythema

_____ 9. Polydactyly of fingers

_____ 10. Blindness due to injury, initial encounter

Neoplasm Table

Instructions: Use the ICD-10-CM Neoplasm Table to assign codes. Verify codes in the ICD-10-CM tabular list.

_____ 11. Carcinoma of right palatine tonsil

_____ 12. Metastatic ovarian cancer to the liver

_____ 13. Stomach cancer

_____ 14. Lipoma of muscle, right forearm

_____ 15. Osteosarcoma, left femoral head

_____ 16. Neurofibromatosis

_____ 17. Hodgkin's sarcoma

_____ 18. Chronic lymphocytic leukemia of B-cell type

_____ 19. Intrathoracic reticulosarcoma

_____ 20. Adenocarcinoma of rectum and anus

Table of Drugs and Chemicals

Instructions: Use the ICD-10-CM Table of Drugs and Chemicals to assign codes. Verify codes in the ICD-10-CM tabular list. Add the seventh character for *initial encounter* to each applicable code.

_____ 21. Allergic reaction to Benadryl

_____ 22. Accidental food poisoning from lobster

_____ 23. Accidental poisoning from ingesting toilet deodorizer

_____ 24. Adverse effect of acetaminophen

_____ 25. Suicide attempt, Ambien

_____ 26. Accidental overdose of prednisone

_____ 27. Rash due to therapeutic use of penicillin

_____ 28. Underdosing of Synthroid in patient with enlarged thyroid

_____ 29. Dizziness due to accidental overdose of Valerian tincture

_____ 30. Suicide attempt due to carbon monoxide poisoning

Index of External Causes of Injuries

Instructions: Use the ICD-10-CM Index of External Causes of Injuries to assign codes. Verify codes in the ICD-10-CM tabular list. Add the seventh character for *initial encounter* to each applicable code.

_____ 31. Patient suffered mental cruelty

_____ 32. Snowmobile occupant injured in nontraffic accident

_____ 33. Altitude sickness

_____ 34. Patient participated in a brawl, and blood alcohol level was 85 mg/100 ml

_____ 35. Law enforcement officer injured during administration of capital punishment

_____ 36. Patient's wedding band constricted ring finger, left hand

_____ 37. Patient injured in earthquake

_____ 38. Patient fell out of window and sustained minor injuries

_____ 39. Patient was using nail gun and nailed hand to roof

_____ 40. Malnourished adolescent was living in an abandoned house

ASSIGNMENT 6.5 – ICD-10-CM TABULAR LIST OF DISEASES AND INJURIES

Objectives

At the conclusion of this assignment, the student should be able to:

1. Identify major topic headings in the ICD-10-CM Tabular List of Diseases and Injuries.

2. Explain the organization of 3-character disease categories within an ICD-10-CM chapter.

3. Differentiate among ICD-10-CM categories, subcategories, and codes.

4. Assign valid ICD-10-CM codes to disease statements.

Overview

The ICD-10-CM Tabular List of Diseases and Injuries is a chronological list of codes contained within 22 chapters, which are based on body system or condition. ICD-10-CM codes are organized within _major topic headings_ (printed in bold uppercase letters) that are followed by groups of 3-character disease categories within a chapter. _Categories, subcategories, and codes_ contain a combination of letters and numbers, and all categories contain 3 characters. A 3-character category that has no further subdivision is a valid code. Subcategories contain either 4 or 5 characters. Codes may contain 3, 4, 5, 6, or 7 characters; the final level of subdivision is a code and all codes in the ICD-10-CM tabular list are boldfaced. Codes that have an applicable seventh character are referred to as codes (not subcategories), and codes that have an applicable seventh character are considered invalid without the seventh character.

ICD-10-CM utilizes the character "X" as a fifth character _placeholder_ for certain 6-character codes to allow for future expansion without disturbing the 6-character structure (e.g., T36.0X1A, an initial encounter for accidental poisoning by penicillin). When a placeholder exists, the X must be entered in order for the code to be considered a valid code.

Certain ICD-10-CM categories contain applicable _seventh characters_, which are required for all codes within the category. The seventh character must always be located in the seventh-character data field. If a code that requires a seventh character is not 6 characters in length, the placeholder X is entered to fill in the empty character(s) (e.g., M48.46XS).

Injury, Poisoning, and Certain Other Consequences of External Causes and _External Causes of Morbidity_ are incorporated into ICD-10-CM's Tabular List of Diseases and Injuries as Chapter 19 (S and T codes) and Chapter 20 (V-Y codes), respectively. External cause codes are also reported for environmental events, industrial accidents, injuries inflicted by criminal activity, and so on. While assigning the codes does not directly impact reimbursement to the provider, reporting them can expedite insurance claims processing because the circumstances related to an injury are indicated.

Factors Influencing Health Status and Contact with Health Services are incorporated into ICD-10-CM's Tabular List of Diseases and Injuries as Chapter 21 (Z codes), which is the last chapter of the ICD-10-CM tabular list. The Z codes are reported for patient encounters when a circumstance other than disease or injury is documented (e.g., well child visit).

Instructions

Use the ICD-10-CM Index to Diseases and Injuries to assign codes. Then, verify codes in the ICD-10-CM tabular list.

Multiple Coding and Combination Coding

NOTE:

Add the seventh character for initial encounter to each applicable code.

_____ 1. Parasitic infestation of eyelid due to pediculus capitis

_____ 2. Post-infectious encephalitis due to measles (20 years ago)

_____ 3. Peripheral neuropathy in hyperthyroidism

_____ 4. Cerebral degeneration due to Fabry's disease

_____ 5. Myotonic cataract due to Thomsen's disease

_____ 6. Acute and chronic conjunctivitis, right eye

_____ 7. Xanthelasma of the left upper eyelid due to lipoprotein deficiency

_____ 8. Cholesteatoma, right middle ear and attic

_____ 9. Varicose vein with inflammation, left lower extremity, complicating third-trimester pregnancy

_____ 10. Psoriatic arthropathy and parapsoriasis

_____ 11. Diabetes with ketoacidosis

_____ 12. Detached retina with giant tear

_____ 13. Rheumatic fever with heart involvement

_____ 14. Acute lung edema with heart disease

_____ 15. Atherosclerosis of the extremities with intermittent claudication

_____ 16. Emphysema with acute and chronic bronchitis

_____ 17. Acute gastric ulcer with perforation and hemorrhage

_____ 18. Diverticulosis with diverticulitis

_____ 19. Acute and chronic cholecystitis

_____ 20. Closed fractures of left fibula and tibia shafts

Injury, Poisoning, and Certain Other Consequences of External Causes and External Causes of Morbidity

> **NOTE:**
>
> Add the seventh character for initial encounter to each applicable code.

_____ 21. Second-degree burn, right upper arm and shoulder

_____ 22. Burns of mouth, pharynx, and esophagus

_____ 23. Third-degree burn, trunk

_____ 24. Open fracture of coccyx with cauda equina spinal cord injury

_____ 25. Bennett's fracture, left hand, closed

_____ 26. Fifth cervical vertebra fracture, closed

_____ 27. Scarring due to third-degree burn of left arm

_____ 28. Hemiplegia due to old cerebral infarction

_____ 29. Pain due to left upper arm injury from car accident (10 years ago)

_____ 30. Brain damage due to old cerebral abscess

Factors Influencing Health Status and Contact with Health Services

_____ 31. Exercise counseling

_____ 32. Personal history of alcoholism

_____ 33. Counseling for parent-child conflict

_____ 34. Screening for bilateral breast cancer

_____ 35. Postsurgical follow-up exam

_____ 36. Adult health checkup

_____ 37. Routine child (age 2) health checkup

_____ 38. Fitting of artificial eye, right

_____ 39. Flu shot

_____ 40. Family history of breast cancer

ASSIGNMENT 6.6 – DIAGNOSTIC CODING AND REPORTING GUIDELINES FOR OUTPATIENT SERVICES

Objectives

At the conclusion of this assignment, the student should be able to:

1. List and explain the diagnostic coding and reporting guidelines for outpatient services.

2. Assign ICD-10-CM codes to diagnostic statements by interpreting the diagnostic coding and reporting guidelines for outpatient services.

3. Interpret abbreviations and lab values to assign ICD-10-CM diagnosis codes appropriately.

Overview

Diagnostic coding and reporting guidelines for outpatient services were developed by the federal government, and they were approved for use by hospitals and providers for coding and reporting hospital-based outpatient services and provider-based office visits. When reviewing the coding guidelines, remember that *encounter* and *visit* are used interchangeably when describing outpatient and physician office services.

Instructions

Assign ICD-10-CM codes to the following diagnostic statements and patient cases. When multiple codes are assigned, sequence them properly according to coding conventions and guidelines. Refer to diagnostic coding and reporting guidelines for outpatient services in your textbook, and verify codes in the ICD-10-CM tabular list.

 NOTE:

Add the seventh character for initial encounter to each applicable code.

Coding Diagnostic Statements

_____ 1. Fever, difficulty swallowing, acute tonsillitis

_____ 2. Chest pain, rule out arteriosclerotic heart disease

_____ 3. Hypertension, acute bronchitis, family history of lung cancer

_____ 4. Lipoma, subcutaneous tissue of left thigh

_____ 5. Audible wheezing, acute exacerbation of asthma

_____ 6. Routine annual gynecological visit and exam with Pap smear

_____ 7. Laceration of right forearm. Pain, left ankle and left wrist. Possible left ankle fracture. Possible left wrist fracture

_____ 8. Pregnancy visit (normal female at second trimester, first pregnancy)

_____ 9. Renal calculi with hematuria

_____ 10. Status post colostomy

_____ 11. Fever, acute otitis media

_____ 12. Epstein-Barr mononucleosis

_____ 13. Severe nausea and vomiting, gastroenteritis due to salmonella food poisoning

_____ 14. Congestive heart failure with bilateral right leg edema

_____ 15. Elevated fasting blood glucose level of 145 mg/dL

_____ 16. Gastroesophageal reflux disease

_____ 17. Severe headache, stuffy nose, allergic sinusitis

_____ 18. Epigastric abdominal pain, fever, vomiting, tachycardia, acute pancreatitis

_____ 19. Pyogenic arthritis of right knee due to *H. influenzae* infection

_____ 20. Acute pericarditis due to tuberculosis

Coding Patient Cases

1. **PATIENT CASE #1**

   HISTORY: The patient is an 87-year-old white male who has coronary artery disease and morbid obesity. He recently had a kidney stone removed. He claims that his only symptom of the stone was persistent back pain. Since the surgery, he has been doing fairly well.

   PHYSICAL EXAMINATION: The exam showed a well-developed, morbidly obese male who does not appear to be in any distress, but has considerable problems with mobility and uses a cane to ambulate. VITAL SIGNS: Blood pressure today is 120/80, pulse is 80 per minute, and weight is 204 pounds. He has no pallor. He has rather pronounced shaking of the arms, which he claims is not new. NECK: No jugular venous distention. HEART: Very irregular. LUNGS: Clear. EXTREMITIES: There is edema of both legs.

   ASSESSMENT:

   1. Coronary artery disease
   2. Exogenous obesity
   3. Degenerative joint disease involving multiple joints
   4. History of congestive heart failure
   5. Atrial fibrillation
   6. History of myocardial infarction

   PLAN: The patient will return to the clinic in four months.

---

2. **PATIENT CASE #2**

   S: No change in gait instability. When the patient had to lie quietly with neck extended, gait instability was much worse for 20 to 30 minutes after the test. Medications: Warfarin, digoxin, verapamil.

   O: Alert. Ataxic gait with foot slapping and instability in tandem walking. Mild distal weakness and wasting. Barely detectable DTRs. Impaired vibratory sense below the hips. Impaired position sense in toes. Head CT shows diffuse atrophic changes. EMG: Distal demyelinating axonal neuropathy.

   A: Gait disorder with central/peripheral components in the context of cervical spondylosis and peripheral neuropathy.

   P: Have patient obtain a B12/folate test. Reassess in one month.

---

3. **PATIENT CASE #3**

   CHIEF COMPLAINT: Feels tired all the time and has no energy.

   HISTORY OF PRESENT ILLNESS: The patient is an 80-year-old man with the following diagnoses: hyperlipidemia, coronary artery disease, cerebrovascular disease, esophageal reflux, and anxiety with depression. The patient was last seen in July of this year for the above problems. The patient is new to our clinic and is requesting follow-up for the fatigue and lack of energy, in addition to the problems noted above.

   PHYSICAL EXAMINATION: The patient is 57 inches tall and weighs 184 pounds. Blood pressure is 122/70. Pulse is 60 per minute. Respiratory rate is 18 per minute. HEENT: Basically within normal limits. The patient wears glasses. Hearing aids are present bilaterally. NECK: Supple. Trachea is midline. LUNGS: Clear to auscultation and percussion. HEART: Regular, without murmur or ectopic beats noted.

ABDOMEN: Slightly obese and nontender. Bowel sounds were normal. EXTREMITIES: The lower extremity pulses were present. He has good circulation with some very mild edema around the ankles.

ASSESSMENT:

1. Hyperlipidemia

2. Coronary artery disease

3. Cerebrovascular disease

4. Esophageal reflux

5. Anxiety with depression

PLAN: The patient will be referred to Psychiatry. I will see him again in three months.

---

4. **PATIENT CASE #4**

   HISTORY OF PRESENT ILLNESS: The patient is an 88-year-old male veteran with chronic constipation, mild dementia, and positive PPD test with negative x-ray. He complains of soreness around the anal region and incontinence of stool and sometimes urine.

   PHYSICAL EXAMINATION: The patient is alert and well-oriented today. Vital signs as per the nursing staff. CHEST: Clear. HEART: Normal sinus rhythm. ABDOMEN: Soft and benign. RECTAL: The anal area and surrounding perianal area is erythematous and there is a tear going from the rectum to the anal region. Slight oozing of blood was noted. Rectal exam was done, and I could not feel any masses in the rectum; however, the exam was painful for the patient.

   ASSESSMENT: Anal tear with hemorrhoids.

   PLAN: Sitz bath. Protective ointment around the area. Surgical consult. Give donut ring to the patient to keep pressure off the area.

---

5. **PATIENT CASE #5**

   S: The 44-year-old female patient is still having pain in the right hip area. She has a new complaint of pain and pressure in the right orbital area.

   O: Blood pressure today was 132/82. Pulse was 76 and regular. Temperature was 100.6 degrees. Pain and tenderness in the right frontal sinus region. The eyes appear slightly puffy. Examination of the right hip reveals point tenderness in the region of the head of the femur.

   A: Orbital pain. Right hip pain; rule out trochanteric bursitis.

   P: The patient will be sent for a sinus x-ray and right hip x-ray. I suspect the patient has a sinus infection due to the symptoms and fever. If the x-ray of the hip does not reveal any other pathology, will offer cortisone injection to the patient for relief of the right hip pain.

ASSIGNMENT 6.7 – MULTIPLE CHOICE REVIEW

1. Which are considered crosswalks of codes?
   a. codes assigned from ICD-10-CM only
   b. general equivalence mappings
   c. morphology and topology codes
   d. official coding guidelines

2. ICD-10-CM far exceeds ICD-9-CM in the number of codes provided, having been expanded to
   a. add third characters for some codes.
   b. include health-related procedures and services.
   c. mandate assignment of sixth characters only.
   d. provide increased specificity at all code levels.

3. Diagnostic coding and reporting guidelines for outpatient services are used for coding and reporting
   a. hospital inpatient encounters.
   b. procedures and services.
   c. provider-based office encounters.
   d. third-party payer encounters.

4. Review the ICD-10-CM Index to Diseases and Injuries entry (below), and identify the subterm.
   a. aqueduct of Sylvius
   b. Stenosis
   c. Stricture
   d. with spina bifida

> **ICD-10-CM INDEX TO DISEASES AND INJURIES**
>
> **Stricture (*see also Stenosis*)**
>   aqueduct of Sylvius (congenital) Q03.0
>   with spina bifida —*see* Spina bifida, by site, with
>   hydrocephalus

5. Which code is reported for *primary malignant neoplasm of cecum?*
   a. C18.0
   b. C7a.021
   c. C78.5
   d. D12.0

6. The patient's final diagnosis is *mucopolysaccharidosis cardiopathy.* The coder locates main term *cardiopathy and* subterm *mucopolysaccharidosis* in the ICD-10-CM index, which has codes E76.3 *[I52]* next to the subterm. After verification in the tabular list
   a. code E76.3 only is reported.
   b. code I52 only is reported.
   c. codes E76.3 and I52, in that order, are reported.
   d. codes I52 and E76.3, in that order, are reported.

7. The "X" character in an ICD-10-CM code is called a(n)
   a. eponym.
   b. modifier.
   c. placeholder.
   d. qualifier.

8. Includes notes appear below ICD-10-CM _____ to further define, or give examples of, the content of the category.
   a. 3-character code titles
   b. chapter headings
   c. subcategory descriptions
   d. tabular list classifications

9. An ICD-10-CM *Excludes1* note is interpreted as
   a. code also.   c. not coded here.
   b. *see* or *see also.*   d. use additional code.

10. Certain conditions have both an underlying etiology and multiple body system manifestations due to the underlying etiology. In ICD-10-CM, the _____ is sequenced first.
    a. etiology   c. pointer
    b. manifestation   d. sign or symptom

11. ICD-10-CM codes can have up to _____ characters.
    a. 4   c. 6
    b. 5   d. 7

12. In ICD-10-CM, the word "and" is interpreted to mean
    a. and.   c. or.
    b. and/or.   d. probable.

13. In ICD-10-CM, the word "with" is interpreted to mean
    a. "associated with" only.
    b. "associated with" or "due to."
    c. "due to" only.
    d. possible, probable, and rule out.

14. The _____ routinely associated with a disease should *not* be assigned as additional codes except when otherwise instructed by ICD-10-CM.
    a. etiologies and manifestations
    b. findings and prognoses
    c. procedures and services
    d. signs and symptoms

15. Impetigo with otitis externa, left ear.
    a. H62.42   c. L01.00, H62.42
    b. L01.00   d. L01.09

16. Hypertensive heart disease with left ventricular heart failure.
    a. I11.0   c. I50.1
    b. I11.0, I50.1   d. I50.9

17. Atrophic glossitis. Patient has long-term dependence on cigarettes.
    a. K14.0, F17.218
    b. K14.4, F17.218
    c. K14.8, F17.218, Z72.0
    d. K14.9, F17.218, Z87.891

18. Methicillin-resistant *Staphylococcus aureus* polyarthritis.
    a. B95.62, M00.00
    b. M00.09
    c. M00.09, B95.62
    d. M13.0, B95.62

19. Paranoid dementia.
    a. F03.90   c. R41.0
    b. F05   d. R41.81

20. Ankle fracture, right (initial encounter).
    a. M84.471A   c. S82.831A
    b. S82.301A   d. S82.891A

CPT Coding

INTRODUCTION

This chapter familiarizes students with coding procedures according to CPT. Students will code procedural statements and case studies by applying CPT coding conventions, principles, and rules.

ASSIGNMENT 7.1 – CPT INDEX

Objectives

At the conclusion of this assignment, the student should be able to:

1. Identify the word in a procedural statement that would be considered the main term in the CPT index.
2. Locate main terms in the CPT index.

Instructions

In each of the following procedural statements, underline the word that would be considered the main term in the CPT index according to type, which is indicated by the name of the heading located above each set of procedures.

Identification of Main Terms in CPT Index

1. Ankle amputation
2. Lower arm biopsy
3. Bone marrow aspiration
4. Laparoscopic jejunostomy
5. Bladder neck resection

Identification of Procedure or Service as Main Term in CPT Index

6. Postpartum dilation and curettage
7. Clamp circumcision of newborn
8. Arthrotomy of toe, interphalangeal joint
9. Gastrotomy with vagotomy
10. Bladder aspiration

Identification of Organ or Other Anatomic Site as Main Term in CPT Index

11. Artery angioplasty

12. Excision of heel spur

13. Repair of diaphragm laceration

14. Excision of cyst of pericardium

15. Excision of epiphyseal bar of radius

Identification of Condition as Main Term in CPT Index

16. Toe polydactyly reconstruction

17. Drainage of hip hematoma

18. Drainage of cyst of liver

19. Destruction of kidney calculus

20. Repair of sliding inguinal hernia

Identification of Synonym as Main Term in CPT Index

21. Albarran test

22. Binding globulin, testosterone-estradiol

23. Digital slit-beam radiograph

24. Urine test for epinephrine

25. Energies, electromagnetic

Identification of Eponym as Main Term in CPT Index

26. Dwyer procedure

27. Kasai procedure

28. Waldius procedure

29. Bloom-Singer prosthesis

30. Ober-Yount procedure

Identification of Abbreviation as Main Term in CPT Index

31. Manual sedimentation rate of RBCs

32. MRA of the leg

33. Urine pH

34. Standard EEG

35. Complete MRI of the heart

ASSIGNMENT 7.2 – EVALUATION AND MANAGEMENT (E/M) CODING

Objectives

At the conclusion of this assignment, the student should be able to:

1. Use the CPT index to locate E/M codes.

2. Verify codes in the E/M section of CPT.

Instructions

Assign CPT Evaluation and Management codes to the following services. (Refer to Figures 7-8A through 7-8D in the textbook for assistance.)

1. Subsequent hospital care, expanded _____
2. Subsequent nursing facility care, problem focused _____
3. Initial office visit, level 2 _____
4. Office consultation, low level of medical decision making _____
5. Initial inpatient hospital visit, level 2 _____
6. Initial home visit, detailed _____
7. Follow-up home visit, comprehensive _____
8. Observation care discharge _____
9. Initial observation care, comprehensive _____
10. Emergency department (ED) visit, detailed _____

ASSIGNMENT 7.3 – ANESTHESIA CODING

Objectives

At the conclusion of this assignment, the student should be able to:

1. Use the CPT index to locate Anesthesia codes.
2. Verify codes in the Anesthesia section of CPT.

Instructions

Assign CPT Anesthesia codes to the following procedures. Be sure to include the provider-type modifier and the physical status modifier, which indicates information about the patient's physical status in relation to anesthesia services provided (00000-AA-P1). Where appropriate, assign one or more of the four codes (99100–99140) from the Medicine section that report qualifying circumstances for anesthesia.

1. Coronary angioplasty of two vessels; patient has severe coronary artery disease. _____
2. Amniocentesis; patient has petit mal epilepsy. _____
3. Extracorporeal shock wave lithotripsy; patient has controlled hypertension. _____
4. Percutaneous liver biopsy; patient has chronic alcoholism. _____
5. Debridement of third-degree burns of right arm, 6 percent body surface area; patient is two years old and otherwise healthy. _____
6. Total hip replacement, open procedure; patient has controlled diabetes mellitus. _____
7. Biopsy of clavicle; patient is postoperative mastectomy two years ago and is undergoing biopsy procedure for suspected metastatic bone cancer. _____
8. Hand cast application; patient is otherwise healthy. _____
9. Arthroscopic procedure of the ankle joint; patient has generalized arthritis. _____
10. Total cystectomy; patient has bladder cancer, which is localized. _____

ASSIGNMENT 7.4 – SURGERY CODING

Objectives

At the conclusion of this assignment, the student should be able to:

1. Use the CPT index to locate Surgery codes.
2. Verify codes in the Surgery section of CPT.

Instructions

Assign codes to the following procedural statements using the CPT index. Be sure to verify the code(s) in the CPT Surgery section.

 NOTE:

Convert inches to centimeters when calculating wound size. The formula is: inches × 2.54. Or, go to **www.manuelsweb.com/in_cm.htm** and use the online conversion calculator.

1. Excision, 1-inch benign lesion, left leg _____
2. Simple repair of 2-inch laceration on the right foot _____
3. Layer closure of 3-inch stab wound of the neck _____
4. Excision, half-inch malignant lesion, left first finger _____
5. Intermediate repair of 5-inch laceration of the right thigh _____
6. Open reduction with internal fixation of fracture of great toe phalanx _____
7. Closed reduction of nasal bone fracture with stabilization _____
8. Surgical elbow arthroscopy with removal of loose body _____
9. Segmental osteotomy of the mandible _____
10. Trigger finger release _____
11. Tracheobronchoscopy through existing tracheostomy incision _____
12. Secondary rhinoplasty with major reconstruction of nasal tip to correct results of an initial rhinoplasty done elsewhere _____
13. Surgical thoracoscopy with excision of pericardial tumor _____
14. Total pulmonary decortication _____
15. Extraplural enucleation of empyema _____
16. Direct repair of cerebral artery aneurysm _____
17. Femoral-popliteal bypass graft _____
18. Coronary artery bypass graft (using two arterial grafts) _____
19. Complete cardiac MRI without contrast _____
20. Insertion of dual-chamber pacemaker with electrodes _____
21. Complete cleft lip repair, primary bilateral, one-stage procedure _____
22. Laparoscopic cholecystectomy with exploration of the common duct _____
23. Umbilectomy _____
24. Pancreatectomy with Whipple procedure _____

25. Percutaneous drainage of subdiaphragmatic abscess (image-guided)   _____

26. Inguinal hernia repair without hydrocelectomy; the patient is a 14-month-old male   _____

27. Cystourethroscopy with fulguration of large (6.5 cm) bladder tumor   _____

28. Manometric studies through pyelostomy tube   _____

29. Nephrorrhaphy of right kidney wound   _____

30. Injection of contrast for voiding urethrocystography   _____

31. Laser removal of three condylomata from penis   _____

32. Incisional biopsy of the prostate   _____

33. Marsupialization of Bartholin's gland cyst   _____

34. Total bilateral salpingectomy and oophorectomy   _____

35. Antepartum care, 10 visits   _____

36. Burr holes with evacuation and drainage of subdural hematoma   _____

37. Craniotomy for repair of cerebrospinal fluid leak and rhinorrhea   _____

38. Thoracic laminectomy with exploration, two vertebrae   _____

39. Percutaneous biopsy of spinal cord   _____

40. Neuroplasty of the sciatic nerve   _____

41. Evisceration of eye with implant   _____

42. Laser iridectomy for glaucoma   _____

43. Total dacryocystectomy   _____

44. Removal of bilateral cerumen impaction   _____

45. Successful cochlear implant   _____

ASSIGNMENT 7.5 – RADIOLOGY CODING

Objectives

At the conclusion of this assignment, the student should be able to:

1. Use the CPT index to locate Radiology codes.
2. Verify codes in the Radiology section of CPT.

Instructions

Assign codes to the following procedural statements using the CPT index. Be sure to verify the code(s) in the CPT Radiology section.

1. Complete radiographic examination of the mandible   _____

2. Urography, retrograde   _____

3. Pelvimetry   _____

4. Orthoroentgenogram, scanogram   _____

5. Chest x-ray, two views, with fluoroscopy   _____

6. X-ray of the facial bones, four views   _____

7. CAT scan of the abdomen, with contrast   _____

8. Gastroesophageal reflux study   _____

9. X-ray of the cervical spine, two views   _____

10. Colon x-ray, single-contrast using barium   _____

ASSIGNMENT 7.6 – PATHOLOGY AND LABORATORY CODING

Objectives

At the conclusion of this assignment, the student should be able to:

1. Use the CPT index to locate Pathology and Laboratory codes.

2. Verify codes in the Pathology and Laboratory section of CPT.

Instructions

Assign codes to the following procedural statements using the CPT index. Be sure to verify the code(s) in the CPT Radiology and Laboratory section.

1. Red blood cell count, automated   _____

2. Blood gases, pH only   _____

3. Glucose-6-phosphate dehydrogenase screen   _____

4. Glucose tolerance test, three specimens   _____

5. KOH prep   _____

6. HIV antibody and confirmatory test   _____

7. HDL cholesterol   _____

8. Rapid test for infection, screen, each antibody   _____

9. Herpes simplex virus, quantification   _____

10. Urine dip, nonautomated, without microscopy   _____

ASSIGNMENT 7.7 – MEDICINE CODING

Objectives

At the conclusion of this assignment, the student should be able to:

1. Use the CPT index to locate Medicine codes.

2. Verify codes in the Medicine section of CPT.

Instructions

Assign codes to the following procedural statements using the CPT index. Be sure to verify the code(s) in the CPT Medicine section.

1. Right heart catheterization, for congenital cardiac anomalies   _____

2. Medical testimony   _____

3. Services requested between 10:00 PM and 8:00 AM in addition to basic service, normal office hours 9:00 AM to 6:00 PM   _____

4. Acupuncture, one or more needles, with electrical stimulation   _____

5. Hypnotherapy _____

6. Psychological test administration and scoring by technician, two tests, 30 minutes _____

7. Wheelchair management with propulsion training, 15 minutes _____

8. Massage therapy, 15 minutes _____

9. Nonpressurized inhalation treatment for acute airway obstruction _____

10. Educational videotapes provided to patient _____

ASSIGNMENT 7.8 – ASSIGNING CPT MODIFIERS

Objectives

At the conclusion of this assignment, the student should be able to:

1. Identify the phrase in a procedure statement that indicates a modifier is to be assigned.

2. Use the CPT Appendix to locate modifiers.

3. Assign the modifier that describes the special circumstances associated with a procedural statement.

Instructions

Assign the CPT code and appropriate modifier to the following procedural statements. Before assigning the modifier, underline the phrase in each procedure statement that indicates a modifier is to be assigned. (Refer to Table 7-1 of the textbook for assistance in assigning modifiers.)

1. Vasovasostomy discontinued after anesthesia due to heart arrhythmia, hospital outpatient _____

2. Decision for surgery during initial office visit, level 4 _____

3. Expanded office visit for follow-up of mastectomy; new onset diabetes was discovered and treatment initiated _____

4. Cholecystectomy, postoperative management only _____

5. Hospital outpatient hemorrhoidectomy by simple ligature discontinued prior to anesthesia due to severe drop in blood pressure _____

6. Total urethrectomy including cystotomy, female, surgical care only _____

7. Simple repair of 2-inch laceration of the right foot, discontinued due to near-syncope, physician's office _____

8. Tonsillectomy and adenoidectomy, age 10, and laser wart removal from the patient's neck while in the operating room _____

9. Repeat left medial collateral ligament repair, same surgeon _____

10. At the patient's request, bilateral correction of bunion deformity was performed. _____

11. A patient undergoes simple repair of multiple skin lacerations and of left foot and toes and intermediate repair of left heel laceration. The patient is discharged home after suturing, bandaging, and placement of the left foot in a soft cast. Codes 12041 and 12002 are reported. Which modifier, if any, is added to code 12002? _____

12. An 80-year-old male patient undergoes bilateral posterior packing of the nasal cavity. Is a modifier added to code 30905? _____

13. A patient undergoes magnetic resonance imaging (MRI), lower left leg. Dr. Miller interprets the MRI and documents a report. Which modifiers are added to CPT code 73718?   _____

14. On April 2, the patient underwent incision and drainage (I&D) of a Bartholin's gland abscess. The abscess recurred two weeks later, and on April 29, the patient underwent repeat I&D by the same surgeon. Code 56420 was reported for the April 2 procedure. Which modifier is added to code 56420 for the procedure performed on April 29?   _____

15. A male patient underwent biopsy of the prostate gland on October 20, as performed by Dr. Smith. The global period for this surgical procedure is zero days. The pathology results were of uncertain behavior. Per the pathologist's recommendation, the patient underwent repeat biopsy to obtain a larger sample on November 13, performed by Dr. Jones. Code 55700 was reported for the October 20 procedure. Which modifier is added to code 55700 for the procedure performed on November 13?   _____

ASSIGNMENT 7.9 – CODING PATIENT CASES

Objectives

At the conclusion of this assignment, the student should be able to:

1. Use the CPT index to locate procedure and service codes.

2. Verify codes in the appropriate section of CPT.

3. Assign modifier(s) when special circumstances are documented in a patient case.

Instructions

Code the following case studies using the CPT index. Be sure to verify the code(s) in the appropriate section of CPT. Assign Procedure and Service codes *only* for each patient case. Do *not* code diagnoses. Refer to textbook Figures 7-8A through 7-8D for assistance with E/M code selection and Table 7-1 for assistance with assigning modifiers.

1. **PATIENT CASE #1**

   HISTORY OF PRESENT ILLNESS: The patient is a 37-year-old female who has complaints of severe fatigue, sore throat, headache, and acute bilateral ear pain. The symptoms have been gradually increasing over the past 7 to 10 days, to the point where she is not able to sleep at night due to coughing and intense bilateral ear pain. She was referred to me by her primary care provider for further evaluation and medical treatment.

   PHYSICAL EXAMINATION: GENERAL: The patient appears tired and ill. HEENT: Eyes are within normal limits. Bilateral otoscopic examination shows erythematous, inflamed tympanic membranes with question of perforation on the right. Throat is red and tonsils appear mildly swollen. NECK: There is mild cervical lymphadenopathy. HEART: Within normal limits. LUNGS: Generally clear. The rest of the exam was within normal limits. LABORATORY: Rapid strep was negative. Poly Stat Mono test was positive.

   ASSESSMENT: Mononucleosis, pharyngitis, bilateral otitis media, and probable sinusitis.

   PLAN: CBC with differential. Sinus x-ray to rule out sinusitis. The patient will be placed on a Z-Pak and prednisone taper. Tussionex for cough. The patient is to be off work for the next 10 days, and is to return to this office in seven days; sooner if she does not begin to feel better or if symptoms worsen.

2. **PATIENT CASE #2**

   OPERATIVE PROCEDURE: Cystoscopy.

   PREOPERATIVE DIAGNOSES:

   1. Benign prostatic hypertrophy.

   2. Rule out stricture of the urethra.

   3. Rule out bladder lesions.

   POSTOPERATIVE DIAGNOSIS:

   1. Benign prostatic hypertrophy.

   2. Cystitis.

   POSTOPERATIVE CONDITION: Satisfactory.

   OPERATIVE PROCEDURE AND FINDINGS: The established patient was placed in the lithotomy position. Genital area was prepped with Betadine and draped in the usual sterile fashion. About 10 cc of 2 percent Xylocaine jelly was introduced into the urethra and a cystoscopy was performed using a #16 French flexible cystoscope. The urethra was grossly normal. The prostate gland was moderately enlarged. There was mild inflammation of the bladder mucosa, but there were no gross tumors or calculi seen in the bladder at this time. Cystoscope was removed. The patient tolerated the procedure well and left the procedure room in good condition.

   ---

3. **PATIENT CASE #3**

   S: Chronic fatigue. No acute complaints. This established female patient purchased an Advantage BG and sugars are 97 to 409; no pattern. (She did not bring copies of her glucose levels as requested.) Eats two meals a day; history of noncompliance. The patient was seen in GYN Clinic this morning. Has GI upset with oral estrogen and doctor recommended estrogen patch. Seen in ophthalmology in July; no retinopathy. Last mammography was in June. Noncompliant with six-month follow-up of calcified cluster in the right breast, upper outer quadrant. Four-year history of small, tender irregularity in the right breast five o'clock position. Feet: The patient still has occasional pain with over-the-counter (OTC) B12 pills. No change in respiration; refuses to attempt to quit smoking. Self-catheterizes neurogenic bladder.

   O: Obese white female in no acute distress. Lump found on breast self-exam, right. Left breast reveals no mass, no nodes, nipple okay. Right breast reveals tender spots at eight and ten o'clock, mobile. Patient believes this has been the same for the past four years. Patient routinely does breast self-exam. Heart reveals regular sinus rhythm.

   A: Diabetes mellitus on oral therapy, poorly controlled. Chronic small airway disease. Nicotine dependent. Obesity. Menopause. Rule out breast disease.

   P: Hemoglobin today. Fasting lipid profile today. Repeat both labs in three months. Schedule mammogram today. Counseled patient on the importance of keeping the mammography appointment and close watch of the masses. Return to clinic in six weeks if mammogram is okay. Will start estrogen patch 0.5 mg/24 hours, #8. All other meds refilled today.

   ---

4. **PATIENT CASE #4**

HISTORY: This 55-year-old male patient presented today for evaluation of ulcers of the lower left leg, in the region of the tibia and in the calf area. The patient reports discomfort with these areas. The patient agreed to be seen at the insistence of his wife and because of increasing pain in the areas of the ulcerations. The patient is a known diabetic with poor compliance and blood sugars are usually high. We discussed his blood sugar monitoring schedule, and his wife indicates that the patient is very stubborn about monitoring his blood sugars. The patient could benefit from an intensive education session regarding diabetes, diabetic care, and preventing or slowing disease progression. He is either in complete denial of his diagnosis or is simply not making the effort to take care of himself; either way, the situation needs to be addressed.

PHYSICAL EXAMINATION: The exam was limited to the lower extremities. The left lower leg shows stasis dermatitis with two ulcerations in the region of the calf. One is approximately 1 cm in diameter and the other is approximately 1.5 cm in diameter. There are varicosities present as well as mild edema noted. There is a small, shallow ulcer in the mid-tibia region as well. The right lower leg has mild edema but is free of ulcers at this time.

DIAGNOSES:

1. Stasis dermatitis with ulcerations.
2. Dependent edema.
3. Diabetes mellitus, uncontrolled.

PLAN: The patient underwent wound irrigation and application of Silvadene cream to the ulcerations. Wounds were dressed with sterile gauze and wrapped with Kerlix. The patient will return in one week for reevaluation. If there is no improvement in the ulcerations, an Unna boot will be the next step. Additionally, we will arrange for intensive diabetic education for this patient.

---

5. **PATIENT CASE #5**

PREOPERATIVE DIAGNOSIS: Pilonidal cyst.

POSTOPERATIVE DIAGNOSIS: Pilonidal cyst, cellulitis.

OPERATION: Pilonidal cystectomy, cyst tract exploration and irrigation.

HISTORY: The patient is a 42-year-old white male who has had intermittent flare-ups of the pilonidal cyst. He was seen in the office two days ago with an acute flare-up with acute pain and pressure. He reported he was running a fever. He was scheduled for office surgery for removal and presents today for the above.

PROCEDURE: The patient was premedicated with 10 mg of Versed. The patient was brought to the procedure room and placed in the jackknife position. The lower sacrum and coccygeal areas were prepped with Betadine, and the operative field was draped in a sterile fashion. Local anesthetic was administered with topical Hurricaine spray, and 1 percent Xylocaine was then injected into the margins of the wound. An incision was made into the area of the obvious pilonidal cyst formation and approximately 15 cc of foul, purulent drainage was expressed from the wound. The contents of the cyst were excised, labeled, and sent for pathology. There was cellulitis extending circumferentially around the cyst, extending approximately 1.5 cm outside the area of the cyst. Exploration of the sinus tract was performed and the tract extended down approximately 2.5 cm. It was felt at this time that no sutures would be required, and the tract was irrigated with normal saline and flushed with antibiotic solution. The wound was then packed and dressed. The patient tolerated the procedure well. The patient was observed for 30 minutes following the procedure, after which he was instructed on wound care and signs of infection. The patient was released to the care of his wife. He was given a prescription for Keflex 500 mg p.o. b.i.d. and Darvocet N-100, #20, 1 p.o. q.4h. as needed for pain. He will return to the office in two days for reevaluation.

ASSIGNMENT 7.10 – CPT CODE VERIFICATION

Objectives

At the conclusion of this assignment, the student should be able to:

1. Validate coding accuracy based on coding information.

2. Analyze results and make recommendations.

Overview

CPT codes are assigned for a variety of outpatient services. Auditing of the codes assigned can be done as a tool to verify correct code assignment.

Instructions

Below is a table of 10 health records with information from the coding statement that was used to assign CPT code(s). Analyze the information provided in the table (using your coding manual) to verify that the code assigned is correct. If the code is correct, enter it again in the coding verification column. If the code is incorrect, locate and enter the correct code in the coding verification column. Provide an analysis of your findings: What percentage of the codes was correct? What percentage was incorrect based on the 10 charts that were reviewed? What recommendations could you provide to the coder(s) of these charts? Prepare a double-spaced, word-processed document that is at least one-half page in length.

Health Record Number	Coding Statement	Code Assigned	Coding Verification
25899	Office visit level 3, established patient	99213	
60159	Flexible diagnostic bronchoscopy	31624	
30121	Biopsy of the oropharynx	42800	
11133	CT scan of the thoracic spine with contrast	72128	
45456	Hepatic panel	82040, 82247, 82248, 84075, 84155, 84450, 84460	
55667	Routine ECG tracing only	93000	
91912	Application of figure-of-eight cast	29049	
34343	Initial posterior nasal packing	30905	
55578	Extensive excision of a pilonidal cyst	11770	
12332	Fitting of bifocals	92340	

ASSIGNMENT 7.11 – RELATIVE VALUE UNITS

Objectives

At the conclusion of this assignment, the student should be able to:

1. Discuss the purpose of relative value units (RVUs).

2. Determine RVUs for CPT and HCPCS level II codes.

Overview

Relative value units (RVUs) are values assigned by the Centers for Medicare and Medicaid Services (CMS) to each CPT and HCPCS level II code. RVUs represent the cost of providing a service, and include the following payment components: physician work (physician's time and intensity in providing the service), practice expense (overhead costs involved in providing a service), and malpractice expense (malpractice expenses). Medicare physician fee schedule payments are based on payment components multiplied by conversion factors and geographical adjustments.

Instructions

1. Go to **www.aapc.com**, click on Practice Management, and scroll down and click on the CPT RVU Calculator.

2. Enter the following CPT and HCPCS level II codes below the CPT Code column of the CPT Work RVU Calculator:

   - 99203
   - 99213
   - 99221
   - 99231
   - 99468
   - 99285
   - 99304
   - 99307
   - G0008
   - G0402

3. For each code, enter the number 1 in the Number of Units column.

4. Click the Calculate link, and print the results.

5. Using your CPT and HCPCS level II coding manuals, locate each code description to identify the services provided. Review the RVUs assigned to each code. Which code would generate the highest payment amount? Which code would generate the lowest payment amount?

ASSIGNMENT 7.12 – MULTIPLE CHOICE REVIEW

1. The CPT coding manual contains _____ sections.
   a. three
   b. four
   c. five
   d. six

2. Instructions provided at the beginning of each section, which define terms particular to that section and provide explanation for codes and services that apply to that section, are called
   a. guidelines.
   b. instructional notes.
   c. qualifiers.
   d. special reports.

3. Rather than using unlisted surgery CPT codes, Medicare and other third-party payers require providers to
   a. assign ICD-10-PCS procedure codes.
   b. attach a special report.
   c. perform a known procedure.
   d. report HCPCS level II codes.

4. CPT modifiers are used to indicate that
   a. special report need not be attached to the claim.
   b. the description of the procedure performed has been altered.
   c. the provider should receive a higher reimbursement rate.
   d. the technique of the procedure was performed differently.

5. Which component is included in the surgical package?
   a. assistant surgeon services
   b. epidural or spinal anesthesia
   c. prescription pain medications
   d. uncomplicated postoperative care

6. Which modifier is reported if a third-party payer requires a second opinion for a surgical procedure?
   a. -26 (professional component)
   b. -32 (mandated services)
   c. -59 (distinct procedural service)
   d. -62 (two surgeons)

7. The time frame during which all postoperative services are included in the surgical package is the global
   a. billing.   c. period.
   b. package.   d. surgery.

8. Use your CPT coding manual to locate code 11300, and identify the technique used to remove epidermal or dermal lesions; it is called
   a. destruction.   c. repair.
   b. excision.   d. shaving.

9. Use your CPT coding manual to locate and review coding notes that apply to Repair (Closure) codes (located prior to code 12001 in the Integumentary subsection of the Surgery section). The proper way to report the repair of multiple lacerations at the same anatomic site is to
   a. add together the length of each laceration and report a single code.
   b. code each individual laceration based on the length of each wound.
   c. code each individual laceration based on the most complicated repair.
   d. report individual codes for each laceration if they involved trauma.

10. Use your CPT coding manual to locate and review coding notes on the first page of the Musculoskeletal System subsection in the Surgery section to identify the term for "the attempted reduction or restoration of a fracture or joint dislocation by the application of manually applied forces." The term is
    a. fixation.   c. traction.
    b. manipulation.   d. treatment.

11. CPT codes that are optional and are used for tracking performance measurements are called
    _____ codes.
    a. Category I   c. Category III
    b. Category II   d. Category IV

12. A bullet located to the left of a code number identifies
    a. a revised code description.   c. new procedures and services.
    b. codes exempt from modifier -51.   d. revised guidelines and notes.

13. An anesthesiologist provided general anesthesia services to a 70-year-old female with mild systemic disease who underwent total knee replacement. Which physical status modifier would be reported with procedure code 01402?
    a. -P1   c. -P3
    b. -P2   d. -P4

14. A series of very specific blood chemistry studies (e.g., code 80047) ordered at one time is called a(n)
    a. assay.   c. report.
    b. panel.   d. study.

15. A CRNA provided general anesthesia services to a healthy patient who underwent an appendectomy. The CRNA did not receive medical direction from a physician. Which HCPCS Level II modifier would be reported with procedure code 00944?
    a. -QS   c. -QY
    b. -QX   d. -QZ

16. When assigning an evaluation and management code, a presenting problem that runs a definite and prescribed course, is transient in nature, and is not likely to alter the patient's permanent health status, the problem is considered
    a. low severity.   c. minor.
    b. minimal.   d. moderate severity.

17. A patient is admitted to the hospital through the emergency department for treatment and is then held for a period of eight hours to be monitored. This patient received hospital _____ evaluation and management services.
    a. critical care   c. observation
    b. inpatient   d. outpatient

18. A 92-year-old female patient received general anesthesia services during total left hip arthroplasty. Which qualifying circumstance code would be reported in addition to procedure code 01214?
    a. 99100   c. 99135
    b. 99116   d. 99140

19. Which evaluation and management service is reported for the care of patients who live in a boarding home?
    a. consultation services
    b. domiciliary care
    c. home services
    d. nursing facility services

20. Use your CPT coding manual to review the Medicine section guidelines, and identify the CPT code assigned to supplies and materials.
    a. 99202   c. 99070
    b. 99000   d. 99199

HCPCS Level II Coding

INTRODUCTION

This chapter familiarizes students with coding procedures, services, and supplies according to HCPCS level II. Students will code procedural statements and case studies by applying HCPCS level II coding conventions, principles, and rules.

ASSIGNMENT 8.1 – HCPCS LEVEL II INDEX

Objectives

At the conclusion of the assignment, the student should be able to:

1. Identify the word in a service or procedural statement that would be considered the main term in the HCPCS level II index.
2. Locate main terms in the HCPCS level II index.

Instructions

In each of the following statements, underline the word that would be considered the main term in the HCPCS level II index.

1. Breast pump
2. Functional outcome assessment
3. Dialysate solution
4. External defibrillator electrode
5. Fracture orthotic devices
6. Liquid gas system
7. High osmolar contrast material
8. Pneumatic nebulizer administration set
9. Pneumococcal vaccination administration
10. Wheelchair controller

ASSIGNMENT 8.2 – HCPCS LEVEL II CODING

Objectives

At the conclusion of this assignment, the student should be able to:

1. Locate main terms in the HCPCS level II index.
2. Identify codes in the HCPCS level II index and verify them in the tabular section.

Instructions

Assign HCPCS level II codes to the following procedures and services:

Transportation Services Including Ambulance (A0021–A0999)

1. Advanced life support, Level 2 _____

2. Ambulance transport of newborn from
   rural hospital to a children's specialty hospital _____

3. Patient received basic life support (BLS) during
   emergency transport via ambulance _____

4. Patient received life-sustaining oxygen in ambulance
   during transport to hospital _____

5. Wheelchair van transporting patient from assisted
   living facility to doctor's office _____

Medical and Surgical Supplies (A4000–A8999)

6. Physician gave patient injection using a sterile 3 cc syringe
   with needle _____

7. One pint of pHisoHex solution _____

8. Diaphragm for contraceptive use _____

9. Replacement adapter for breast pump _____

10. One pound of paraffin _____

11. Male external catheter with adhesive coating _____

12. Two-way indwelling Foley catheter _____

13. Ostomy belt _____

14. Reusable enema bag with tubing _____

15. One pair of apnea monitor electrodes _____

16. Rubber pessary _____

17. Tracheostomy care kit for new tracheostomy _____

18. Automatic blood pressure monitor _____

19. Ammonia test strips for dialysis (50 count) _____

20. Patient with diabetes was fitted with a pair of shoes custom-molded
    from casts of the patient's feet _____

Enteral and Parenteral Therapy (B4000–B9999)

21. Parenteral nutrition supply kit; home mix, one day _____

22. Enteral formula via feeding tube (100 calories/1 unit), manufactured blenderized natural foods with intact nutrients _____

23. Enteral infusion pump with alarm _____

24. Gravity-fed enteral feeding supply kit (one day) _____

25. Parenteral nutrition administration kit (one day) _____

Outpatient PPS (C Codes) (C1000–C9999)

26. Brachytherapy seed, high-dose rate iridium 192 _____

27. Cardiac event recorder (implantable) _____

28. Implantable joint device _____

29. Patient underwent left breast MRI without contrast, followed by left breast MRI with contrast _____

30. Short-term hemodialysis catheter _____

31. Single-chamber implantable cardioverter-defibrillator _____

Durable Medical Equipment (E0100–E8002)

32. "Patient helper" trapeze bars, attached to bed, with grab bar _____

33. Adult oxygen tent _____

34. Bilirubin light with photometer _____

35. Nebulizer with compressor _____

36. Folding walker with adjustable height _____

37. Four-lead TENS unit _____

38. Free-standing cervical traction stand _____

39. Heavy-duty, extra-wide hospital bed with mattress to accommodate patient who weighs 460 pounds _____

40. Heparin infusion pump for hemodialysis _____

41. Jug urinal (male) _____

42. Lambswool sheepskin heel pad for decubitus prevention _____

43. Low-intensity ultrasound osteogenesis stimulator _____

44. Metal bed pan _____

45. Nonelectronic communication board _____

46. Patient was fitted with a pair of underarm wooden crutches with pads, tips, and handgrips _____

47. Portable paraffin bath (unit) _____

48. Portable sitz bath _____

49. Quad cane with tips _____

50. Raised toilet seat _____

51. Power wheelchair accessory, lithium-based battery, each _____

52. Replacement brake attachment for wheeled walker _____

53. Ultraviolet light therapy 6-foot panel, with bulbs, timer, and eye protection   _____

54. Variable height hospital bed with mattress and side rails   _____

55. Wheelchair anti-tipping device   _____

Procedures/Professional Services (Temporary) (G0008–G9999)

56. Automated CBC (complete) with automated WBC differential count   _____

57. Patient received maintenance hemodialysis (outpatient dialysis facility)   _____

58. Individual smoking cessation counseling (10 minutes)   _____

59. Initial E/M evaluation for patient with peripheral neuropathy with loss of protective sensation (LOPS)   _____

60. PET imaging for initial diagnosis of breast cancer   _____

Alcohol and/or Drug Abuse Treatment Services (H0001–H9999)

61. Behavioral health counseling and therapy, 30 minutes   _____

62. Partial hospitalization for mental health crisis, 18 hours   _____

63. Psychiatric health facility services (one day)   _____

64. Respite care services, not in the home (*per diem*)   _____

65. Thirty minutes of activity therapy   _____

J Codes Drugs (J0100–J9999)

66. Injection of baclofen, 10 mg   _____

67. Injection of prochlorperazine, 10 mg   _____

68. Injection of doripenem, 20 mg   _____

69. Parental tacrolimus, 15 mg   _____

70. Oral aprepitant, 10 mg   _____

Temporary Codes Assigned to DME Regional Carriers (MACs) (K0000–K9999)

71. Complete front caster assembly for wheelchair with two semi-pneumatic tires   _____

72. IV hanger (each)   _____

73. Leg strap (for wheelchair)   _____

74. Lightweight portable motorized wheelchair   _____

75. Replacement alkaline battery, 1.5 volt, for patient-owned external infusion pump   _____

Orthotics (L0100–L4999)

76. Cervical wire frame, semi-rigid, for occipital/mandibular support   _____

77. Custom-fabricated thoracic rib belt   _____

78. HALO procedure; cervical halo incorporated into Milwaukee orthosis   _____

79. Neoprene heel and sole elevation lift (one inch)   _____

80. Posterior solid ankle plastic AFO, custom fabricated _____

81. Spenco foot insert _____

Prosthetics (L5000–L9999)

82. Below-knee disarticulation prosthesis, molded socket, shin, with SACH foot _____

83. Electric hand, myoelectrical controlled, adult _____

84. Partial foot prosthesis, shoe insert with longitudinal arch, toe filler _____

85. Preparatory prosthesis for hip disarticulation-hemipelvectomy; pylon, no cover, solid ankle cushion heel foot, thermoplastic, molded to patient model _____

86. Silicone breast prosthesis _____

Other Medical Services (M0000–M0301)

87. Intragastric hypothermia using gastric freezing _____

88. Cellular therapy _____

89. Chemical endarterectomy (IV chelation therapy) _____

90. Fabric wrapping of abdominal aneurysm _____

91. Prolotherapy _____

Laboratory Services (P0000–P9999)

92. Catheterization for collection of specimen (one patient) _____

93. Bacterial culture, urine (quantitative) (sensitivity study) _____

94. Platelets, each unit _____

95. Two units whole blood for transfusion _____

Q Codes: Temporary Codes Assigned by CMS (Q0000–Q9999)

96. Chemotherapy administration by push _____

97. Collagen skin test _____

98. Oral magnetic resonance contrast agent, 100 ml _____

99. Injection, sermorelin acetate, 1 mcg _____

100. KOH preparation _____

101. Pinworm examination _____

Diagnostic Radiology Services (R0000–R9999)

102. Portable x-ray service transportation to nursing home, one trip, one patient seen _____

103. Transportation of portable ECG to nursing facility, one patient seen _____

104. Transportation of portable x-ray service to patient's home, two patients seen (husband and wife) _____

Temporary National Codes Established by Private Payers (S0000–S9999)

105. Allogenic cord-blood-derived stem cell transplant   _____

106. Echosclerotherapy   _____

107. Gastrointestinal fat absorption study   _____

108. Global fee for extracorporeal shock wave lithotripsy
(ESWL) treatment of kidney stone   _____

109. Harvesting of multivisceral organs from cadaver with
preparation and maintenance of allografts   _____

110. Vaginal birth after Caesarean (VBAC) classes   _____

Temporary National Codes Established by Medicaid (T1000–T9999)

111. Family training and counseling for child development, 15 minutes   _____

112. Human breast milk processing, storage, and distribution   _____

113. Intramuscular medication administration by home health LPN   _____

114. Private-duty nursing, 30 minutes   _____

115. Waiver for utility services to support medical equipment   _____

Vision Services (V0000–V2999)

116. Bifocal lenses, bilateral, 5.25 sphere, 2.12 cylinder   _____

117. Deluxe frame   _____

118. Photochromatic tint for two lenses   _____

119. Processing, preserving, and transporting corneal tissue   _____

120. Reduction of ocular prosthesis   _____

Hearing Services (V5000–V5999)

121. Assessment for hearing aid   _____

122. Binaural behind-the-ear hearing aid   _____

123. Digitally programmable monaural hearing aid, analog   _____

124. Dispensing fee, Bilateral Contra Lateral Routing of Signal (BICROS)   _____

125. Telephone amplifier   _____

ASSIGNMENT 8.3 – CODING DRUGS USING HCPCS LEVEL II

Objectives

At the conclusion of this assignment, the student should be able to:

1. Interpret the HCPCS level II Table of Drugs.

2. Assign HCPCS level II codes to procedure or service statements that contain drugs.

Instructions

Code the following statements using the Table of Drugs in HCPCS level II. Be sure to verify the code(s) in the HCPCS level II tabular section.

NOTE:

Drugs in the HCPCS level II Table of Drugs are listed by the generic or chemical name. (Drugs are listed by the trade name only if no generic or chemical name is available.) If you search for a drug by its trade name in the table, you are instructed to "see" the generic or chemical name. For assistance with identifying generic or chemical drug names, go to **www.rxlist.com**.

_____ 1. Tetracycline 250 mg injection

_____ 2. Ancef 500 mg IV

_____ 3. Clonidine HCl, 1 mg

_____ 4. Botulinum toxin type B, 100 units

_____ 5. Injection, morphine sulfate, 10 mg

_____ 6. Kenalog-40 20 mg

_____ 7. Streptokinase 250,000 IU IV

_____ 8. Ranitidine HCl injection, 25 mg

_____ 9. 50 units of insulin for administration through insulin pump

_____10. Lasix 20 mg IM

ASSIGNMENT 8.4 – HCPCS LEVEL II NATIONAL MODIFIERS

Objectives

At the conclusion of this assignment, the student should be able to:

1. Locate HCPCS level II national modifiers in the coding manual.

2. Assign HCPCS level II national modifiers to special circumstances associated with procedures, services, and supplies.

Instructions

Match the modifier in the left column to its appropriate description in the right column.

_____ 1. AH   a. Left hand, thumb

_____ 2. E4   b. Technical component

_____ 3. FA   c. Four patients served

_____ 4. NU   d. Registered nurse (RN)

_____ 5. RC   e. Lower right eyelid

_____ 6. SB   f. New equipment

_____ 7. TA   g. Clinical psychologist

_____ 8. TC   h. Right coronary artery

_____ 9. TD   i. Left foot, great toe

_____10. UQ   j. Nurse midwife

Enter the appropriate modifier for each description.

11. Intern   _____

12. Court-ordered   _____

13. Monitored anesthesia services   _____

14. Replacement of DME item   _____

15. RN   _____

16. Right coronary artery   _____

17. Primary physician   _____

18. Left hand, 5th digit   _____

19. Dressing for 2 wounds   _____

20. Adult program, geriatric   _____

21. Medicare Secondary Payer   _____

22. CLIA-waived test   _____

23. Administered subcutaneously   _____

24. Mental health program   _____

25. Replacement of a DME, prosthetic item   _____

26. Rental   _____

27. Special payment rate, weekends   _____

28. Follow-up services   _____

29. Great toe, left foot   _____

30. Substance abuse program   _____

31. Patient with mild systemic disease   _____

32. Specialty physician   _____

33. New equipment   _____

34. Lower right eyelid   _____

35. Thumb, left hand   _____

36. Related to trauma   _____

37. Outside providers' customary service area   _____

38. Ambulance transport from physician's office   _____

39. Patient pronounced dead after ambulance called   _____

40. Emergency services   _____

ASSIGNMENT 8.5 – CODING PATIENT CASES

Objectives

At the conclusion of this assignment, the student should be able to:

1. Use the HCPCS level II index to locate procedure and service codes.

2. Verify codes in the appropriate section of HCPCS.

3. Assign modifier(s) when special circumstances are documented in a patient case.

Instructions

Code the following case studies using the HCPCS level II index. Be sure to verify the code(s) in the appropriate section of HCPCS level II. Assign the HCPCS level II procedure and service codes *only* for each patient case. Do *not* code diagnoses or assign CPT codes.

1. **PATIENT CASE #1**

   S: The patient is an 89-year-old white female resident of the county nursing facility. I was asked to see her today because the nursing staff had noticed the patient was having difficulty breathing and was coughing up purulent material. A chest x-ray was ordered, and the mobile x-ray service arrived and took the x-ray while I was seeing my other patients.

   O: The patient appears ill. Temperature is 100.7. CHEST: Scattered rhonchi throughout all lung fields, with severely diminished breath sounds in the left lower lung. Expiratory and inspiratory wheezes present. HEART: Within normal limits. ABDOMEN: No tenderness on palpation. EXTREMITIES: Mild dependent edema is noted; otherwise within normal limits.

   A: The chest x-ray revealed a density consistent with left lower lobe pneumonia.

   P: The patient was given an injection of Zithromax 500 mg. The cough does not seem to be bothersome to the patient right now, so the nursing staff will wait and watch. The nursing staff is to monitor her for any signs of increased fever, lethargy, or medication reaction. They are to encourage fluids and keep the patient up in a chair as much as possible when she is not sleeping. They are to contact me immediately if the patient's symptoms worsen.

2. **PATIENT CASE #2**

   S: This 45-year-old male construction worker was seen in the office today on an emergency basis because he stepped on a sharp edge of steel and lacerated his right foot. He states he cannot recall his last tetanus shot.

   O: Examination of the right foot reveals a laceration of approximately 3.5 cm at the lateral edge of the foot which extends medially across the heel. PROCEDURE: The right heel was cleansed with pHisoHex and prepped with Betadine. The wound edges were infiltrated with 1 percent Xylocaine. After adequate anesthesia was obtained, the laceration was repaired with 3-0 nylon sutures. The wound was dressed with gauze and secured with paper tape.

   A: Laceration of right heel, repaired in the office.

   P: The patient was given a tetanus shot today. He was given instructions on wound care and signs of infection, and was also given reference sheets on the same. He is to be non-weightbearing for the next three days, and was given a pair of wooden crutches. He will return to the office in three days for reevaluation. The patient was also reminded to call immediately if pain increases or if he shows any signs of fever.

3. **PATIENT CASE #3**

   MAMMOGRAPHY CLINIC NOTE: The patient is a 72-year-old female who presented today for bilateral diagnostic digital breast tomosynthesis (3D) mammography for screening. Patient has remained up to date with mammograms, and records shows compliance with yearly screening exams. The patient stated that when performing a self-breast exam about five days ago, a lump was felt in the upper outer quadrant of the left breast. The technician asked the patient to identify the location of the lump, and it was marked with a BB for mammography. The patient was asked to wait until the radiologist had read the initial mammograms. Upon interpretation, there indeed was a suspicious lesion in the upper outer quadrant of the left breast, approximately 1.5 cm. The patient was then asked to undergo additional radiographic views of the left breast for further investigation of the lesion, specifically digital breast tomosynthesis (3D) mammography for diagnostic screening. The patient waited while mammography results were interpreted, the radiologist met with the patient to discuss the documented results. It is felt that the lesion is consistent with malignancy, and the patient was counseled by the nurse practitioner regarding the results of the mammography. We contacted the surgeon's office, and the patient was scheduled tomorrow for biopsy and further evaluation as needed.

---

4. **PATIENT CASE #4**

S: The patient presents today for annual physical exam with Pap. Patient is now 34, has two healthy children, and is doing well except for some complaints of fatigue and recent weight gain.

O: VITAL SIGNS: Blood pressure is 124/72. Pulse is 64 and regular. Respiratory rate is 20. Temperature is 98.8. Weight is 156, which is up 12 pounds since her last visit. HEENT: Within normal limits. The patient wears glasses. NECK: No thyromegaly or lymphadenopathy. HEART: Regular sinus rhythm. CHEST: Clear breath sounds throughout all lung fields. ABDOMEN: No tenderness or organomegaly. PELVIC: Normal external genitalia. Vagina is pink and rugated. Pap specimen was obtained without difficulty. RECTAL: Exam was deferred. EXTREMITIES: Pulses were full and equal. NEUROLOGIC: No complaints; exam within normal limits. LABORATORY: Lab performed in the office today included a CBC with differential, thyroid panel, and complete metabolic panel.

A: Fatigue and weight gain in an otherwise healthy 34-year-old female.

P: Will await the results of the blood work and call the patient to discuss them. Instructed the patient to take a daily multivitamin and drink at least two glasses of milk daily. Discussed dietary modifications to help stop weight gain. If the patient's blood work indicates abnormal thyroid function, will refer to Endocrinology.

---

5. **PATIENT CASE #5**

PROSTHESIS CLINIC NOTE: This 32-year-old male patient presents today because of complaints of discomfort from his right ocular prosthesis. The prosthesis is relatively new and may need some modification. Upon examination, the patient appeared otherwise generally well. The right eye prosthesis was removed and given to the technician for evaluation. The right eye socket had a very small patch of irritated tissue in the upper medial wall. The technician resurfaced and polished the prosthesis, and after refitting, the patient reported a noticeable improvement in his level of comfort. The patient and I then discussed the psychological struggles he has had with the loss of his eye, but overall he feels more optimistic and states he believes he will be able to fully resume normal level of activity.

ASSIGNMENT 8.6 – CODING VERIFICATION

Objectives

At the conclusion of this assignment, the student should be able to:

1. Validate coding accuracy based on coding information.
2. Analyze results and make recommendations.

Overview

HCPCS level II codes can be utilized to capture procedures and services that do not have a CPT level I code. Auditing of HCPCS level II code(s) will provide the opportunity for analysis to provide recommendations that will improve code reporting and reimbursement.

Instructions

Use your HCPCS level II coding manual or log in to **www.EncoderPro.com**, and analyze the codes assigned below for each coding statement to determine if the code is correct. If correct, record it again in the coding verification column; if the code is incorrect, locate and enter the correct code in the coding verification column. Provide an analysis of your findings: What percentage of the codes was correct? What percentage was incorrect based on the 10 charts that were reviewed? What recommendations or suggestions can you provide based on your verification process? Provide your thoughts in a double-spaced, word-processed document that is at least one-half page in length.

Health Record Number	Procedure/Service	HCPCS Level II Code Assigned	Coding Verification
585598	Azathioprine oral 50 mg	J7501	
111454	20 mg of methylprednisolone acetate	J1030	
313258	Digoxin 0.3 mg	J1160	
899784	Zidovudine, 10 mg	S0104	
123456	Prochlorperazine, 10 mg	Q0164	
778541	200 mg of fluconazole	J1450	
549786	3 mg of hydromorphone	J1170	
343437	2 mg of Urecholine	J0520 x 2	
777845	6 mg of pegfilgrastim	J2440	
233233	500 mg of cefazolin sodium	J0690	

 NOTE:

Navigate the HCPCS level II coding website to research information needed for your summary. This will help you learn how to locate information using the Internet as a research tool and using websites, which often requires using tool bars and pull-down menus.

ASSIGNMENT 8.7 – MULTIPLE CHOICE REVIEW

1. HCPCS level II codes are developed and maintained by the _____.
   a. American Medical Association
   b. CMS HCPCS Workgroup
   c. Medicare Administrative Contractors
   d. PDAC and DMEPOS dealers

2. Which organization is responsible for developing and maintaining the HCPCS level II codes?
   a. AMA
   b. CMS
   c. HHS
   d. WHO

3. Which is a member of the CMS HCPCS Workgroup?
   a. American Hospital Association
   b. American Medical Association
   c. Centers for Disease Control and Prevention
   d. Centers for Medicare and Medicaid Services

4. Which organization is responsible for providing suppliers and manufacturers with assistance in determining HCPCS level II codes to be used?
   a. BCBSA
   b. DMEPOS
   c. DMERC
   d. PDAC

5. Which HCPCS level II codes are used by state Medicaid agencies and mandated by state law to separately identify mental health services?
   a. G codes
   b. H codes
   c. K codes
   d. S codes

6. The first alphabetic character in a HCPCS code identifies the code
   a. as one established for Medicare.
   b. as one unique to Medicaid.
   c. section of HCPCS level I.
   d. section of HCPCS level II.

7. Drugs are listed in the HCPCS Table of Drugs according to
   a. dosage to be used.
   b. generic name.
   c. route of administration.
   d. brand name.

8. A regional MAC will receive claims that contain which HCPCS level II codes?
   a. A, J, Q, V
   b. B, E, K, L
   c. C, F, H, N, S
   d. D, G, M, P, R

9. If a provider is not registered with a regional MAC, a patient will receive medical equipment when the
   a. local hospital dispenses the equipment.
   b. patient places an order for the equipment.
   c. physician refers the patient to another doctor.
   d. prescription is taken to a local DMEPOS dealer.

10. If a particular service has both a CPT code and a HCPCS level II code, the provider will
    a. assign only the CPT code.
    b. follow instructions provided by the payer.
    c. report both codes on the CMS-1500 claim.
    d. report only the HCPCS code.

11. If a HCPCS drug code description states "per 50 mg" and is administered in an 80 mg dose, which quantity (e.g., units) is reported on the CMS-1500 claim?
    a. 1
    b. 2
    c. 50
    d. 80

12. HCPCS level II is considered a _____ system.
    a. coding
    b. nomenclature
    c. payment
    d. reimbursement

13. Which would be assigned to report DMEPOS on insurance claims?
    a. CPT codes
    b. HCPCS level II codes
    c. ICD-10-CM codes
    d. ICD-10-PCS codes

14. How many regional MACs are assigned by CMS to process DME claims?
    a. two
    b. three
    c. four
    d. five

15. Which is an example of durable medical equipment (DME)?
    a. blood glucose monitor
    b. irrigation solution
    c. IV pain medication
    d. liquid oxygen

16. New permanent HCPCS level II codes are implemented annually on
    a. January 1.
    b. March 1.
    c. June 1.
    d. October 1.

17. Which code range is assigned to "temporary" HCPCS procedures or professional services?
    a. A4206–A9999
    b. C1300–C9899
    c. E0100–E9999
    d. G0008–G9156

18. Which modifier is used to describe the services of a clinical psychologist?
    a. -AH   c. -AP
    b. -AM   d. -AS

19. Which modifier is used to describe the right upper eyelid?
    a. -E1   c. -E3
    b. -E2   d. -E4

20. HCPCS level II codes are organized by type, depending on the purpose of the codes and the entity responsible for establishing and maintaining them. The four types include
    a. Permanent, Vision, Medical, Modifiers.
    b. Miscellaneous, Temporary, Permanent, Drugs.
    c. Diagnostic, Vision, Hearing, Medical.
    d. Permanent national, Miscellaneous, Temporary codes, and Modifiers.

CMS Reimbursement Methodologies

ASSIGNMENT 9.1 – DATA ANALYTICS FOR REIMBURSEMENT

Objectives

At the conclusion of this assignment, the student should be able to:

1. Calculate statistics using data from a report.
2. Verify the accuracy of data included in a report.
3. Analyze data in a report to reach a conclusion.

Overview

Data analytics for revenue management uses information collected about claims and actual costs of health care provided, patient clinical data, patient satisfaction surveys, and research studies to assist health care facilities and providers make decisions about facility size, types of health care services offered, staffing needs, and more. The Centers for Medicare and Medicaid Services (CMS) website (**www.cms.gov**) contains many resources, such as Medicare Utilization for both Part A and Part B services. Data are presented in table format, and they are ranked in order from the highest to the lowest allowed charge and allowed services. Types of data available include HCPCS codes according to specialty and type of service codes.

Instructions

Refer to the Top 10 Current Procedural Terminology (CPT) Codes (Table 9-1). Analyze data in the table by answering the following questions.

TABLE 9-1 Top 10 Current Procedural Terminology (CPT) Codes

Medicare Part B Physician/Supplier National Data Top 10 Current Procedural Terminology (CPT) Codes			
Rank by Charges	CPT Code	Allowed Charges	Number of Services
1	99214	$ 8,174,871,557	81,303,417
2	99213	$ 6,789,770,914	100,262,062
3	99232	$ 3,572,583,474	50,943,179
4	99223	$ 2,309,147,150	11,770,703
5	66984	$ 2,254,500,991	3,103,372

(continues)

TABLE 9-1 *(continued)*

Rank by Charges	CPT Code	Allowed Charges	Number of Services
		Medicare Part B Physician/Supplier National Data	
		Top 10 Current Procedural Terminology (CPT) Codes	
6	99233	$ 2,253,815,789	22,283,347
7	99285	$ 1,674,265,887	9,879,083
8	88305	$ 1,377,477,046	19,853,914
9	99204	$ 1,339,445,004	8,569,205
10	99215	$ 1,316,510,822	9,691,728
	TOTALS	$ 31,062,388,634	317,660,010

_____ 1. What CPT level I code is ranked first according to number of services?

_____ 2. What was the total allowed charges for CPT code 99285?

_____ 3. What is the percentage of non-E/M codes in the top 10 ranking?

_____ 4. In his annual meeting, a CFO at a local hospital stated that CMS paid $2.2 million for services in the emergency department under CPT code 99285. Is this correct?

_____ 5. List the highest ranking CPT surgical code and allowed charges. What was the average per-service charge?

ASSIGNMENT 9.2 – CASE-MIX INDEX, RELATIVE WEIGHTS, AND MS-DRG PAYMENTS

Objectives

At the conclusion of this assignment, the student should be able to:

1. Calculate a case-mix index.
2. Interpret the impact of a facility's case-mix index on its reimbursement.

Overview

With implementation of prospective payment systems, **case-mix management** has become an important function of revenue management because it allows health care facilities and providers to determine anticipated health care needs by reviewing data analytics about types and/or categories of patients treated. The term *case mix* describes a health care organization's patient population and is based on a number of characteristics (e.g., age, diagnosis, gender, resources consumed, risk factors, treatments received, type of health insurance). A facility's case mix reflects the diversity, clinical complexity, and resource needs of the patient population.

The *case-mix index* is the relative weight assigned for a facility's patient population, and it is used in a formula to calculate health care reimbursement. If 1.000 represents an average relative weight, a weight lower than 1.000 (such as 0.9271) indicates that less complex resource needs are required of a facility's patient population while a weight higher than 1.000 (such as 1.495) indicates more complex resource needs.

A facility's *case-mix index* is calculated by totaling all relative weights for a period of time and dividing by the total number of patients treated during that period of time. Thus, a facility assigned a lower case-mix index will receive less reimbursement for services provided. Conversely, a facility assigned a higher case-mix index will receive higher reimbursement for services provided. Facilities typically calculate statistics for case-mix management purposes as total relative weight (relative weight × total number of cases) and total payment (reimbursement amount per case × total number of cases).

Instructions

Anywhere Medical Center receives reimbursement for inpatient hospitalizations according to Medicare severity diagnosis-related groups (MS-DRGs) based on principal and secondary diagnosis, surgical procedures performed, age, discharge status, medical complexity (e.g., existence of comorbidities and/or complications), and resource needs. Each MS-DRG has a relative weight associated with it, and that weight is related to the complexity of patient resource needs.

Anywhere Medical Center's case-mix index (relative weight) is 1.108. You have been tasked with calculating the total relative weights and total payments for MS-DRG 295 and MS-DRG 305 during the month of March.

_____ 1. MS-DRG 295 had 194 cases during the month of March, and its relative weight is 0.5513. Calculate the total relative weight for MS-DRG 295, carrying the decimal two places.

_____ 2. MS-DRG 295 has a reimbursement rate of $1,400. Calculate the total payment for MS-DRG 295, carrying the decimal two places.

_____ 3. MS-DRG 305 had 54 cases during the month of March, and its relative weight is 0.7199. Calculate the total relative weight for MS-DRG 305, carrying the decimal two places.

_____ 4. MS-DRG 305 has a reimbursement rate of $1,750. Calculate the total payment for MS-DRG 305, carrying the decimal two places.

_____ 5. Which MS-DRG consumes more resources for patient care purposes?

ASSIGNMENT 9.3 – CALCULATING MEDICARE PHYSICIAN FEE SCHEDULE PAYMENTS

Objectives

At the conclusion of this assignment, the student should be able to:

1. Calculate Medicare payment and write-off amounts for participating and nonparticipating providers.

2. Calculate limiting charges for nonparticipating providers.

3. Calculate amounts owed by patient for participating and nonparticipating providers.

Overview

The *Medicare physician fee schedule (MPFS)* reimburses providers according to predetermined rates assigned to services and is revised by CMS each year.

- *Participating providers (PARs)* typically receive 80 percent of the MPFS amount as payment, with the patient responsible for the remaining 20 percent.

- *Nonparticipating providers (nonPARs)* are subject to a *limiting charge* associated with the MPFS amount, which is calculated by multiplying the MPFS amount by 115 percent and takes into consideration a conversion factor and relative value units. NonPARs typically receive 80 percent of the MPFS limiting charge, less an additional 5 percent. Patients are restricted to paying *no more than* the difference between the MPFS amount calculated as payment to a PAR and the MPFS limiting charge.

The *Medicare Physician Fee Schedule Look-up* tool at **www.cms.gov** provides information about services covered by the MPFS. Data about more than 10,000 physician services can be searched using the tool. Search results are reviewed to determine pricing, limiting charges, conversion factors, and associated relative value units (when relevant) (Figure 9-1). Of significance is that this tool has eliminated the need to calculate limiting charge amounts for non-participating providers.

Instructions

Use Medicare Physician Schedule Look-up tool search results (Figure 9-1) to locate price and charge data, and calculate amounts paid by Medicare and patients. When calculating the provider and patient payments, use mathematical rounding rules.

_____ 1. An established female patient receives a level 3 evaluation and management service from her participating provider. What is the non-facility price for MAC locality 0111205? (Go to Figure 9-1, locate the Non-Facility Price column, and go to row 2 where MAC locality 0111205 data can be found.)

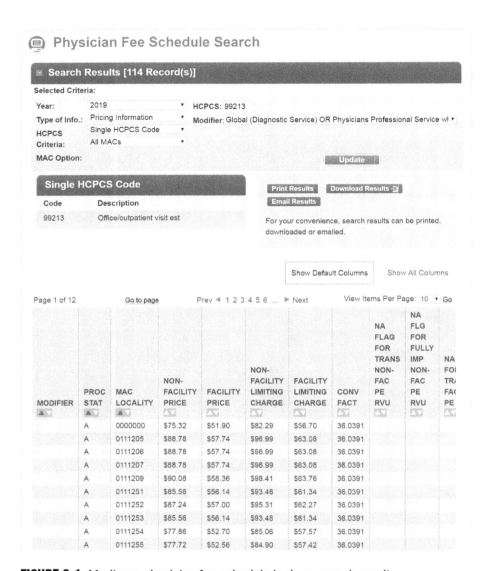

FIGURE 9-1 Medicare physician fee schedule look-up search results.

_____ 2. A participating provider (PAR) charges $125 for a level 3 established patient evaluation and management service. If the non-facility price for MAC locality 0111209 is $90.08, what will the PAR receive as payment from Medicare?

_____ 3. A PAR charges $125 for a level 3 established patient evaluation and management service. If the non-facility price for MAC locality 0111255 is $77.72, what will the PAR receive as payment from the patient?

_____ 4. An established patient receives level 3 evaluation and management services from a nonparticipating provider (nonPAR). What is the non-facility limiting charge for MAC locality 0111205? (Go to Figure 9-1, locate the Non-Facility Limiting Charge column, and go to row 2 where MAC locality 0111205 data can be found.)

_____ 5. A nonPAR charges $125 for a level 3 established patient evaluation and management service. If the non-facility limiting charge for MAC locality 011209 is $98.41, what will the nonPAR receive as payment from patient? (Figure 9-1 contains a column of non-facility limiting charges, which means the limiting charge is not separately calculated. Remember! NonPARs are paid 80 percent of the limiting fee, _less an additional 5 percent._)

ASSIGNMENT 9.4 – DIAGNOSIS-RELATED GROUPS

Objectives

At the conclusion of this assignment, the student should be able to:

1. Interpret a diagnosis-related group (DRG) decision tree.
2. Differentiate between medical partitioning and surgical partitioning DRG decision trees.
3. Determine which DRG is assigned when a secondary diagnosis such as a complication or comorbidity is documented in the patient record.

Overview

Diagnoses and procedures are grouped according to a particular DRG, and DRG decision trees (Figures 9-2 and 9-3) visually represent the process of assigning a DRG within a medical diagnostic category (MDC). The decision trees use a flowchart design to facilitate the decision-making logic for assigning a DRG. (Only ICD-10-CM diagnosis codes are grouped according to a medical partitioning DRG decision tree. ICD-10-PCS surgical procedure codes are grouped according to a surgical partitioning DRG decision tree.)

Instructions

Use Figures 9-2 and 9-3 to answer the following questions.

1. Interpret the DRG decision tree in Figure 9-2 to answer the following questions.

   EXAMPLE: Which neoplasm DRG is assigned to a patient whose provider has documented a complication or comorbidity?
   ANSWER: DRG 10.

   _____ a. Which DRG is assigned when the provider documents "transient ischemia" as the patient's principal diagnosis?
   _____ b. For a patient who has cranial and peripheral nerve disorders and a documented comorbidity, which DRG is assigned?
   _____ c. Which DRG is assigned for a patient whose principal diagnosis is multiple sclerosis?
   _____ d. A patient was diagnosed with trigeminal neuralgia. This is the only diagnosis reported in the record. Which DRG is assigned?
   _____ e. For a patient with cerebrovascular disease that is classified as nonspecific, which DRG is assigned when the patient has a secondary diagnosis of insulin-dependent diabetes mellitus?

2. Interpret the DRG decision tree in Figure 9-3 to answer the following questions.

   _____ a. For a 25-year-old patient who undergoes craniotomy for implantation of a chemotherapeutic agent, which DRG is assigned?
   _____ b. Which DRG is assigned to a 5-year-old patient who underwent a procedure for a ventricular shunt?
   _____ c. A 56-year-old patient underwent a craniotomy and suffered a cerebrovascular accident after the procedure. Which DRG is assigned?
   _____ d. Which DRG is assigned for an otherwise healthy patient who underwent sciatic nerve biopsy?
   _____ e. A patient underwent lumbar laminectomy because of injury from a fall. The patient recently completed a course of chemotherapy for non-Hodgkin's lymphoma. Which DRG is assigned?

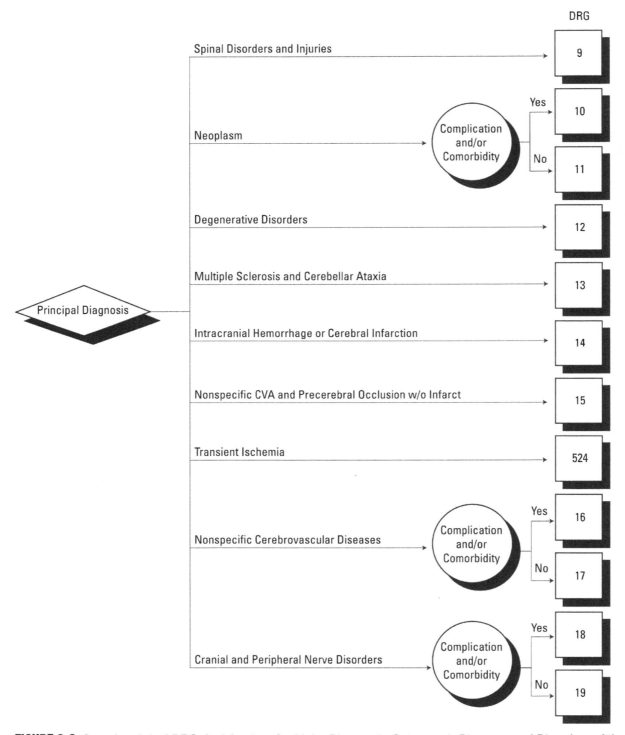

Major Diagnostic Category 1
Diseases and Disorders of the Nervous System

Medical
Partitioning

FIGURE 9-2 Sample original DRG decision tree for Major Diagnostic Category 1: Diseases and Disorders of the Nervous System (Medical Partitioning).

Major Diagnostic Category 1
Diseases and Disorders of the Nervous System

FIGURE 9-3 Sample original DRG decision tree for Major Diagnostic Category 1: Diseases and Disorders of the Nervous System (Surgical Partitioning).

ASSIGNMENT 9.5 – MEDICARE SEVERITY DRGs

Objectives

At the conclusion of this assignment, the student should be able to:

1. Enter data to calculate MS-DRGs (Medicare Severity Diagnosis-Related Groups).
2. Evaluate MS-DRG data (e.g., reimbursement rate, weight).

Overview

Medicare Severity Diagnosis-Related Groups (MS-DRGs) are payment groups designed for the inpatient hospital Medicare population. Patients who have similar clinical characteristics and similar costs are assigned to an MS-DRG. The MS-DRG is linked to a fixed payment amount based on the average cost of patients in the group. Patients can be assigned to an MS-DRG based on diagnosis, surgical procedure, age, and other information (e.g., diagnosis present on admission status, discharge status). Hospitals report such information on the UB-04, and Medicare uses the information to determine inpatient hospital reimbursement. There may be some MS-DRGs that are based on complications or comorbidities (CCs) or major complications or comorbidities (MCCs). Complications are new problems that are the result of an illness, procedure performed, or treatment provided. Comorbidities are co-existing conditions (e.g., diabetes mellitus, hypertension) for which the patient is medically managed during an inpatient hospitalization.

CMS uses MS-DRGs to account for the severity of illness and resource consumption of Medicare beneficiaries. There are three levels of severity in the MS-DRG system based on secondary diagnosis codes:

- MCC–Major Complication/Comorbidity, which reflect the highest level of severity
- CC–Complication/Comorbidity, which is the next level of severity
- Non-CC–Non-Complication/Comorbidity, which does not significantly affect severity of illness and resource use

A weight is assigned to each MS-DRG and reflects the average relative costliness of cases in that group compared with the costliness for the average Medicare case. A reimbursement amount is also assigned to each MS-DRG based on formula calculations that reflect a combination of factors determined (e.g., weight, wage index, and so on).

Instructions

Review each case study to answer the questions in this assignment. All information needed to answer each question is provided in the case studies. (MS-DRG tables below the case studies contain sample data created for this assignment.)

1. John L. Berry is a 70-year-old male, seen and admitted for congestive heart failure. The patient is discharged after developing pneumonia during the hospital stay. Total inpatient days this patient was in the hospital were seven days. Mr. Berry is discharged to his home with follow-up at his internist's office in three days. Discharge diagnoses codes (after review of the record by the coder): I50.9, E10.9, J18.9, and I10. (The pneumonia diagnosis is listed as an MCC when the MS-DRG is calculated.)

MS-DRG	MDC	Type	MS-DRG Title	Weight	Los	Rate
0291	05	Med	Heart Failure & Shock w MCC	1.4943	4.6	$2,241.45
0292	05	Med	Heart Failure & Shock w CC	0.9938	3.7	$1,490.70
0293	05	Med	Heart Failure & Shock w/o CC/MCC	0.6723	2.6	$1,008.45

   a. What is the MS-DRG weight for this patient? _____
   b. What is the major complication or comorbidity (MCC) diagnosis code? _____

2. Sally Parsons is an 85-year-old female admitted after being seen in the emergency department with a painful and swollen lower right leg. She is admitted for further treatment and evaluation. She is found to have an acute hematogenous osteomyelitis of her right tibia and fibula. Discharge diagnoses codes are M86.061, M81.0, and E03.9. Mrs. Parsons has osteoporosis and hypothyroidism, which are treated and evaluated during this inpatient admission.

Mrs. Parsons is discharged to home with IV home health services. (There are no MCCs or CCs when the MS-DRG is calculated.)

MS-DRG	MDC	Type	MS-DRG Title	Weight	Los	Rate
0539	08	Med	Osteomyelitis w MCC	1.8631	6.2	$2,974.65
0540	08	Med	Osteomyelitis w CC	1.3063	4.9	$1,959.45
0541	08	Med	Osteomyelitis w/o CC/MCC	0.9743	3.6	$1,461.45

a. What is the MS-DRG? _____

b. What is the MS-DRG reimbursement rate? _____

3. Lawrence Texfield is a 90-year-old man who is admitted due to his uncontrolled type 2 diabetes with diabetic peripheral angiopathy. He is in the hospital for eight days due to his additional complaint of chest pain on admission day three. He is discharged to home with home health services. Codes assigned after review of the record and physician documentation are E11.51 and I20.9. (There are no MCCs or CCs when the MS-DRG is calculated.)

MS-DRG	MDC	Type	MS-DRG Title	Weight	Los	Rate
637	10	Med	Diabetes w MCC	1.3888	4.2	$2,083.20
638	10	Med	Diabetes w CC	0.8252	3.0	$1,237.80
639	10	Med	Diabetes w/o CC/MCC	0.5708	2.2	$856.20

a. What is the MS-DRG reimbursement rate? _____

4. Maria Martin is a 65-year-old female admitted after falling at home. She is diagnosed with a left upper femur fracture and requires an open reduction with internal fixation (ORIF). After having the operation, she has a cardiac arrest, which converted, and she is found to have cardiomyopathy. Discharge for this patient is to a skilled nursing facility (SNF). ICD-10-CM codes assigned by coder after chart review: S72.009A, I97.121, I42.9, and 0QS704Z. (The cardiac arrest diagnosis is listed as a CC when the MS-DRG is calculated.)

MS-DRG	MDC	Type	MS-DRG Title	Weight	Los	Rate
480	08	Surg	Hip & Femur Procedures Except Major Joint w MCC	3.0694	7.1	$4,064.10
481	08	Surg	Hip & Femur Procedures Except Major Joint w CC	1.9721	4.8	$2,958.15
482	08	Surg	Hip & Femur Procedures Except Major Joint w/o CC/MCC	1.6305	3.9	$2,445.75

a. What is the MS-DRG? _____

b. What is the MS-DRG reimbursement rate? _____

5. Abe Dillon is a 75-year-old male who is admitted for inpatient surgery due to acute obstructive cholecystitis and cholelithiasis. Mr. Dillon underwent cholecystectomy via open approach and was discharged from the hospital after four days to an intermediate care facility. ICD-10-CM codes assigned are K80.13 and 0FT40ZZ. (There are no MCCs or CCs when the MS-DRG is calculated.)

MS-DRG	MDC	Type	MS-DRG Title	Weight	Los	Rate
414	07	Surg	Cholecystectomy Except by Laparoscope w/o CDE w MCC	3.6208	8.8	$5,431.20
415	07	Surg	Cholecystectomy Except by Laparoscope w/o CDE w CC	2.0173	5.8	$3,025.95
416	07	Surg	Cholecystectomy Except by Laparoscope w/o CDE w/o CDE w/o CC/MCC	1.3268	3.5	$1,990.20

a. What is the MS-DRG weight? _____

b. What is the MS-DRG reimbursement rate? _____

ASSIGNMENT 9.6 – AMBULATORY PAYMENT CLASSIFICATIONS

Objectives

At the conclusion of this assignment, the student should be able to:

1. Explain the difference between Medicare status indicators and procedure discounting.

2. Locate and interpret data in an ambulatory payment classification table.

3. Verify procedure and service codes in the appropriate section of the CPT manual.

Overview

Ambulatory payment classifications (APCs) are used by Medicare's outpatient prospective payment system (OPPS) to calculate reimbursement rates for hospital outpatient procedures and services. APC payments are made to hospitals when a Medicare outpatient is discharged from the emergency department or outpatient clinic or when the patient is transferred to another hospital (or other facility) that is not affiliated with the initial hospital where the patient originally received outpatient services. If the patient is admitted to the hospital (as an inpatient) from the hospital's emergency department or outpatient, there is no APC payment; instead, Medicare reimburses the hospital according to its inpatient prospective payment system (IPPS) that uses Medicare severity diagnosis-related groups (MS-DRGs).

Instructions

Analyze each ambulatory payment classification (APC) table, and answer the questions listed below each table (Tables 9-2 through 9-6). Be sure to verify the description of procedure/service code(s) in the CPT manual.

To answer Questions 1–6, refer to Table 9-2.

_____ 1. What is the level I skin repair payment rate?

_____ 2. What is the relative weight for level I skin repair?

_____ 3. What is the Medicare status indicator for level I skin repair?

_____ 4. How many codes are contained in the range for level I skin repair?

TABLE 9-2 Level I Skin Repair

Medicare Status Indicators and Procedure Discounting	
Status Indicator	Description
T	Significant procedure, multiple procedure reduction applies
S	Significant procedure, and is not discounted when you report multiple CPT codes that group to APCs with multiple "S" status indicators
Level I Skin Repair	
Codes in Range	11760
	11950
	11952
	11954
	12001
Status Indicator:	T
Relative Weight:	1.330
Payment Rate:	$98.81
National Adjusted Coinsurance:	$25.67
Minimum Unadjusted Coinsurance:	$18.37

_____ 5. What is the national adjusted coinsurance for level I skin repair?

_____ 6. What is the level I skin repair minimum unadjusted coinsurance?

To answer Questions 7–10, refer to Table 9-3.

_____ 7. What is the payment rate for fine needle biopsy/aspiration?

_____ 8. What is the relative weight for fine needle biopsy/aspiration?

_____ 9. Which code is reported for placement of a needle for intraosseous infusion?

_____ 10. What is the Medicare status indicator for fine needle biopsy/aspiration?

TABLE 9-3 Fine Needle Biopsy/Aspiration

Medicare Status Indicators and Procedure Discounting	
Status Indicator	Description
T	Significant procedure, multiple procedure reduction applies
S	Significant procedure, and is not discounted when you report multiple CPT codes that group to APCs with multiple "S" status indicators
Fine Needle Biopsy/Aspiration	
Codes in Range	10021
	19001
	36680
Status Indicator:	T
Relative Weight:	1.5703
Payment Rate:	$108.16
National Adjusted Coinsurance:	N/A
Minimum Unadjusted Coinsurance:	$21.64

To answer Questions 11–15, refer to Table 9-4.

_____ 11. What is the Medicare status indicator for level II breast surgery?

_____ 12. What is the national adjusted coinsurance for level II breast surgery?

_____ 13. What is the minimum unadjusted coinsurance for level II breast surgery?

_____ 14. What is the payment rate for level II breast surgery?

_____ 15. What is the relative weight for level II breast surgery?

TABLE 9-4 Level II Breast Surgery

Medicare Status Indicators and Procedure Discounting	
Status Indicator	Description
T	Significant procedure, multiple procedure reduction applies
S	Significant procedure, and is not discounted when you report multiple CPT codes that group to APCs with multiple "S" status indicators
Level II Breast Surgery	
Codes in Range	19105
	19303
	19316
	19328
Status Indicator:	T
Relative Weight:	33.9253
Payment Rate:	$2,336.64
National Adjusted Coinsurance:	$581.52
Minimum Unadjusted Coinsurance:	$467.33

To answer Questions 16–20, refer to Table 9-5.

_____ 16. What is the payment rate for cardiac rehabilitation?

_____ 17. What is the national adjusted coinsurance for cardiac rehabilitation?

_____ 18. What is the Medicare status indicator for cardiac rehabilitation?

_____ 19. What is the relative weight for cardiac rehabilitation?

_____ 20. Which code is reported for "intensive cardiac rehabilitation; with or without continuous ECG monitoring with exercise, per session"?

TABLE 9-5 Cardiac Rehabilitation

Medicare Status Indicators and Procedure Discounting	
Status Indicator	Description
T	Significant procedure, multiple procedure reduction applies
S	Significant procedure, and is not discounted when you report multiple CPT codes that group to APCs with multiple "S" status indicators
Cardiac Rehabilitation	
Codes in Range	93797
	93798
	G0422
	G0423
Status Indicator:	S
Relative Weight:	0.9991
Payment Rate:	$68.81
National Adjusted Coinsurance:	$13.86
Minimum Unadjusted Coinsurance:	$13.77

To answer Questions 21–25, refer to Table 9-6.

_____ 21. How many codes are contained in the range for small intestine endoscopy?

_____ 22. What is the relative weight for small intestine endoscopy?

_____ 23. What is the national adjusted coinsurance for small intestine endoscopy?

_____ 24. What is the payment rate for small intestine endoscopy?

_____ 25. What is the minimum unadjusted coinsurance for small intestine endoscopy?

TABLE 9-6 Small Intestine Endoscopy

Medicare Status Indicators and Procedure Discounting	
Status Indicator	Description
T	Significant procedure, multiple procedure reduction applies
S	Significant procedure, and is not discounted when you report multiple CPT codes that group to APCs with multiple "S" status indicators
Small Intestine Endoscopy	
Codes in Range	44360
	44361
	44363
	44364
	44365
Status Indicator:	T
Relative Weight:	10.1857
Payment Rate:	$701.55
National Adjusted Coinsurance:	$152.78
Minimum Unadjusted Coinsurance:	$140.31

ASSIGNMENT 9.7 – MULTIPLE CHOICE REVIEW

1. The Resource-Based Relative Value Scale (RBRVS) system is also known as
   a. Clinical Laboratory Fee Schedule.
   b. Long-Term Care Diagnosis-Related Groups.
   c. Medicare Physician Fee Schedule.
   d. Resource Utilization Groups.

2. Which reimbursement system establishes rates in advance of services and is based on reported charges from which a *per diem* rate is determined?
   a. fee-for-service cost-based
   b. prospective price-based
   c. prospective cost-based
   d. retrospective reasonable cost

3. Review the following ambulance fee schedule and calculate the Medicare payment rate in year 6 (for an ambulance company reasonable charge of $600).
   a. $425
   b. $460
   c. $480
   d. $495

Ambulance Fee Schedule

Year	Ambulance Company (Reasonable) Charge (a)	% of Reasonable Charge (b)	Amount (c)	Ambulance Fee Schedule Rate (d)	Phase In % (e)	Amount (f)	Medicare Payment (g)
		Formula: [(a) × (b) = (c)] + [(d) × (e) = (f)] = Medicare payment (g)					
1.	$600	80%	$480	n/a	n/a	n/a	
2.	$600	80%	$480	$425	20%	$ 85	
3.	$600	60%	$360	$425	40%	$170	
4.	$600	40%	$240	$425	60%	$255	
5.	$600	20%	$120	$425	80%	$340	
6.	$600	0%	$0	$425	100%	$425	

4. Review the following ambulance fee schedule and calculate the amount Medicare paid in year 5 (for an ambulance company reasonable charge of $720).
   a. $425
   b. $460
   c. $484
   d. $576

Ambulance Fee Schedule

Year	Ambulance Company (Reasonable) Charge (a)	% of Reasonable Charge (b)	Amount (c)	Ambulance Fee Schedule Rate (d)	Phase In % (e)	Amount (f)	Medicare Payment (g)
		Formula: [(a) × (b) = (c)] + [(d) × (e) = (f)] = Medicare payment (g)					
1.	$720	80%	$576	n/a	n/a	n/a	
2.	$720	80%	$576	$425	20%	$ 85	
3.	$720	60%	$432	$425	40%	$170	
4.	$720	40%	$288	$425	60%	$255	
5.	$720	20%	$144	$425	80%	$340	
6.	$720	0%	$0	$425	100%	$425	

5. The Deficit Reduction Act of 1984 established the Medicare _____ fee schedule.
   a. ambulance
   b. clinical laboratory
   c. DMEPOS
   d. physician

6. Sally Brown registered as an outpatient at the hospital for three encounters: chest x-ray, gait training physical therapy, and excision of lesion from right upper arm. Ambulatory patient classification (APC) reimbursement will be based on the
   a. APC that provides the hospital with the highest reimbursement amount possible.
   b. assignment of multiple APCs that reflect all services provided, with discounting.
   c. calculation of four APC rates after codes are assigned to calculate the payment.
   d. reimbursement determined by the APC that the primary care provider documents.

7. An *episode of care* in the home health prospective payment system (HHPPS) is _____ days.
   a. 21   c. 60
   b. 30   d. 90

8. In which year was the inpatient prospective payment system implemented?
   a. 1973   c. 1983
   b. 1976   d. 1986

9. Which type of hospital is excluded from the inpatient prospective payment system?
   a. cancer   c. osteopathic
   b. coronary   d. university

10. The IPPS window requires outpatient preadmission services provided by a hospital up to _____ prior to a patient's inpatient admission to be covered by the IPPS MS-DRG payment.
    a. 12 hours   c. 48 hours
    b. 36 hours   d. 72 hours

11. Which is a relative value unit (RVU) in the Medicare physician fee schedule payment system?
    a. geographic location   c. physician experience
    b. payroll expenditures   d. practice expense

12. Medicare Part B radiology services payments vary according to
    a. cost of supplies.   c. relative value units.
    b. place of service.   d. time with the patient.

13. The physician fee schedule for CPT code 99214 is $75. Calculate the nonPAR *limiting charge* for this service.
    a. $56.25   c. $75.00
    b. $71.25   d. $81.94

14. The physician fee schedule for CPT code 99214 is $75. Calculate the nonPAR *limiting charge* that Medicare will reimburse for this service.
    a. $56.25   c. $75.00
    b. $71.25   d. $81.94

15. The intent of establishing a limiting charge for nonPARs is to
    a. increase the patient case load of Medicare PARs.
    b. protect Medicare enrollees financially.
    c. penalize providers who do not participate in Medicare.
    d. reduce fraud and abuse of the Medicare system.

16. Jeffrey Border received care from his participating physician, who charged $300 for services provided. (Mr. Border has already met his Medicare Part B deductible.) Mr. Border has primary coverage with his employer group health plan (EGHP). The EGHP's allowed charge for the service was $260, of which 80 percent was paid by the EGHP ($208). The Medicare physician fee schedule for the procedure is $240. Using the rules to determine the amount of Medicare secondary benefits, calculate the Medicare secondary payment.

    a. $32
    b. $42
    c. $52
    d. $92

17. Which is classified as a nonphysician practitioner?

    a. laboratory technician
    b. medical assistant
    c. physician assistant
    d. radiologic technologist

18. Which publication communicates new or changed policies and procedures that will be incorporated into a specific CMS manual?

    a. coverage determinations
    b. Medicare summary notice
    c. MPFS look-up tool
    d. transmittals

19. When an office-based service is performed in a health care facility, payment is affected by the use of

    a. additional CPT modifier(s).
    b. a case-mix adjustment.
    c. ICD-10-PCS procedure code(s).
    d. a site of service differential.

20. Medicare Secondary Payer (MSP) refers to situations in which the Medicare program does not have primary responsibility for paying a beneficiary's medical expenses. For which of the following payers would Medicare be considered primary?

    a. BCBS EGHP
    b. homeowner liability insurance
    c. Medicaid
    d. workers' compensation

Coding Compliance Programs, Clinical Documentation Improvement, and Coding for Medical Necessity

## CHAPTER 10

ASSIGNMENT 10.1 – CHOOSING THE FIRST-LISTED DIAGNOSIS

Objectives

At the conclusion of this assignment, the student should be able to:

1. Define *first-listed diagnosis* as it is reported on the CMS-1500 claim.

2. Identify the first-listed diagnosis upon review of conditions, diagnoses, and signs or symptoms.

Instructions

Review each case and underline the first-listed diagnosis.

> **EXAMPLE:** The patient was seen in the office to rule out cervical radiculopathy. The patient has a recent history of pain in both scapular regions along with spasms of the left upper trapezius muscle. The patient has limited range of motion, neck and left arm. X-rays reveal significant cervical osteoarthritis. FIRST-LISTED DIAGNOSIS: <u>Cervical osteoarthritis</u>.

 NOTE:

> Do not select differentiated diagnoses, such as "rule out cervical radiculopathy," as the answer because such diagnoses are not coded and reported on the CMS-1500 claim for outpatient cases. Also, do not report symptoms such as spasms of the left upper trapezius muscle and limited range of motion, neck and left arm, because they are due to the cervical osteoarthritis that is reported as the first-listed diagnosis in Block 21, #1, of the CMS-1500 claim.

1. Pain, left knee. History of injury to left knee 20 years ago. The patient underwent arthroscopic surgery and medial meniscectomy, right knee (10 years ago). Probable arthritis, left knee.

2. The patient was admitted to the emergency department (ED) with complaints of severe chest pain. Possible myocardial infarction. EKG and cardiac enzymes revealed normal findings. Diagnosis upon discharge was gastroesophageal reflux disease.

3. A female patient was seen in the office for follow-up of hypertension. The nurse noticed upper arm bruising on the patient and asked how she sustained the bruising. The physician renewed the patient's hypertension prescription, hydrochlorothiazide.

4. A 10-year-old male was seen in the office for sore throat. The nurse swabbed the patient's throat and sent swabs to the hospital lab for a strep test. The physician documented "likely strep throat" on the patient's record.

5. The patient was seen in the outpatient department to have a lump in his abdomen evaluated and removed. The surgeon removed the lump, and the pathology report revealed that the lump was a lipoma.

ASSIGNMENT 10.2 – LINKING DIAGNOSES WITH PROCEDURES/SERVICES

Objectives

At the conclusion of this assignment, the student should be able to:

1. Define *medical necessity*.

2. Link diagnoses with procedures/services to justify medical necessity.

Instructions

Match the diagnosis in the right-hand column with the procedure/service in the left-hand column that justifies medical necessity.

_____ 1. allergy test	a. bronchial asthma
_____ 2. EKG	b. chest pain
_____ 3. inhalation treatment	c. family history, cervical cancer
_____ 4. Pap smear	d. fractured wrist
_____ 5. removal of ear wax	e. hay fever
_____ 6. sigmoidoscopy	f. hematuria
_____ 7. strep test	g. impacted cerumen
_____ 8. urinalysis	h. fibroid tumor
_____ 9. biopsy	i. rectal bleeding
_____10. x-ray, radius and ulna	j. sore throat

ASSIGNMENT 10.3 – NATIONAL COVERAGE DETERMINATIONS

Objectives

At the conclusion of this assignment, the student should be able to:

1. Define *national coverage determinations*.

2. Locate national coverage determination policies at the CMS website.

3. Interpret national coverage determination policies to determine whether Medicare will reimburse for procedures/services provided.

Instructions

Assign ICD-10-CM and CPT or HCPCS level II (procedure/service) codes to the following outpatient scenarios. (Do *not* assign ICD-10-PCS procedure codes.) Go to **www.cms.gov/mcd,** click on the INDEXES link, click the plus sign next to National Coverage, and then click on the NCDs Listed Alphabetically link below the National Coverage Determinations (NCDs) heading to review the item/service description and determine indications and limitations of coverage for each case. Indicate whether the procedure/service is covered by Medicare. (The title of each NCD is underlined to facilitate its location in the NCD website.)

_____ 1. A 65-year-old white female underwent <u>apheresis (therapeutic pheresis)</u> of red blood cells for the treatment of Guillain-Barré syndrome.

_____ 2. A 70-year-old male underwent <u>blood glucose testing</u> to monitor his diabetes mellitus.

_____ 3. A 45-year-old female with a mental disability underwent Roux-en-Y gastric bypass (RYGBP) (<u>bariatric surgery for treatment of co-morbid conditions related to morbid obesity</u>) surgery for treatment of morbid obesity. The patient also has hypertension and uncontrolled diabetes mellitus.

_____ 4. A 75-year-old female participated in <u>cardiac rehabilitation programs for congestive heart failure</u> for three months immediately following inpatient hospital discharge for congestive heart failure.

_____ 5. A 72-year-old female underwent an annual screening mammogram, bilateral (<u>mammograms</u>).

ASSIGNMENT 10.4 – CODING FROM CASE SCENARIOS

Objectives

At the conclusion of this assignment, the student should be able to:

1. Select diagnoses, procedures, and services upon review of case scenarios.
2. Assign ICD-10-CM, CPT, and HCPCS level II codes (and appropriate modifiers) to diagnoses, procedures, and services.

Instructions

Assign ICD-10-CM codes to diagnoses and CPT or HCPCS level II codes to procedures and services in each case scenario. Be sure to report CPT and HCPCS modifiers where appropriate.

1. A 35-year-old established patient came to the office for excessive menstruation and irregular menstrual cycle. The physician provided a level 3 E/M service and performed a cervical biopsy.

   CPT/HCPCS Level II Codes   **ICD-10-CM Codes**

   _____   _____

2. The patient was referred by his primary care physician to see Dr. Pearson because of severe back pain. Dr. Pearson feels the patient should have surgery, but the patient states the pain is relieved by regular chiropractic care and doesn't want to have back surgery. After a problem-focused examination and a complete radiologic examination of the lumbosacral spine, including bending views, I consulted with Dr. Pearson and concluded the patient's degenerative disc disease is probably doing as well with a chiropractor as with orthopedic treatment. I did not recommend surgery at this time.

   CPT/HCPCS Level II Codes   **ICD-10-CM Codes**

   _____   _____

3. The patient underwent a colon x-ray, double-contrast which included barium and air contrast. The request form noted severe abdominal pain and diarrhea for the past two weeks. The radiology impression was diverticulitis of the colon.

   CPT/HCPCS Level II Codes   **ICD-10-CM Codes**

   _____   _____

4. The patient presented for follow-up of COPD. At this time the patient is experiencing no significant cough, no sputum, no fever, and no respiratory distress. However, there is dyspnea only with exertion, which is accompanied by angina. A level 4 E/M service was provided during which the physician spent approximately 30 minutes with the patient. Chest is clear, no wheeze or rales. Chest x-rays, frontal and lateral, were taken to determine status of COPD. No additional treatment is required at this time.

CPT/HCPCS Level II Codes   **ICD-10-CM Codes**

_____   _____

5. A surgeon is called to the hospital by the emergency department physician to see a 59-year-old male who presented with an abdominal mass, left lower quadrant. The surgeon performed a comprehensive examination, admitted the patient, and scheduled an exploratory laparotomy.

CPT/HCPCS Level II Codes   **ICD-10-CM Codes**

_____   _____

ASSIGNMENT 10.5 – CODING FROM SOAP NOTES AND OPERATIVE REPORTS

Objectives

At the conclusion of this assignment, the student should be able to:

1. Interpret SOAP notes and the contents of operative reports to identify diagnoses, procedures, and services that should be reported on the CMS-1500 claim.

2. Assign ICD-10-CM, CPT, and HCPCS level II codes (and appropriate modifiers) to diagnoses, procedures, and services.

Instructions

Review the following SOAP notes and operative reports to select the diagnoses, procedures, and services that should be reported on the CMS-1500 claim. Then assign ICD-10-CM codes to diagnoses and CPT or HCPCS level II codes (and appropriate modifiers) to procedures and services. (The level of service is indicated for each visit.)

1. **PATIENT CASE #1**

   S: A new patient was seen today in the GI clinic for a level 2 E/M service, which was 20 minutes in length. Patient complains of one week of severe epigastric pain and burning, especially after eating.

   O: On examination there is extreme guarding and tenderness, epigastric region, with no rebound. Bowel sounds are normal. BP 110/70.

   A: Rule out gastric ulcer.

   P: The patient is to have upper gastrointestinal series. Start on Zantac and eliminate alcohol, fried foods, and caffeine. Return to clinic in one week.

   CPT/HCPCS Level II Codes   **ICD-10-CM Codes**

   _____   _____

2. **PATIENT CASE #2**

S: The patient returned to the clinic this month for a level 2 E/M service, which was 15 minutes in length. Patient underwent an upper gastrointestinal series last month, which revealed areas of acute gastric ulceration. Patient is still experiencing epigastric pain.

O: Upper gastrointestinal series revealed areas of ulceration.

A: Acute gastric ulcer.

P: Omeprazole 10 mg q.d. Return for follow-up visit in three weeks.

CPT/HCPCS Level II Codes	ICD-10-CM Codes
_____	_____

3. **PATIENT CASE #3**

S: The new 52-year-old male patient was seen in the orthopedic clinic today for an urgent level 3 E/M service, which was 30 minutes in length. He was walking up his driveway when he slipped and fell, landing on his left arm and striking his head against the car. He was unconscious for less than 10 minutes, experienced dizziness and vomiting, and felt severe pain in his left arm. The patient's wife was actually coming here today for follow-up of her rheumatoid arthritis, and asked that we evaluate her husband's injuries.

O: Examination of the head reveals a 2.5 cm superficial laceration of the scalp, temporal region, left side. Examination of the left arm reveals restriction of motion and acute pain upon palpation and with attempted range of motion of the upper arm and shoulder. The patient underwent a skull x-ray to rule out fracture and x-ray of the left arm and shoulder for evaluation of the pain. The patient was taken to the radiography department where x-ray was negative for skull fracture, revealing only swelling in the area of the laceration. An x-ray of the left arm and shoulder, however, revealed an undisplaced fracture of the proximal left humerus at the greater tuberosity.

A: Concussion. Superficial laceration of scalp, 2.5 cm. Nondisplaced fracture of proximal left humerus at the greater tuberosity.

P: The patient underwent simple repair of the scalp laceration with sutures. The left arm was manipulated slightly to achieve proper anatomic alignment of the proximal humerus. The arm and shoulder were immobilized with sling and binder. The patient was given pain medication, and the patient's wife was instructed on how to perform neuro checks every two hours on the patient for the next 24 hours. The patient will be seen back in the clinic in two days. The patient and wife were instructed to contact the office if any problems arise in the meantime.

CPT/HCPCS Level II Codes	ICD-10-CM Codes
_____	_____

4. **PATIENT CASE #4**

S: An established patient was seen today for a level 2 E/M service, which was 15 minutes in length. The patient complains of rectal discomfort, rectal bleeding, and severe itching.

O: Rectal examination reveals multiple soft external hemorrhoids.

A: Multiple soft, thrombosed external hemorrhoids.

P: Suppositories are to be used after each bowel movement. The patient will return to the office in four weeks for reevaluation.

CPT/HCPCS Level II Codes	ICD-10-CM Codes
_____	_____

5. **PATIENT CASE #5**

S: A 53-year-old new patient was seen today for a level 2 E/M service, which was 20 minutes in length. The female patient presents with complaints of polyuria, polydipsia, and weight loss.

O: Urinalysis by dip, automated, with microscopy reveals elevated glucose level.

A: Possible diabetes.

P: The patient is to have a glucose tolerance test and return in three days for her blood work results and applicable management of care.

CPT/HCPCS Level II Codes   ICD-10-CM Codes

_____   _____

6. **PATIENT CASE #6**

PREOPERATIVE DIAGNOSIS: Pterygium of the right eye

POSTOPERATIVE DIAGNOSIS: Pterygium of the right eye

PROCEDURE PERFORMED: Pterygium excision with conjunctival autograft of the right eye

ANESTHESIA: General endotracheal anesthesia

PROCEDURE: After the patient was prepped and draped in the usual sterile fashion, attention was directed to his right eye under the operating microscope. The area of the pterygium was viewed and an injection of lidocaine with Marcaine was placed subconjunctivally to infiltrate the area of the pterygium and surrounding conjunctiva. Then, using a combination of sharp and blunt dissection with 57 Beaver blade Westcott scissors, the pterygium was lifted away from the cornea, making a plane to the cornea to achieve clarity to the cornea. Next, an area was marked with a hand-held cautery nasally through the conjunctiva. A muscle hook was inserted to identify the medial rectus muscle. Then, using Westcott scissors, the head and body of the pterygium were removed noting where the medial rectus muscle was at all times. Cautery was used to achieve hemostasis. An area of conjunctiva superior to the area of the prior pterygium under the lid was isolated and an incision was made through the conjunctiva. This section of conjunctiva was then transposed and placed into position over the area of the prior pterygium, thus forming an autograft. This was sutured into place with multiple single 8-0 Vicryl sutures. The autograft was noted to be in good position. Hemostasis was noted to be well achieved. The cornea was noted to be smooth and clear in the area of the prior pterygium with the epithelial defect secondary to removal of the pterygium. Maxitrol drops were placed. The patient's eye was patched. The patient tolerated the procedure well without complications and is to follow up in our office tomorrow.

CPT/HCPCS Level II Codes   ICD-10-CM Codes

_____   _____

7. **PATIENT CASE #7**

PREOPERATIVE DIAGNOSIS: Subcutaneous mass, posterior scalp

POSTOPERATIVE DIAGNOSIS: Subcutaneous mass, posterior scalp

PROCEDURE PERFORMED: Excision, subcutaneous mass, posterior scalp

ANESTHESIA: General

PROCEDURE: After instillation of 1 percent Xylocaine, a transverse incision was made directly over this elongated posterior scalp lesion. Hemostasis was obtained with electrocautery and suture ligature. A fatty tumor was encountered and sharp dissection used in completely excising this lesion. Hemostasis was obtained with ties, suture ligatures, and electrocautery. The 3 cm lesion was removed in its entirety. The wound was irrigated and the incision closed in layers. The skin was closed with a running nylon suture for hemostasis.

CPT/HCPCS Level II Codes   ICD-10-CM Codes

_____   _____

8. **PATIENT CASE #8**

PREOPERATIVE DIAGNOSIS: Ventral hernia

POSTOPERATIVE DIAGNOSIS: Ventral hernia

PROCEDURE PERFORMED: Repair of ventral hernia with mesh

ANESTHESIA: General

PROCEDURE: The vertical midline incision was opened. Sharp and blunt dissection was used in defining the hernia sac. The hernia sac was opened and the fascia examined. The hernia defect was sizable. Careful inspection was utilized to uncover any additional adjacent fascial defects. Small defects were observed on both sides of the major hernia and were incorporated into the main hernia. The hernia sac was dissected free of the surrounding subcutaneous tissues and retained. Prolene mesh was then fashioned to size and sutured to one side with running #0 Prolene suture. Interrupted Prolene sutures were placed on the other side and tagged untied. The hernia sac was then sutured to the opposite side of the fascia with Vicryl suture. The Prolene sutures were passed through the interstices of the Prolene mesh and tied into place, ensuring that the Prolene mesh was not placed under tension. Excess mesh was excised. Jackson-Pratt drains were placed, one on each side. Running subcutaneous suture utilizing Vicryl was placed, after which the skin was stapled.

CPT/HCPCS Level II Codes   **ICD-10-CM Codes**

_____   _____

9. **PATIENT CASE #9**

PREOPERATIVE DIAGNOSIS: Intermittent exotropia, alternating fusion with decreased stereopsis

POSTOPERATIVE DIAGNOSIS: Intermittent exotropia, alternating fusion with decreased stereopsis

PROCEDURE PERFORMED: Bilateral lateral rectus recession of 7.0 mm

ANESTHESIA: General endotracheal anesthesia

PROCEDURE: The patient was brought to the operating room and placed in the supine position and prepped and draped in the usual sterile fashion for strabismus surgery. Both eyes were exposed to the surgical field. After adequate anesthesia, one drop of 2.5 percent Neosynephrine was placed in each eye for vasoconstriction. Forced ductions were performed on both eyes, and the lateral rectus was found to be normal. An eye speculum was placed in the right eye and surgery was begun on the right eye. An inferotemporal fornix incision was performed. The right lateral rectus muscle was isolated on a muscle hook. The muscle insertion was isolated, and checked ligaments were dissected back. After a series of muscle hook passes using the Steven's hook and finishing with two passes of a Green's hook, the right lateral rectus was isolated. The epimesium, as well as Tenon's capsule, was dissected from the muscle insertion and the checked ligaments were lysed. The muscle was imbricated on a 6-0 Vicryl suture with an S29 needle with locking bites at either end. The muscle was detached from the globe, and a distance of 7.0 mm posterior to the insertion of the muscle was marked. The muscle was then reattached 7.0 mm posterior to the original insertion using a cross-swords technique. The conjunctiva was closed using two buried sutures. Attention was then turned to the left eye where an identical procedure was performed. At the end of the case the eyes seemed slightly exotropic in position in the anesthetized state. Bounce back tests were normal. Both eyes were dressed with tetracaine drops and Maxitrol ointment. There were no complications. The patient tolerated the procedure well, was awakened from anesthesia without difficulty, and was sent to the recovery room. The patient was instructed in the use of topical antibiotics, and detailed postoperative instructions were provided. The patient will be followed up within a 48-hour period in my office.

CPT/HCPCS Level II Codes   **ICD-10-CM Codes**

_____   _____

10. **PATIENT CASE #10**

   PREOPERATIVE DIAGNOSIS: Right trigger thumb

   POSTOPERATIVE DIAGNOSIS: Right trigger thumb

   OPERATION: Right trigger thumb release, midlateral incision technique

   ANESTHESIA: Local digital block

   ESTIMATED BLOOD LOSS: Minimal

   DESCRIPTION OF PROCEDURE: A local digital block anesthetic was administered to allow the patient to actively flex the thumb after release. After exsanguination of the extremity, a tourniquet cuff on the right upper arm was inflated. A longitudinal skin incision was marked along the radial side of the metacarpophalangeal crease, approximately 1 cm from the midline and measuring 2.5 cm in length.

   The skin incision was made with a #15 blade scalpel. Care was taken to extend the incision only through the dermal layer, and skin hooks were used for retraction. Blunt dissection was performed to identify the radial digital nerve. The nerve was retracted away from the flexor tendon and protected throughout the procedure. Blunt dissection was continued to expose the first annular pulley and its boundaries. Retraction allowed full visualization of the pulley to perform the longitudinal release. The patient was asked to flex and extend the thumb to confirm the absence of triggering. The wound was irrigated, and the skin was closed with nonabsorbable suture. The patient tolerated the procedure well and was discharged to the outpatient observation area in good condition.

   CPT/HCPCS Level II Codes   **ICD-10-CM Codes**

   _____   _____

ASSIGNMENT 10.6 – DRG CODING VALIDATION REVIEW

Objectives

At the conclusion of this assignment, the student should be able to:

1. Explain the impact of diagnosis-related group (DRG) coding validation review on claims denials.

2. List steps hospitals follow to respond to payer DRG coding validation reviews.

3. Appropriately respond to DRG coding validation reviews to confirm or appeal results.

Overview

DRG coding validation review is vital to revenue cycle management because it permits the recovery of otherwise lost revenue to the facility or overpayments received by the hospital (that are paid back to the payer). Inpatient DRG coding validation reviews are performed by payers to confirm the accuracy of hospital coding and reimbursement. As part of this review process, payers conduct coding, level of care, readmission, and transfer audits. The hospital health information management department completes the following steps as a result of the third-party payer DRG coding validation review:

1. Identify the reason for the UB-04 claims change or denial.

2. Implement effective claims denial management, based on established policies.

3. Review facility documents to determine whether the claims change or denial is justified.

4. Prepare a letter of appeal to obtain appropriate reimbursement if review results in disagreement with the payer's decision.

5. Follow up to ensure appropriate reimbursement has been received by the hospital.

The hospital inpatient claims denial analysis evaluates the accuracy of ICD-10-CM/PCS codes and DRG assignment by assessing whether patient record documentation and official coding guidelines support code and DRG assignment.

Medicare Administrative Contractor
DRG Coding Validation Review
123 Main Street
Anywhere, US 12345
(101) 555-1234

May 15, YYYY

Dear Health Information Manager:

Coding and diagnostic-related group (DRG) validation review was conducted on this case to ensure that the diagnostic and procedural codes reported resulted in appropriate DRG assignment as compared with documentation in the medical record. Upon review of the above case, we have determined that the admission was medically necessary and appropriate. However, based on a review of submitted medical records and any other information available, the DRG assignment was changed from **682** to **683**.

Upon review of the medical record and any additional information provided, we determined that secondary diagnosis code **K85.90 (acute pancreatitis)** was not supported.

If you disagree with our determination, you may appeal. Please submit your appeal request in writing within 60 days from receipt of this notice to the address listed above.

Sincerely,

Mary Pat Simpson

Supervisor, DRG Coding Validation Review

DRG Coding Validation Review Outcome Report

Facility Name:	Memorial Hospital	**Review Date:**	5/1/YYYY
Patient Last Name:	Smith	**Provider Notification Date:**	5/1/YYYY
Patient First Name:	Linda J.	**Patient DOB:**	9/1/YYYY
Subscriber ID #:	321654987	**Patient Gender:**	Female
Claim Number:	ABC123	**Discharge Status:**	06
Admission Date:	3/4/YYYY	**Account Number:**	987654123
Discharge Date:	3/15/YYYY	**Med Rec Number:**	654321
		Review Type:	DRG Coding Validation

Diagnosis Codes	Submitted	Revised	Procedure Codes	Submitted	Revised
Principal:	N17.9		**First:**	05HM33Z	
	K85.90	DELETE		05HN33Z	
	I12.0				
	Z94.0				
	E87.2				
	E87.6				
	N18.6				
Billed DRG:	682 (Renal failure with MCC)		**Revised DRG:**	683 (Renal failure with CC)	

Rationale: A secondary diagnosis code of **K85.90 (acute pancreatitis)** was reported on the claim. There is no clinical documentation in the medical record to support the coding of this condition. The patient had no abdominal pain. Therefore, the recommendation has been made to delete code **K85.90** from the profile. This will result in a change from the billed DRG **682** to the revised DRG **683**.

FIGURE 10-1 DRG coding validation review letter from Medicare administrative contractor to hospital.

MDC 011 Diseases & Disorders of the Kidney & Urinary Tract					
Renal Failure					
MCC	CC	DRG	CMS Weight	Reimbursement Amount	Average Length of Stay
Yes	n/a	682	1.4989	$11,111.72	6.0
No	Yes	683	0.9191	$ 6,850.94	4.2
No	No	684	0.6181	$ 4,607.30	2.9
Yes	n/a	698	1.5661	$11,673.68	6.3

DRG 682 Renal failure w MCC
DRG 683 Renal failure w CC
DRG 684 Renal failure w/o CC/MCC
DRG 698 Other kidney & urinary tract diagnoses w MCC

Principal	Diagnosis
E88.3	Tumor lysis syndrome
I12.0	Hypertensive chronic kidney disease with stage 5 chronic kidney disease or end stage renal disease
I12.9	Hypertensive chronic kidney disease with stage 1 through stage 4 chronic kidney disease, or unspecified chronic kidney disease
I13.11	Hypertensive heart and chronic kidney disease without heart failure, with stage 5 chronic kidney disease, or end stage renal disease
N17.0	Acute kidney failure with tubular necrosis
N17.1	Acute kidney failure with acute cortical necrosis
N17.2	Acute kidney failure with medullary necrosis
N17.8	Other acute kidney failure
N17.9	Acute kidney failure, unspecified
N18.1	Chronic kidney disease, stage 1
N18.2	Chronic kidney disease, stage 2 (mild)
N18.30	Chronic kidney disease, stage 3 unspecified (moderate)
N18.4	Chronic kidney disease, stage 4 (severe)
N18.5	Chronic kidney disease, stage 5
N18.6	End stage renal disease
N18.9	Chronic kidney disease, unspecified
N19	Unspecified kidney failure
R34	Anuria and oliguria
T79.5xxA	Traumatic anuria, initial encounter

FIGURE 10-2 MS-DRG 682–684, 698 definitions data.

Discharge Summary

Patient Last Name:	Smith	**Patient DOB:**	9/1/YYYY
Patient First Name:	Linda J.	**Patient Gender:**	Female
Admission Date:	3/4/YYYY	**Account Number:**	987654123
Discharge Date:	3/15/YYYY	**Patient Record Number:**	654321
Attending Physician:	Donald Templeton, M.D.		

This 72-year-old female patient was admitted to the hospital through the emergency department with a chief complaint of weakness.

Discharge Diagnoses:

- Stage 5 chronic kidney disease (CKD) (current baseline creatinine level of 1.4–1.6)
- Kidney replaced by transplant, 1999
- Acute kidney failure
- Hypertension

Hospital Course (including key diagnostic test results): This is a 30-year-old female with past medical history significant for congenital (chronic) renal failure (stage 5), status post kidney transplant in 1999, and hypertension who presented on March 4 with one day of severe weakness. Patient was found to have hypokalemia (potassium level of 2.5), metabolic acidosis (bicarbonate level of 6), BUN of 49, and creatinine level of 6.78. There is concern for kidney transplant rejection. Initial elevated lipase and amylase of unclear etiology, which was initially thought not to be acute pancreatitis. However, the patient's continued elevated lipase and amylase lab values along with nausea and vomiting suggests possible pancreatitis; patient had no abdominal pain upon exam; patient was "nothing by mouth" for first part of her inpatient admission, labs were repeated, and IV hydration administered.

Patient was started on 1/2 normal saline with bicarb and given several amps of bicarb. A right internal jugular central catheter was placed. Nephrology felt urgent dialysis was not required but requested placement of Hohn central venous catheter. Fluids were changed to D5W with potassium for hypernatremia hyperchloremia. Creatinine trended down and stabilized at 4.5, raising concern for graft (transplant) rejection. Prednisone increased to 20 milligrams daily (which is to continue upon discharge) and creatinine began trending down again. Tacrolimus levels were adjusted with goal 6–8 ng/ml. When electrolytes stabilized, intravenous hydration was stopped. For prophylaxis, patient is to continue diflucan 200 mg. Mag-Ox 1200 mg twice daily continued. NaHC03 650 mg twice daily started. Nephrology is supposed to call patient with follow up appointment day and time. Power line catheter removed by interventional radiology on March 14. Hypokalemia: potassium was repleted. Patient has a chronically leaking G-tube, requiring 2L of lactated ringers nightly through the G tube. Patient is to continue this regimen. Procedures: successful percutaneous placement of left-sided and right-signed power line, jugular veins, for infusion of intravenous fluids.

Key Exam Findings at Discharge:

Vitals: Blood pressure 137/74, pulse 63, temperature 36.2 oc (97.2 °F), temperature source temporal (forehead), respiratory rate 18, height 1.499 m (4' 11.02"), weight 77.837 kg (171 1b, 9.6 oz), SpO2 97.00%.

Admission Weight: 73.936 kg (163 lb). **Discharge Weight:** 77.837 kg (171 lb 9.6 oz).

Pending Test Results: None.

Consulting Providers: nephrology.

Discharged Condition: good.

Discharge Medications, Instructions, and Follow-up Plans: as per After Visit Summary.

Disposition: Home with home health care services.

Signed: Donald Templeton, MD On: 3/15/YYYY at: 10:43AM

FIGURE 10-3 Discharge summary from patient's record.

Instructions

The hospital received a letter (Figure 10-1) from the Medicare administrative contractor about a DRG coding validation review that was recently conducted. Review the letter from the contractor and the related DRG data (Figure 10-2) and discharge summary from the patient's record (Figure 10-3), and answer each question below:

1. The reason that the *DRG coding validation review letter from Medicare administrative contractor to hospital* (Figure 10-1) was sent to the hospital is because the
   a. hospital fraudulently submitted a claim that included invalid code(s).
   b. overpayment received by the third-party payer needs to be paid back.
   c. payer disagrees with the assignment of code(s) and resultant DRG.
   d. recovery of lost revenue to hospitals triggered the review process.

2. Inpatient DRG coding validation reviews are performed by third-party payers to
   a. confirm the accuracy of hospital coding and reimbursement.
   b. ensure that hospitals receive the maximum reimbursement possible.
   c. identify reasons for claims denials of inpatient hospital admissions.
   d. reduce payer liability for reimbursement of hospitals inpatient stays.

3. Third-party payers conduct coding, level of care, readmission, and transfer audits as part of the _____ process.
   a. appeal of changed or denied claims
   b. DRG coding validation review
   c. hospital claims denial management
   d. initial UB-04 claims submission

4. As a result of the *DRG coding validation review letter from Medicare administrative contractor to hospital* (Figure 10-1), the payer
   a. changed the assignment of DRG 682 to DRG 683.
   b. determined that the stay was not medically necessary.
   c. revised multiple ICD-10-CM and ICD-10-PCS codes.
   d. scheduled an on-site review of patient records.

5. As a result of the *DRG coding validation review letter from Medicare administrative contractor to hospital* (Figure 10-1) and a review of *MS-DRG 682–684, 698 definitions data* (Figure 10-2), which reimbursement amount can the hospital now expect to receive from the payer?
   a. $4,607.30   c. $11,111.72
   b. $6,850.94   d. $11,673.68

6. As a result of the *DRG coding validation review letter from Medicare administrative contractor to hospital* (Figure 10-1) and a review of *MS-DRG 682–684, 698 definitions data* (Figure 10-2), the reimbursement the hospital would receive was less than originally determined because the weight of new DRG 683 was _____.
   a. 0.6181   c. 1.4989
   b. 0.9191   d. 1.5661

7. The *DRG coding validation review letter from Medicare administrative contractor to hospital* (Figure 10-1) stated that "upon review of the medical record and any additional information provided, we determined that secondary diagnosis code K85.90 (acute pancreatitis) was not supported." What step should be taken in response to the payer's decision?
   a. Check with the hospital's billing department to verify that the original reimbursement amount was received.
   b. Determine the specific reason that the payer changed the DRG on the submitted UB-04 claim.
   c. Review the patient record to determine whether the exclusion of acute pancreatitis (K85.90) is justified.
   d. Write a letter of appeal to the third-party payer to collect the initially calculated reimbursement amount.

8. The *DRG coding validation review letter from Medicare administrative contractor to hospital* (Figure 10-1) stated that "upon review of the medical record and any additional information provided, we determined that secondary diagnosis code K85.90 (acute pancreatitis) was not supported." Upon review of the *Discharge summary from patient's record* (Figure 10-3), the payer's decision was

   a. correct because the provider did not include "acute pancreatitis" in the list of discharge diagnoses, which is located at the top of the discharge summary.

   b. correct because the provider documented, "Initial elevated lipase and amylase of unclear etiology, which was initially thought not to be acute pancreatitis."

   c. incorrect because the provider documented, "Patient was found to have hypokalemia (potassium level of 2.5), metabolic acidosis (bicarbonate level of 6), BUN of 49, and creatinine level of 6.78."

   d. incorrect because the provider documented, "However, the patient's continued elevated lipase and amylase lab values along with nausea and vomiting suggests possible pancreatitis; patient had no abdominal pain upon exam; patient was "nothing by mouth" for first part of the inpatient admission, labs were repeated, and IV hydration administered."

9. The hospital initially reported the following ICD-10-CM/PCS codes and diseases/procedures on the UB-04, which resulted in assignment of DRG 682. A review MS-DRG 682–684 definitions data (Figure 10-2) indicates columns for major comorbidity or complication (MCC) and comorbidity or complication (CC). Which was the MCC that resulted in the hospital's original assignment of DRG 682?

N17.9	Acute kidney failure, unspecified
K85.90	Acute pancreatitis without necrosis or infection, unspecified
I12.0	Hypertensive chronic kidney disease with stage 5 chronic kidney disease or end stage renal disease
Z94.0	Kidney transplant status
E87.2	Acidosis
E87.6	Hypokalemia
N18.6	End stage renal disease
05HM33Z	Insertion of Infusion Device into Right Internal Jugular Vein, Percutaneous Approach
05HN33Z	Insertion of Infusion Device into Left Internal Jugular Vein, Percutaneous Approach

   a. K85.90

   b. N17.9

   c. Z94.0

   d. 05HM33Z, 05HN33Z

10. Review of the discharge summary from the patient's record (Figure 10-3) indicates an alternate principal diagnosis (instead of N17.9, acute kidney failure, unspecified), based on provider documentation, "This is a 30-year-old female with past medical history significant for congenital (chronic) renal failure (stage 5), status post kidney transplant in 1999, and hypertension who presented on March 4 with one day of severe weakness. Patient was found to have hypokalemia (potassium level of 2.5), metabolic acidosis (bicarbonate level of 6), BUN of 49, and creatinine level of 6.78. There is concern for kidney transplant rejection." Which ICD-10-CM code and disease could be considered the principal diagnosis (instead of N17.9, acute kidney failure, unspecified)?

   a. E87.2 (acidosis)

   b. E87.6 (hypokalemia)

   c. T86.11 (kidney transplant rejection)

   d. Z94.0 (kidney transplant status)

ASSIGNMENT 10.7 – MULTIPLE CHOICE REVIEW

1. A patient was seen today for pain in his right foot. During the evaluation, the physician also documented that the patient was last seen for pneumonia four months ago. How is the pneumonia reported on the CMS-1500 claim?
   a. as the ICD-10-CM code for "status post pneumonia"
   b. by reporting modifier -25 with the appropriate E/M code
   c. the pneumonia history is not documented on the claim
   d. by using an E/M code that reflects an extended evaluation

2. A secondary diagnosis is also known as a _____ condition.
   a. coexisting
   b. complicating
   c. reference
   d. verified

3. An acceptable reason to delay a documentation entry in the patient record is to
   a. authenticate provided services.
   b. change an erroneous entry.
   c. provide additional information for clarification.
   d. substantiate medical necessity of care provided.

4. Local coverage determinations (LCDs) contain
   a. auditing instructions.
   b. coding guidelines.
   c. covered and noncovered codes.
   d. reimbursement rates.

5. An *Advance Beneficiary Notice (ABN)* is required by _____ for all outpatient and physician office procedures/services that are not covered.
   a. Medicaid
   b. Medicare
   c. TRICARE
   d. worker's compensation

6. The objective section of a SOAP note includes the
   a. chief complaint and the patient's description of the presenting problem.
   b. diagnostic statement and the physician's rationale for the diagnosis.
   c. documentation of measurable observations made during a physical exam.
   d. statement of the physician's future plans for work-up and management.

7. Which of the following belongs in the "review of systems" section of the history and physical examination report?
   a. Blood pressure 113/70; pulse 80 and regular; temperature 97.9; respiratory rate 18.
   b. No complaints of nausea, vomiting, diarrhea, bloody stools, reflux, or constipation.
   c. Patient has a long-standing history of atrial fibrillation and is on Coumadin therapy.
   d. The patient's mother died from leukemia when the patient was 25; father is living and well.

8. After a fall at home, a 77-year-old woman was brought to the emergency department and received level 3 E/M services. The patient sustained a 2 cm laceration of the thigh and a small, 0.5 cm laceration of the wrist. The thigh wound was closed with sutures and the wrist laceration underwent adhesive closure. The patient was discharged from the emergency department in satisfactory condition.

   Select the appropriate CPT and HCPCS procedure code(s) and modifier(s) for this case.
   a. 12001, G0168-59
   b. 99283-25, 12001
   c. 99283-25, 12001, G0168-59
   d. 99283-25, 12001-59, G0168-59

9. A patient was seen in the physician's office with complaints of rapid heartbeat. The patient has no known history of cardiac problems. The physician ordered an electrolyte panel. After receiving the results, the physician ordered a repeat potassium level.

   Select the appropriate CPT code(s) and modifier(s) for this case.
   a. 80051, 84132
   b. 80051, 84132, 84132
   c. 80051, 84132-59
   d. 80051, 84132-91

10. A 42-year-old male was referred to an ophthalmologist for evaluation of two lesions of his left eye and was scheduled for surgery. The patient presented for surgery and was prepped and draped in the usual sterile fashion. The patient underwent two separate procedures: the first was excision of a chalazion of the left lower eyelid. The second procedure was incisional biopsy of left upper eyelid lesion including lid margin.

Select the appropriate CPT code(s) and modifier(s) for this case.
a. 67800, 67810
b. 67800, 67810-59
c. 67800-E2, 67810-59-E1
d. 67800-E2, 67810-E1

11. A 58-year-old male presented for screening colonoscopy. The patient received premedication per protocol. The scope was inserted and advanced, but despite multiple attempts, could not pass beyond the splenic flexure. For the patient's comfort, the procedure was terminated.

Select the appropriate CPT code(s) and modifier(s) for this case.
a. 45330
b. 45330-21
c. 45378
d. 45378-52

12. A patient was admitted to the day surgery unit to undergo a laparoscopic cholecystectomy. The patient was prepped and draped in the usual sterile fashion for laparoscopy. Upon laparoscopic examination, the patient's gallbladder was noted to be extremely friable, and there was also question of obstruction or torsion of the common bile duct. The decision was made to perform an open cholecystectomy. The patient still had excellent general anesthetic response, and the open procedure was begun. The gallbladder was removed without much difficulty. The surgeon also performed exploration of the common bile duct and although it had appeared abnormal under laparoscopic viewing, the common bile duct was normal and free of stone or obstruction. The patient tolerated the procedure well.

Select the appropriate CPT code for this case.
a. 47562-57
b. 47562
c. 47600
d. 47610

13. This 39-year-old male patient was seen by General Surgery and scheduled for removal of a worrisome lump behind the right knee. The patient stated he had no idea how long it had been there; he noticed it while trying to "rub out" a cramp of his calf muscle. The patient underwent excision of what was identified as a Baker's cyst of the left popliteal fossa. The patient tolerated the procedure well and was understandably relieved by the definitive benign diagnosis.

Select the appropriate CPT code for this case.
a. 27334
b. 27345
c. 27347
d. 27360

14. HISTORY: The established patient is a very vibrant 82-year-old woman seen today for routine evaluation during this level 2 E/M service.

Select the appropriate CPT code for this case.
a. 99202
b. 99203
c. 99211
d. 99212

15. The patient is a 40-year-old male who is known to me and was seen in the office today on an urgent basis for a level 2 E/M service because he believed he had collapsed his right lung. He has a history of collapsed lung and was confident it had happened again. On examination, the patient's breath sounds on the right were nonexistent. An emergency two-view (frontal and lateral) chest x-ray was performed which demonstrated the collapsed lung on the right. The patient was sent to the local hospital emergency department. The on-call surgeon was contacted and met the patient in the emergency department, where a right tube thoracoscopy was performed.

Select the appropriate CPT code(s) and modifier(s) for the office visit only for this case.
a. 99212-57, 71046
b. 99213-57, 71046
c. 99241, 71046
d. 99281, 71046

16. The patient presents to the office for a level 3 E/M service after a five-year absence with complaints of abdominal pain, diarrhea, and rectal bleeding, which began three weeks ago. An examination revealed a tense abdomen with some guarding in the right upper quadrant. Tomorrow, the patient will undergo a flexible sigmoidoscopy to rule out colon cancer.

Select the appropriate CPT code(s) and modifier(s) for this case.

a. 99202   c. 99203

b. 99202-57   d. 99203-57

17. On 08/12/YY, a patient underwent an exploratory laparotomy, left partial hepatic resection for malignant hepatoma and a cholecystectomy.

Select the CPT code for the first-listed procedure in this case.

a. 47120   c. 47125

b. 47122   d. 47141

18. A 65-year-old patient underwent bronchoscopy and biopsy for a left lower lobe lung mass. The biopsy was sent to pathology immediately and revealed adenocarcinoma of the left lower lobe. The patient then underwent a left lower lobectomy and thoracic lymphadenopathy.

Select the CPT code for the first-listed procedure in this case.

a. 31625   c. 32663

b. 32480   d. 38746

19. A 33-year-old patient with a strong family history of breast cancer underwent excision of a right breast mass in the outpatient surgery center. The pathology report was returned immediately and revealed a malignant neoplasm, central portion of the right breast. The patient then underwent a right modified radical mastectomy.

Select the CPT code and modifier for the therapeutic procedure in this case.

a. 19120-RT   c. 19302-RT

b. 19301-RT   d. 19307-RT

20. An 80-year-old patient was admitted to the outpatient surgery center for dilation of a urethral stricture with insertion of urethral stent. A cystourethroscope was inserted through the urethral meatus and advanced through the urethra into the bladder. It was able to pass through the site of stricture successfully, although with some difficulty. Examination of the urethra showed the area of stricture. Examination of the bladder revealed the bladder appeared to be essentially unremarkable. A urethral stent was introduced into the urethra and placed at the point of stricture. Improved urinary flow was immediately noted. The procedure was concluded, and the patient tolerated the procedure well.

Select the CPT code for the first-listed procedure in this case.

a. 52000   c. 52281

b. 52005   d. 52282

CMS-1500 and UB-04 Claims

INTRODUCTION

This chapter familiarizes students with special instructions that apply to completion of CMS-1500 claims.

ASSIGNMENT 11.1 – NATIONAL PROVIDER IDENTIFIER (NPI) STANDARD

Objectives

At the conclusion of this assignment, the student should be able to:

1. Discuss electronic file interchange (EFI).
2. Discuss the national provider identifier (NPI).

Overview

The Centers for Medicare and Medicaid Services (CMS) has many resources available on its website related to the NPI: overview, fact sheets, tip sheets, PowerPoint presentation, and a question resource sheet, just to list a few. The NPI replaced the PIN and UPIN used in the past by health care providers. One advantage of the NPI is that it will provide identification for all health care plans and insurance payers.

Instructions

Access the Centers for Medicare and Medicaid Services website to answer questions about its content. Write your answers in the space provided at the end of each question.

1. Go to **www.cms.gov,** click on the Regulations and Guidance link, and click on the National Provider Identifier Standard (NPI) link below the HIPAA Administrative Simplification heading. Then, click on the EFI link, and scroll down and click on the EFI Summary PDF file to answer the following questions about electronic file interchange (EFI).

   a. What is electronic file interchange (EFI)?

   _____

   b. Why was the EFI implemented?

   _____

2. Go to **www.cms.gov**, click on the Regulations and Guidance link, and click on the National Provider Identifier Standard (NPI) link below the Health Insurance Portability and Accountability Act (HIPAA) Administrative Simplification heading.

   a. What is the purpose of the national provider identifier (NPI)?

   _____

   b. Who must use the NPI, and when?

   _____

ASSIGNMENT 11.2 – MEDICALLY UNLIKELY EDITS (MUE) PROJECT

Objective

At the conclusion of this assignment, the student should be able to:

1. Define and provide examples of medical unlikely edits (MUE).
2. Discuss the MUE project.

Overview

The Centers for Medicare and Medicaid Services (CMS) has resources available on its website related to the MUE project. As outlined in the chapter text, the MUE project is a method that CMS has implemented to improve claim accuracy and decrease errors in billing.

Instructions

Access the website for the Centers for Medicare and Medicaid Services (**www.cms.gov**). Once at the site, click on the Medicare link, click on the National Correct Coding Initiative Edits link below the Coding heading, and click on the MUE link. Review the following questions related to information on the site. Write your answers in the space provided at the end of each question.

1. Why did CMS develop MUEs?

   _____

2. What is an MUE?

   _____

3. When were MUEs implemented?

   _____

4. To whom are inquiries about a specific claim addressed?

   _____

5. To whom should inquiries about the rationale for an MUE value be addressed?

   _____

NOTE:

Navigate the CMS website to research information needed to answer the questions in this assignment. This will help you learn how to locate information using the Internet as a research tool and using websites. It will also require you to find and verify information on a table.

ASSIGNMENT 11.3 – IDENTIFYING CMS-1500 CLAIMS COMPLETION ERRORS

Objectives

At the conclusion of this assignment, the student should be able to:

1. Explain the importance of accurate CMS-1500 claims completion.

2. Identify CMS-1500 claims completion errors.

Overview

The CMS-1500 claim is generated by using medical practice management software, which helps ensure accuracy of claims completion. It is important to ensure that submitted CMS-1500 claims are free of errors, such as formats required for entering dates, codes, and so on.

 NOTE:

When completing this assignment, refer to optical scanning guidelines located in Chapter 11 in your textbook.

Instructions

1. The CMS-1500 claims in Figures 11-1 to 11-3 contain errors.

2. Review each claim to identify the errors.

3. Circle each error.

HEALTH INSURANCE CLAIM FORM

APPROVED BY NATIONAL UNIFORM CLAIM COMMITTEE (NUCC) 02/12

FIGURE 11-1 Chris P. Cream CMS-1500 with optical scanning errors.

HEALTH INSURANCE CLAIM FORM

APPROVED BY NATIONAL UNIFORM CLAIM COMMITTEE (NUCC) 02/12

| | PICA | | | | | | | | | | | | PICA | | |

| 1. MEDICARE (Medicare#) ☐ | MEDICAID (Medicaid#) ☐ | TRICARE (ID#/DoD#) ☐ | CHAMPVA (Member ID#) ☐ | GROUP HEALTH PLAN (ID#) ☐ | FECA BLKLUNG (ID#) ☐ | OTHER ☒ (ID#) | 1a. INSURED'S I.D. NUMBER (For Program in Item 1) **42915750** |

2. PATIENT'S NAME (Last Name, First Name, Middle Initial)
BRIGHT, BRITTANY

3. PATIENT'S BIRTH DATE MM **04** DD **07** YY **1988**   SEX M ☐ F ☒

4. INSURED'S NAME (Last Name, First Name, Middle Initial)
WRIGHT, BRITTANY

5. PATIENT'S ADDRESS (No., Street)
8731 NOVELS AVENUE

6. PATIENT RELATIONSHIP TO INSURED
Self ☒ Spouse ☐ Child ☐ Other ☐

7. INSURED'S ADDRESS (No., Street)

CITY **ANYWHERE**   STATE **NY**

8. RESERVED FOR NUCC USE

CITY   STATE

ZIP CODE **12345**   TELEPHONE (Include Area Code) ( )

ZIP CODE   TELEPHONE (Include Area Code) ( )

9. OTHER INSURED'S NAME (Last Name, First Name, Middle Initial)

10. IS PATIENT'S CONDITION RELATED TO:

11. INSURED'S POLICY GROUP OR FECA NUMBER

a. OTHER INSURED'S POLICY OR GROUP NUMBER

a. EMPLOYMENT? (Current or Previous) ☐ YES ☒ NO

a. INSURED'S DATE OF BIRTH MM **04** DD **07** YY **1988**   SEX M ☐ F ☒

b. RESERVED FOR NUCC USE

b. AUTO ACCIDENT? ☐ YES ☒ NO   PLACE (State)

b. OTHER CLAIM ID (Designated by NUCC)

c. RESERVED FOR NUCC USE

c. OTHER ACCIDENT? ☐ YES ☒ NO

c. INSURANCE PLAN NAME OR PROGRAM NAME
US HEALTH

d. INSURANCE PLAN NAME OR PROGRAM NAME

10d. CLAIM CODES (Designated by NUCC)

d. IS THERE ANOTHER HEALTH BENEFIT PLAN? ☐ YES ☒ NO   If yes, complete items 9, 9a and 9d.

READ BACK OF FORM BEFORE COMPLETING & SIGNING THIS FORM.
12. PATIENT'S OR AUTHORIZED PERSON'S SIGNATURE I authorize the release of any medical or other information necessary to process this claim. I also request payment of government benefits either to myself or to the party who accepts assignment below.

SIGNED **SIGNATURE ON FILE**   DATE _____

13. INSURED'S OR AUTHORIZED PERSON'S SIGNATURE I authorize payment of medical benefits to the undersigned physician or supplier for services described below.

SIGNED **SIGNATURE ON FILE**

14. DATE OF CURRENT ILLNESS, INJURY, or PREGNANCY (LMP) MM **10** DD **31** YY **YYYY**   QUAL. **431**

15. OTHER DATE QUAL.   MM   DD   YY

16. DATES PATIENT UNABLE TO WORK IN CURRENT OCCUPATION FROM MM DD YY TO MM DD YY

17. NAME OF REFERRING PROVIDER OR OTHER SOURCE

17a.
17b. NPI

18. HOSPITALIZATION DATES RELATED TO CURRENT SERVICES FROM MM DD YY TO MM DD YY

19. ADDITIONAL CLAIM INFORMATION (Designated by NUCC)

20. OUTSIDE LAB? ☐ YES ☒ NO $ CHARGES

21. DIAGNOSIS OR NATURE OF ILLNESS OR INJURY Relate A-L to service line below (24E)   ICD Ind. **0**

A. **J45909**   B. _____   C. _____   D. _____
E. _____   F. _____   G. _____   H. _____
I. _____   J. _____   K. _____   L. _____

22. RESUBMISSION CODE   ORIGINAL REF. NO.

23. PRIOR AUTHORIZATION NUMBER

24. A. DATE(S) OF SERVICE						B. PLACE OF SERVICE	C. EMG	D. PROCEDURES, SERVICES, OR SUPPLIES (Explain Unusual Circumstances) CPT/HCPCS	MODIFIER	E. DIAGNOSIS POINTER	F. $ CHARGES	G. DAYS OR UNITS	H. EPSDT Family Plan	I. ID. QUAL.	J. RENDERING PROVIDER ID. #
MM **10**	DD **31** From YY **YYYY**	MM	DD	YY		**11**		**99212**	**24**	**A**	**55**	**1**		NPI	
														NPI	
														NPI	
														NPI	
														NPI	
														NPI	

25. FEDERAL TAX I.D. NUMBER **111234562**   SSN ☐ EIN ☐

26. PATIENT'S ACCOUNT NO. **11-B**

27. ACCEPT ASSIGNMENT? (For govt. claims, see back) ☒ YES ☐ NO

28. TOTAL CHARGE $ **55 00**

29. AMOUNT PAID $

30. Rsvd for NUCC Use

31. SIGNATURE OF PHYSICIAN OR SUPPLIER INCLUDING DEGREES OR CREDENTIALS (I certify that the statements on the reverse apply to this bill and are made a part thereof.)

DONALD L GIVINGS MDMMDDYYYY
SIGNED   DATE

32. SERVICE FACILITY LOCATION INFORMATION

a.   b.

33. BILLING PROVIDER INFO & PH # (**101**) **1115555**
DONALD L GIVINGS MD
11350 MEDICAL DRIVE
ANYWHERE NY 12345-6541

a. **1234567890**   b.

NUCC Instruction Manual available at: www.nucc.org   **PLEASE PRINT OR TYPE**

FIGURE 11-2 Brittany Bright CMS-1500 with optical scanning errors.

HEALTH INSURANCE CLAIM FORM

APPROVED BY NATIONAL UNIFORM CLAIM COMMITTEE (NUCC) 02/12

Courtesy of the Centers for Medicare & Medicaid Services, www.cms.gov, claim data created by author.

PICA		PICA

CARRIER

1. MEDICARE (Medicare#)	MEDICAID (Medicaid#)	TRICARE (ID#/DoD#)	CHAMPVA (Member ID#)	GROUP HEALTH PLAN (ID#) [X]	FECA BLKLUNG (ID#)	OTHER (ID#)	1a. INSURED'S I.D. NUMBER (For Program in Item 1)
							321987456

2. PATIENT'S NAME (Last Name, First Name, Middle Initial)	3. PATIENT'S BIRTH DATE MM DD YY / SEX	4. INSURED'S NAME (Last Name, First Name, Middle Initial)
DUNNETT, ANTHONY. L	7 30 1990 M [X] F	DUNNETT, ANTHONY, L

5. PATIENT'S ADDRESS (No., Street)	6. PATIENT RELATIONSHIP TO INSURED	7. INSURED'S ADDRESS (No., Street)
555 MILKY WAY	Self [X] Spouse Child Other	

CITY	STATE	8. RESERVED FOR NUCC USE	CITY	STATE
ANYWHERE	NY			

ZIP CODE	TELEPHONE (Include Area Code)	ZIP CODE	TELEPHONE (Include Area Code)
12345	( )		( )

PATIENT AND INSURED INFORMATION

9. OTHER INSURED'S NAME (Last Name, First Name, Middle Initial)	10. IS PATIENT'S CONDITION RELATED TO:	11. INSURED'S POLICY GROUP OR FECA NUMBER
		411

a. OTHER INSURED'S POLICY OR GROUP NUMBER	a. EMPLOYMENT? (Current or Previous) YES [X] NO	a. INSURED'S DATE OF BIRTH MM DD YY / SEX
		07 30 1990 M [X] F

b. RESERVED FOR NUCC USE	b. AUTO ACCIDENT? YES [X] NO PLACE (State)	b. OTHER CLAIM ID (Designated by NUCC)

c. RESERVED FOR NUCC USE	c. OTHER ACCIDENT? YES [X] NO	c. INSURANCE PLAN NAME OR PROGRAM NAME
		METROPLITAN

d. INSURANCE PLAN NAME OR PROGRAM NAME	10d. CLAIM CODES (Designated by NUCC)	d. IS THERE ANOTHER HEALTH BENEFIT PLAN? YES [X] NO If yes, complete items 9, 9a and 9d.

READ BACK OF FORM BEFORE COMPLETING & SIGNING THIS FORM.

12. PATIENT'S OR AUTHORIZED PERSON'S SIGNATURE I authorize the release of any medical or other information necessary to process this claim. I also request payment of government benefits either to myself or to the party who accepts assignment below.

SIGNED **SIGNATURE ON FILE**   DATE

13. INSURED'S OR AUTHORIZED PERSON'S SIGNATURE I authorize payment of medical benefits to the undersigned physician or supplier for services described below.

SIGNED **SIGNATURE**

14. DATE OF CURRENT ILLNESS, INJURY, or PREGNANCY (LMP) MM DD YY QUAL. 431	15. OTHER DATE QUAL. MM DD YY	16. DATES PATIENT UNABLE TO WORK IN CURRENT OCCUPATION MM DD YY FROM TO
04 01 YYYY		

17. NAME OF REFERRING PROVIDER OR OTHER SOURCE	17a.	18. HOSPITALIZATION DATES RELATED TO CURRENT SERVICES MM DD YY FROM TO
	17b. NPI	

19. ADDITIONAL CLAIM INFORMATION (Designated by NUCC)	20. OUTSIDE LAB? YES [X] NO $ CHARGES

21. DIAGNOSIS OR NATURE OF ILLNESS OR INJURY Relate A-L to service line below (24E)   ICD Ind.

A. R350	B.	C.	D.
E.	F.	G.	H.
I.	J.	K.	L.

22. RESUBMISSION CODE   ORIGINAL REF. NO.

23. PRIOR AUTHORIZATION NUMBER

PHYSICIAN OR SUPPLIER INFORMATION

24. A. DATE(S) OF SERVICE From MM DD YY To MM DD YY	B. PLACE OF SERVICE	C. EMG	D. PROCEDURES, SERVICES, OR SUPPLIES (Explain Unusual Circumstances) CPT/HCPCS MODIFIER	E. DIAGNOSIS POINTER	F. $ CHARGES	G. DAYS OR UNITS	H. EPSDT Family Plan	I. ID. QUAL.	J. RENDERING PROVIDER ID. #
1	04 01 YYYY	11		99214	A	350 00	1		NPI	
2									NPI	
3									NPI	
4									NPI	
5									NPI	
6									NPI	

25. FEDERAL TAX I.D. NUMBER SSN EIN	26. PATIENT'S ACCOUNT NO.	27. ACCEPT ASSIGNMENT? (For govt. claims, see back)	28. TOTAL CHARGE	29. AMOUNT PAID	30. Rsvd for NUCC Use
111234524 [X]	11-C	[X] YES NO	$ 350 00	$	

31. SIGNATURE OF PHYSICIAN OR SUPPLIER INCLUDING DEGREES OR CREDENTIALS (I certify that the statements on the reverse apply to this bill and are made a part thereof.)	32. SERVICE FACILITY LOCATION INFORMATION	33. BILLING PROVIDER INFO & PH # (101) 1111234
ERIN A HELPER MD MMDDYYYY SIGNED DATE	a. b.	ERIN A HELPER MD 101 MEDIC STREEET ANYWHERE NY 12345-9874 a. b.

NUCC Instruction Manual available at: www.nucc.org   **PLEASE PRINT OR TYPE**

FIGURE 11-3 Anthony Dunnett CMS-1500 with optical scanning errors.

ASSIGNMENT 11.4 – COMPLETING THE UB-04 CLAIM

Objectives

At the conclusion of this assignment, the student should be able to:

1. Explain the purpose of the UB-04 claim.

2. Complete the UB-04 claim, following claims completion instructions.

Overview

The *UB-04 claim* contains data entry blocks called form locators (FLs) that are similar to the CMS-1500 claim blocks used to input information about procedures or services provided to a patient. Although some institutions manually complete the UB-04 claim and submit it to third-party payers for reimbursement, others perform data entry of UB-04 information using commercial software.

However, most institutions do not complete the UB-04 because it is automatically generated from chargemaster data entered by providers (e.g., nurses, therapists, laboratory, and so on). Data are transmitted to the facility's billing department by providers who circle procedure/service CPT/ HCPCS codes on a paper-based chargemaster (after which keyboarding specialists enter the codes into the facility's computer) or select codes using a hand-held computer, such as a personal digital assistant (PDA) (and click to transmit the codes).

Instructions

Complete a separate UB-04 claim for each case study. Blank UB-04 claims can be copied from Appendix I of the textbook, or claims can be printed from the online Student Resources for this product. Sign up or sign in at **www.cengage.com** to search for and access this product and its online resources. Enter 9876543211 as the NPI for Alfred State Medical Center in FL56. For the purpose of this assignment, enter data in the following UB-04 form locators:

- FL1
- FL2
- FL3a
- FL3b
- FL4
- FL5
- FL6
- FL8b
- FL9a
- FL9b
- FL9c
- FL9d

- FL10
- FL11
- FL12 (DATE)
- FL42
- FL43
- FL44
- FL45
- FL46
- FL47
- CREATION DATE
- TOTALS
- FL50

- FL51
- FL52
- FL53
- FL56
- FL58
- FL59
- FL60
- FL66 (0 for ICD-10-CM)
- FL67
- FL71
- FL76
- FL80

 NOTE:

Enter letter Y (for Yes) in Form Locator 53 ASG. BEN. (assignment of benefits) on each completed UB-04 claim. The patient in each outpatient case has agreed to the assignment of benefits so that the provider is reimbursed directly by the payer.

Outpatient Case #1

Alfred Medical Center • 548 N Main St • Alfred NY 14802	**Outpatient Case #1**
(607) 555-1234 EIN: 871349061 TOB: 131	

PATIENT NAME	PATIENT CONTROL NO.	DATE/TIME OF OUTPATIENT VISIT	SOURCE OF ADMISSION
Mary Sue Patient	859451563867	0605YYYY 1300	Physician referral

PATIENT ADDRESS	TELEPHONE NO.	BIRTH DATE	GENDER
10 Main St, Alfred NY 14802	(607) 555-2345	10-15-1980	Female (F)

MARITAL STATUS	MEDICAL RECORD NUMBER	PRIMARY PAYER	DISCHARGE HOUR	PATIENT STATUS
Single (S)	123456	BLUECROSS BLUESHIELD	1350	Discharged Home

RESPONSIBLE PARTY	RESPONSIBLE PARTY ADDRESS	HEALTH INSURANCE ID NUMBER (HICN)
Mary Sue Patient	10 Main St, Alfred NY 14802	63596365

PATIENT RELATIONSHIP TO INSURED	EMPLOYMENT STATUS	NAME OF EMPLOYER
Self (18)	Employed Full Time (1)	City College, Alfred NY

GROUP NAME	GROUP NO.	PRIMARY PAYER MAILING ADDRESS	HEALTH PLAN ID
Commercial	506G	P.O. Box 761, Buffalo NY 14201	123456789

RESPONSIBLE PHYSICIAN	RESPONSIBLE PHYSICIAN NPI	TYPE OF ADMISSION
Terry Smith, M.D.	2376902906	Elective (3)

CASE SUMMARY	DIAGNOSES	ICD CODE
Patient was registered in the outpatient clinic and underwent venipuncture for repeat T3 and T4 update laboratory test for hypothyroidism. Patient discharged home, to be followed by primary physician.	Hypothyroidism	E03.9

CHARGE DESCRIPTION MASTER

ALFRED MEDICAL CENTER
548 N MAIN ST
ALFRED NY 14802

Printed on 06/05/YYYY

DEPARTMENT CODE: 01.955   DEPARTMENT: Laboratory

SERVICE CODE	SERVICE DESCRIPTION	REVENUE CODE	CPT CODE	CHARGE	RVU
8650002	T3 and T4 uptake, THBR	0301	84479	74.50	0.90
8650013	Venipuncture	0309	36415	24.95	0.50

Outpatient Case #2

Alfred Medical Center • 548 N Main St • Alfred NY 14802	**Outpatient Case #2**
(607) 555-1234 EIN: 871349061 TOB: 131	

PATIENT NAME	PATIENT CONTROL NO.	DATE/TIME OF OUTPATIENT VISIT	SOURCE OF ADMISSION
James World	645791254301	0401YYYY 0400	Physician referral

PATIENT ADDRESS	TELEPHONE NO.	BIRTH DATE	GENDER
7416 Light Street, Anywhere NY 12345	(101) 111-7700	03-08-1992	Male (M)

MARITAL STATUS	MEDICAL RECORD NUMBER	PRIMARY PAYER	DISCHARGE HOUR	PATIENT STATUS
Single (S)	746381	Aetna	0600	Discharged Home

RESPONSIBLE PARTY	RESPONSIBLE PARTY ADDRESS	HEALTH INSURANCE ID NUMBER (HICN)
James World	7416 Light Street, Anywhere NY 12345	32569841

PATIENT RELATIONSHIP TO INSURED	EMPLOYMENT STATUS	NAME OF EMPLOYER
Self (18)	Employed Full Time (1)	Security R Us

GROUP NAME	GROUP NO.	PRIMARY PAYER MAILING ADDRESS	HEALTH PLAN ID
Commercial	2114	Aetna, PO Box 45, Stillwater PA 12345	7485713659

RESPONSIBLE PHYSICIAN	RESPONSIBLE PHYSICIAN NPI	TYPE OF ADMISSION
Sejal Raja, M.D.	5548732106	Elective (3)

CASE SUMMARY	DIAGNOSES	ICD CODE
Patient was registered in the outpatient clinic and underwent ECG with interpretation. Patient discharged home, to be followed by primary physician.	Cardiac Arrhythmia (Unspecified)	I49.9

CHARGE DESCRIPTION MASTER

ALFRED MEDICAL CENTER
548 N MAIN ST
ALFRED NY 14802

Printed on 04/01/YYYY

DEPARTMENT CODE: 01.953   DEPARTMENT: Radiology

SERVICE CODE	SERVICE DESCRIPTION	REVENUE CODE	CPT CODE	CHARGE	RVU
8650400	ECG with interpretation	0730	93000	75.00	0.85

Outpatient Case #3

```
Alfred Medical Center • 548 N Main St • Alfred NY 14802        Outpatient Case #3
(607) 555-1234      EIN: 871349061      TOB: 131
```

PATIENT NAME	PATIENT CONTROL NO.	DATE/TIME OF OUTPATIENT VISIT	SOURCE OF ADMISSION
Audry Waddoups	846279461307	0809YYYY 0900	Physician referral

PATIENT ADDRESS	TELEPHONE NO.	BIRTH DATE	GENDER
8990 Date St, Anywhere NY 12345	(101) 124-5789	10-19-1972	Female (F)

MARITAL STATUS	MEDICAL RECORD NUMBER	PRIMARY PAYER	DISCHARGE HOUR	PATIENT STATUS
Married (M)	976431	Health Net	1200	Discharged Home

RESPONSIBLE PARTY	RESPONSIBLE PARTY ADDRESS	HEALTH INSURANCE ID NUMBER (HICN)
John Waddoups	8990 Date St, Anywhere NY 12345	316497

PATIENT RELATIONSHIP TO INSURED	EMPLOYMENT STATUS	NAME OF EMPLOYER
Spouse (01)	Employed Full Time (1)	Lifetime Books

GROUP NAME	GROUP NO.	PRIMARY PAYER MAILING ADDRESS	HEALTH PLAN ID
Commercial	348	Health Net, PO Box 9900, New York NY 12300	1024867932

RESPONSIBLE PHYSICIAN	RESPONSIBLE PHYSICIAN NPI	TYPE OF ADMISSION
Tina Betker, M.D.	4567890123	Elective (3)

CASE SUMMARY	DIAGNOSES	ICD CODE
Patient was registered in the outpatient clinic and underwent evaluation. Patient discharged home, to be followed by primary physician.	Asthma (Acute) with exacerbation	J45.901

CHARGE DESCRIPTION MASTER

```
ALFRED MEDICAL CENTER                          Printed on 08/09/YYYY
548 N MAIN ST
ALFRED NY 14802
```

DEPARTMENT CODE:	01.900		DEPARTMENT:	Outpatient Services		

SERVICE CODE	SERVICE DESCRIPTION	REVENUE CODE	CPT CODE	CHARGE	RVU
8650016	Outpatient office visit, level 2, new patient	0500	99202	65.00	0.65

Outpatient Case #4

Alfred Medical Center • 548 N Main St • Alfred NY 14802	**Outpatient Case #4**
(607) 555-1234 EIN: 871349061 TOB: 131	

PATIENT NAME	PATIENT CONTROL NO.	DATE/TIME OF OUTPATIENT VISIT	SOURCE OF ADMISSION
Todd Terry	546987254361	02-07-YYYY 1400	Physician referral

PATIENT ADDRESS	TELEPHONE NO.	BIRTH DATE	GENDER
115 Glenn Street, Anywhere NY 12345	(101) 555-8457	12-30-1985	Male (M)

MARITAL STATUS	MEDICAL RECORD NUMBER	PRIMARY PAYER	DISCHARGE HOUR	PATIENT STATUS
Married (M)	648570	Tricare	2000	Discharged Home

RESPONSIBLE PARTY	RESPONSIBLE PARTY ADDRESS	HEALTH INSURANCE ID NUMBER (HICN)
Todd Terry	115 Glenn Street, Anywhere NY 12345	342870

PATIENT RELATIONSHIP TO INSURED	EMPLOYMENT STATUS	NAME OF EMPLOYER
Self (18)	Employed Full Time (1)	US Navy

GROUP NAME	GROUP NO.	PRIMARY PAYER MAILING ADDRESS	HEALTH PLAN ID
		Tricare, PO Box 2107, Tricity SC 76654	1144886250

RESPONSIBLE PHYSICIAN	RESPONSIBLE PHYSICIAN NPI	TYPE OF ADMISSION
Arnold Young, M.D.	0123458760	Elective (3)

CASE SUMMARY	DIAGNOSES	ICD CODE
Patient was registered in the outpatient clinic and underwent 45-minute psychotherapy evaluation. Patient discharged home, to be followed by primary physician.	Post-traumatic stress disorder, chronic	F43.12

CHARGE DESCRIPTION MASTER

ALFRED MEDICAL CENTER
548 N MAIN ST
ALFRED NY 14802

Printed on 02/07/YYYY

DEPARTMENT CODE:	01.950	DEPARTMENT:	Psychiatry

SERVICE CODE	SERVICE DESCRIPTION	REVENUE CODE	CPT CODE	CHARGE	RVU
8650311	Psychotherapy, 45 minutes with patient	0914	90834	350.00	0.70

Outpatient Case #5

Alfred Medical Center • 548 N Main St • Alfred NY 14802	**Outpatient Case #5**

(607) 555-1234   EIN: 871349061   TOB: 131

PATIENT NAME	PATIENT CONTROL NO.	DATE/TIME OF OUTPATIENT VISIT	SOURCE OF ADMISSION
Candy Santos	215478965230	05-01-YYYY 0230	Physician referral

PATIENT ADDRESS	TELEPHONE NO.	BIRTH DATE	GENDER
3902 Hatzel St, Anywhere NY 12345	(101) 111-5128	06-16-1999	Female (F)

MARITAL STATUS	MEDICAL RECORD NUMBER	PRIMARY PAYER	DISCHARGE HOUR	PATIENT STATUS
Single (S)	356478	Medicaid	0500	Discharged Home

RESPONSIBLE PARTY	RESPONSIBLE PARTY ADDRESS	HEALTH INSURANCE ID NUMBER (HICN)
Candy Santos	3902 Hatzel Street, Anywhere NY 12345	241793

PATIENT RELATIONSHIP TO INSURED	EMPLOYMENT STATUS	NAME OF EMPLOYER
Self (18)	Employed Part Time (1)	Fashion Joy

GROUP NAME	GROUP NO.	PRIMARY PAYER MAILING ADDRESS	HEALTH PLAN ID
		Medicaid, PO Box 9800, New York NY 12300	1997458701

RESPONSIBLE PHYSICIAN	RESPONSIBLE PHYSICIAN NPI	TYPE OF ADMISSION
Bill Waters, M.D.	1149678520	Elective (3)

CASE SUMMARY	DIAGNOSES	ICD CODE
Patient was registered in the outpatient clinic and underwent excision of mass of right breast. Patient discharged home, to be followed by primary physician.	Benign neoplasm of right breast	D24.1

CHARGE DESCRIPTION MASTER

ALFRED MEDICAL CENTER
548 N MAIN ST
ALFRED NY 14802

Printed on 05/01/YYYY

DEPARTMENT CODE: 01.957   DEPARTMENT: Surgery

SERVICE CODE	SERVICE DESCRIPTION	REVENUE CODE	CPT CODE	CHARGE	RVU
8650101	Excision of mass, right breast	0314	19120-RT	950.00	1.05

ASSIGNMENT 11.5 – MULTIPLE CHOICE REVIEW

1. The Federal Privacy Act of 1974 prohibits a payer from notifying the provider about payment or rejection of unassigned claims or payments sent directly to the patient or
   a. government.
   b. policyholder.
   c. provider.
   d. third-party payer.

2. Medicare *Conditions of Participation (CoP)* require providers to keep copies of any government insurance claims and copies of all attachments filed by the provider for a period of _____ years, unless state law specifies a longer period.
   a. 3
   b. 5
   c. 7
   d. 10

3. After comparing batched remittance advice notices with claims submitted, if an error in processing is found (e.g., denied claims), which should be done?
   a. Complete new CMS-1500 claims for any denied claims so that the third-party properly processes them.
   b. Discard the batched remittance advice notices and claims because the payer has denied payment.
   c. Mail a copy of the batched remittance advice notices and claims to the provider for reconsideration.
   d. Submit an appeal to the third-party payer for reconsideration of payment for any denied claims.

4. When Block 27 contains an X in the YES box, the provider agrees to
   a. accept assignment and collect a copayment from the patient.
   b. accept assignment and collect deductible/copayment/coinsurance amounts from the patient.
   c. collect deductible and coinsurance payments from the patient.
   d. collect deductible/copayment/coinsurance amounts from the policyholder.

5. Claims are electronically transmitted as data packets and routed from
   a. clearinghouse to provider.
   b. internet service provider to physician.
   c. provider to billing company.
   d. third-party payer to clearinghouse.

6. Medicare supplemental plans usually cover which of the following?
   a. all prescribed pharmaceutical medications
   b. anything that Medicare Part A does not cover
   c. deductible, copayment, coinsurance amounts
   d. health insurance premiums, including deductibles

7. Which is the correct way to enter the amount of $125.75 on the CMS-1500 claim?
   a. $125.75
   b. 125.75
   c. $125 75
   d. 125 75

8. A patient's name on the insurance card reads Marvin L. Blue III. How is this entered on the CMS-1500 claim?
   a. BLUE III, MARVIN, L
   b. BLUE, MARVIN, L III
   c. MARVIN, BLUE, L III
   d. MARVIN, L, BLUE III

9. Which is the proper way to report a patient's birth date of June 16, 1967, on the CMS-1500 claim?
   a. 06-16-67
   b. 06 16 67
   c. 06-16-1967
   d. 06 16 1967

10. Which is a common error that delays claims processing?
    a. aligning paper-based claims so that data is populated in appropriate fields
    b. keyboarding accurate patient identification information
    c. listing dates of services for procedures/services provided
    d. reporting ICD-10-PCS codes when CPT codes are required

11. Which is the proper format for entering the name of a provider in Block 33 of the CMS-1500 claim?
    a. Dr. Howard Hurtz
    b. Dr. Howard Hurtz, M.D.
    c. Howard Hurtz MD
    d. Hurtz, Howard M.D.

12. Which is issued by CMS to individual providers and health care organizations?
    a. EIN
    b. NPI
    c. PIN
    d. UPIN

13. If the patient does not sign Block 13 of the CMS-1500 claim, the payer sends reimbursement to the
    a. billing entity.   c. patient.
    b. facility.   d. provider.

14. When more than one diagnosis reference number is reported on a CMS-1500 claim, the first-listed code is the
    a. condition that has been treated most regularly.
    b. diagnosis with the highest reimbursement rate.
    c. illness most likely to require hospital admission.
    d. reason the patient was treated by the provider.

15. What type of data are required by all payers in Block 24B of the CMS-1500 claim?
    a. date of service   c. type of service
    b. place of service   d. units of service

Commercial Insurance

INTRODUCTION

This chapter familiarizes students with completion of the CMS-1500 claim for primary and secondary commercial payers.

 NOTE:

When the subscriber's employer and a group number are included on the case study, enter an X in the Group Health Plan box in Block 1. If there is no employer or group number, enter an X in the Other box in Block 1.

 NOTE:

When completing CMS-1500 claims for case studies in this workbook, enter just one diagnosis pointer letter in Block 24E.

 NOTE:

When completing claims for patients who have both primary and secondary insurance coverage, enter a P (primary) next to the case number on the primary claim (e.g., 12-A-P), and enter an S (secondary) (e.g., 12-A-S) next to the case number on the secondary claim.

ASSIGNMENT 12.1 – COMMERCIAL PRIMARY CMS-1500 CLAIMS COMPLETION

Objectives

At the conclusion of this assignment, the student should be able to:

1. Assign ICD-10-CM diagnosis and CPT or HCPCS level II procedure/service codes.

2. Prepare commercial insurance CMS-1500 claims.

Instructions

Complete CMS-1500 claims for case studies 12-A and 12-B. Obtain a blank claim by making a copy of the CMS-1500 claim in Appendix I of the textbook. Refer to the CMS-1500 claims completion instructions (primary) in the textbook.

Donald L. Givings, M.D.

Case Study 12-A

11350 Medical Drive ■ Anywhere NY 12345-6541 ■ (101) 111-5555

EIN: 11-1234562
NPI: 1234567890

PATIENT INFORMATION:

Name:	Dawn L. Zapp
Address:	663 Hilltop Drive
City:	Anywhere
State:	NY
Zip Code:	12345
Telephone:	(101) 333-4445
Gender:	Female
Date of Birth:	02-12-1967
Occupation:	Cashier
Employer:	Superfresh Foods
Spouse's Employer:	

INSURANCE INFORMATION:

Patient Number:	12-A
Place of Service:	Office
Primary Insurance Plan:	NorthWest Health
Primary Insurance Plan ID #:	444556666
Group #:	
Primary Policyholder:	Dawn L. Zapp
Policyholder Date of Birth:	02-12-1967
Relationship to Patient:	Self
Secondary Insurance Plan:	
Secondary Insurance Plan ID #:	
Secondary Policyholder:	

Patient Status   ☐ Married   ☐ Divorced   ☒ Single   ☐ Student   ☐ Other

DIAGNOSIS INFORMATION

Diagnosis	Code	Diagnosis	Code
1. Headache		5.	
2. Cough		6.	
3.		7.	
4.		8.	

PROCEDURE INFORMATION

Description of Procedure or Service	Date	Code	Charge
1. Established patient office visit, level 2	05-10-YYYY		$65.00
2.			
3.			
4.			
5.			

SPECIAL NOTES:
   Return visit: 2 weeks

Donald L. Givings, M.D.

11350 Medical Drive ■ Anywhere NY 12345-6541 ■ (101) 111-5555

EIN: 11-1234562
NPI: 1234567890

Case Study 12-B

PATIENT INFORMATION:

Name:	Albert E. Stein
Address:	2011 Shore Drive
City:	Anywhere
State:	NY
Zip Code:	12345
Telephone:	(101) 651-9388
Gender:	Male
Date of Birth:	07-25-1968
Occupation:	Driver
Employer:	Home Decor Today
Spouse's Employer:	

INSURANCE INFORMATION:

Patient Number:	12-B
Place of Service:	Office
Primary Insurance Plan:	Aetna
Primary Insurance Plan ID #:	4291974911
Group #:	
Primary Policyholder:	Albert E. Stein
Policyholder Date of Birth:	07-25-1968
Relationship to Patient:	Self
Secondary Insurance Plan:	
Secondary Insurance Plan ID #:	
Secondary Policyholder:	

Patient Status ☐ Married ☐ Divorced ☒ Single ☐ Employed ☐ Student ☐ Other

DIAGNOSIS INFORMATION

Diagnosis	Code	Diagnosis	Code
1. Annual physical exam		5.	
2.		6.	
3.		7.	
4.		8.	

PROCEDURE INFORMATION

Description of Procedure or Service	Date	Code	Charge
1. Preventive service, established visit	02-23-YYYY		$65.00
2.			
3.			
4.			
5.			

SPECIAL NOTES:

ASSIGNMENT 12.2 – COMMERCIAL PRIMARY/SECONDARY SAME PAYER CMS-1500 CLAIMS COMPLETION

Objectives

At the conclusion of this assignment, the student should be able to:

1. Assign ICD-10-CM diagnosis codes and CPT or HCPCS level II procedure/service codes.
2. Prepare a commercial insurance CMS-1500 claim.

Instructions

Complete the CMS-1500 claim for case study 12-C. Obtain a blank claim by making a copy of the CMS-1500 claim in Appendix I of the textbook. Refer to the textbook CMS-1500 claims completion instructions when third-party payer is the same for primary and secondary health insurance coverage.

ASSIGNMENT 12.3 – COMMERCIAL SECONDARY CMS-1500 CLAIMS COMPLETION

Objectives

At the conclusion of this assignment, the student should be able to:

1. Assign ICD-10-CM diagnosis and CPT or HCPCS level II procedure/service codes.
2. Prepare a commercial insurance secondary payer CMS-1500 claim.

Instructions

Complete a CMS-1500 claim for case study 12-D. Obtain a blank claim by making a copy of the CMS-1500 claim in Appendix I of the textbook. Refer to the CMS-1500 claims completion instructions (secondary) in the textbook.

ASSIGNMENT 12.4 – GROUP HEALTH PLAN CMS-1500 CLAIMS COMPLETION

Objectives

At the conclusion of this assignment, the student should be able to:

1. Assign ICD-10-CM diagnosis and CPT or HCPCS level II procedure/service codes.
2. Prepare a commercial insurance group health plan CMS-1500 claim.

Instructions

Complete a CMS-1500 claim for case study 12-E. Obtain a blank claim by making a copy of the CMS-1500 claim in Appendix I of the textbook. Refer to the CMS-1500 claims completion instructions (group health plans) in the textbook.

Donald L. Givings, M.D.

11350 Medical Drive ■ Anywhere NY 12345-6541 ■ (101) 111-5555

EIN: 11-1234562
NPI: 1234567890

Case Study 12-C

PATIENT INFORMATION:

Name:	Bethany L. Branch
Address:	401 Cartvalley Court
City:	Anywhere
State:	NY
Zip Code:	12345
Telephone:	(101) 333-4445
Gender:	Female
Date of Birth:	05-03-2006
Occupation:	Student (Full time)
Employer:	
Spouse's Employer:	

INSURANCE INFORMATION:

Patient Number:	12-C
Place of Service:	Office
Primary Insurance Plan:	Metropolitan
Primary Insurance Plan ID #:	212224545
Group #:	
Primary Policyholder:	John L. Branch
Policyholder Date of Birth:	10-10-54
Relationship to Patient:	Father
Primary Policyholder's Employer:	Alstom
Secondary Insurance Plan:	Metropolitan
Secondary Insurance Plan ID #:	315661111
Secondary Policyholder:	Karen M. Branch
Policyholder Date of Birth:	12-01-1953
Secondary Policyholder's Employer:	Gateway

Patient Status	☐ Married	☐ Divorced	☒ Single	☒ Student	☐ Other

DIAGNOSIS INFORMATION

Diagnosis	Code	Diagnosis	Code
1. Acute bronchitis		5.	
2. Strep pharyngitis		6.	
3.		7.	
4.		8.	

PROCEDURE INFORMATION

Description of Procedure or Service	Date	Code	Charge
1. Office consultation, level 2	12-04-YYYY		$75.00
2. Rapid strep test	12-04-YYYY		$12.00
3.			
4.			
5.			

SPECIAL NOTES:
Return visit: PRN
Referring physician: James R. Feltbetter, M.D.
NPI: 7778878789

Donald L. Givings, M.D.

Case Study 12-D

11350 Medical Drive ■ Anywhere NY 12345-6541 ■ (101) 111-5555

EIN: 11-1234562
NPI: 1234567890

PATIENT INFORMATION:

Name:	Laurie P. Reed
Address:	579 Vacation Drive
City:	Anywhere
State:	NY
Zip Code:	12345
Telephone:	(101) 333-5555
Gender:	Female
Date of Birth:	06-05-1964
Occupation:	Tutor
Employer:	The Learning Center
Spouse's Employer:	Recycling R US

INSURANCE INFORMATION:

Patient Number:	12-D
Place of Service:	Office
Primary Insurance Plan:	US Health
Primary Insurance Plan ID #:	C748593
Group #:	
Primary Policyholder:	John P. Reed
Policyholder Date of Birth:	09-08-1962
Relationship to Patient:	Spouse
Secondary Insurance Plan:	Cigna
Secondary Insurance Plan ID #:	345679999
Secondary Policyholder:	Laurie P. Reed

Patient Status   ☒ Married   ☐ Divorced   ☐ Single   ☐ Student   ☐ Other

DIAGNOSIS INFORMATION

Diagnosis	Code	Diagnosis	Code
1. Allergic rhinitis		5.	
2.		6.	
3.		7.	
4.		8.	

PROCEDURE INFORMATION

Description of Procedure or Service	Date	Code	Charge
1. Established patient office visit, level 2	10-28-YYYY		$55.00
2.			
3.			
4.			
5.			

SPECIAL NOTES:
    Return visit: PRN Reimbursement of $44.00 from primary payer is documented on EOB.

Donald L. Givings, M.D.

11350 Medical Drive ■ Anywhere NY 12345-6541 ■ (101) 111-5555

EIN: 11-1234562
NPI: 1234567890

Case Study 12-E

PATIENT INFORMATION:

Name:	Sandy Marks
Address:	101 West State Street
City:	Anywhere
State:	NY
Zip Code:	12345
Telephone:	(101) 333-9876
Gender:	Female
Date of Birth:	05-10-1990
Occupation:	Teacher
Employer:	Carnelian Middle School
Spouse's Employer:	

INSURANCE INFORMATION:

Patient Number:	12-E
Place of Service:	Office
Primary Insurance Plan:	Empire Plan
Primary Insurance Plan ID #:	890102568
Group #:	123
Primary Policyholder:	Sandy Marks
Policyholder Date of Birth:	05-10-1990
Relationship to Patient:	Self
Secondary Insurance Plan:	
Secondary Insurance Plan ID #:	
Secondary Policyholder:	

Patient Status   ☐ Married   ☐ Divorced   ☒ Single   ☐ Student   ☐ Other

DIAGNOSIS INFORMATION

Diagnosis	Code	Diagnosis	Code
1. Hypertension		5.	
2.		6.	
3.		7.	
4.		8.	

PROCEDURE INFORMATION

Description of Procedure or Service	Date	Code	Charge
1. New patient office visit, level 3	07-20-YYYY		$75.00
2.			
3.			
4.			
5.			

SPECIAL NOTES:

ASSIGNMENT 12.5 – MULTIPLE CHOICE REVIEW

1. Which is considered a commercial health insurance company?
   a. Medicaid
   b. Medicare
   c. Prudential
   d. TRICARE

2. Another term that can be used to indicate a fee-for-service plan is a(n) _____ plan.
   a. liability
   b. indemnity
   c. prepaid
   d. sliding scale

3. When a patient is covered by a large employer group health plan (EGHP), *and* the patient is also a Medicare beneficiary, _____ is primary.
   a. EGHP
   b. EGHP or Medicare
   c. Medicare
   d. neither EGHP nor Medicare

4. Logan is the daughter of Amy (DOB 3/29/68) and Bill (DOB 11/15/70) and is covered by both parents' health insurance plans. According to the birthday rule, a medical claim for Logan will be submitted to
   a. Amy's plan as primary payer and Bill's plan as secondary payer.
   b. Amy's plan only, as Amy is two years older than Bill.
   c. Bill's plan as primary payer and Amy's plan as secondary payer.
   d. Bill's plan only, as Bill has been employed with his company longer.

5. When the patient is the domestic partner of the primary policyholder, this is indicated on the CMS-1500 claim by
   a. entering "DP" after the patient's name in Block 2.
   b. entering the patient's full name in Block 9.
   c. placing an X in the OTHER box of Block 6.
   d. placing an X in the SINGLE box of Block 8.

6. Reimbursement for income lost as a result of a temporary or permanent illness or injury is covered by _____ insurance.
   a. automobile
   b. disability
   c. health
   d. liability

7. The patient was seen in the provider's office on 12/03/YYYY for an injury sustained four months earlier. What is entered in Block 14 of the CMS-1500 claim?
   a. 04 03 YYYY
   b. 08 03 YYYY
   c. 11 03 YYYY
   d. 12 03 YYYY

8. What is entered in Block 17b of the CMS-1500 claim?
   a. employer identification number (EIN)
   b. national provider identifier (NPI)
   c. provider identification number (PIN)
   d. Social Security number (SSN)

9. Dr. Smith evaluates Marcia Brady during a three-month recheck of diabetes mellitus. Dr. Smith performs venipuncture and sends the patient's blood sample to an outside laboratory for testing of the blood glucose level. Dr. Smith's insurance specialist enters the outside laboratory's _____ in Block 24J because the blood glucose test is reported in Block 24D on that line.
   a. EIN
   b. NPI
   c. SSN
   d. Group #

10. If the patient has paid a copayment on the claim being submitted, this is indicated on the CMS-1500 claim by entering the
    a. amount paid in Block 19.
    b. amount paid in Block 29.
    c. patient's name in Block 13.
    d. letter Y in Block 27.

11. The patient was required to obtain an authorization number before being treated by a specialist. Where is the authorization number entered in the CMS-1500 claim?
    a. Block 10d
    b. Block 17a
    c. Block 19
    d. Block 23

12. When an insurance claim is submitted to an insurance company that covers the treatment of injuries sustained in a motor vehicle accident, the _____ reviews the claim and determines coverage for the injured person.
    a. claims analyst
    b. health care broker
    c. medical adjuster
    d. negligence attorney

13. Beatrice Blue holds a private commercial health care policy and wishes to have payment from the health insurance company sent directly to the provider. How is this reported on the CMS-1500 claim?
    a. Beatrice Blue will sign Block 12.
    b. Beatrice Blue will sign Block 13.
    c. The provider will sign Block 12.
    d. The provider will sign Block 13.

14. Which claims are submitted to cover the cost of medical care for traumatic injuries, lost wages, pain, and suffering?
    a. disability
    b. automobile
    c. liability
    d. medical

15. A balance of $12.55 is due to the patient for services provided by Dr. Brown. What is entered in *Block 30* of the CMS-1500 claim?
    a. Leave blank
    b. 12 55
    c. −12 55
    d. CREDIT

16. When the same commercial payer issues the primary and secondary or supplemental policies, it is *generally* acceptable to submit _____ claim(s).
    a. one
    b. two
    c. three
    d. three or more

17. When laboratory tests are performed in the office, enter an X in the NO box of
    a. Block 9d.
    b. Block 11d.
    c. Block 20.
    d. Block 27.

18. Reimbursement for loss of or damage to a vehicle (e.g., caused by fire, flood, hail, theft, vandalism, or wind) is covered by _____ (automobile) insurance.
    a. collision
    b. comprehensive
    c. liability
    d. medical

19. Which health plan is required to accept employees and their family members?
    a. dental
    b. group
    c. individual
    d. medical

20. Nancy White's employer provides individual and family group health plan coverage, and it pays 80 percent of the annual premium. Nancy selected family coverage for the group health plan, which means the employer pays $12,000 per year (of the $15,000 annual premium). Nancy is responsible for the remaining $3,000 of the annual premium, which means approximately _____ is deducted from each of 26 biweekly paychecks.
    a. $90
    b. $100
    c. $115
    d. $125

BlueCross BlueShield

INTRODUCTION

This chapter familiarizes students with completion of CMS-1500 claims for primary and secondary BlueCross BlueShield payers.

 NOTE:

When the subscriber's employer and a group number are included on the case study, enter an X in the Group Health Plan box in Block 1. If there is no employer or group number, enter an X in the Other box in Block 1.

 NOTE:

When completing CMS-1500 claims for case studies in this workbook, enter just one diagnosis pointer letter in Block 24E.

 NOTE:

When completing claims for patients who have both primary and secondary insurance coverage, enter a P (primary) next to the case number on the primary claim (e.g., 13-A-P), and enter an S (secondary) (e.g., 13-A-S) next to the case number on the secondary claim. When completing claims for patients who have BLUECROSS BLUESHIELD insurance for both primary and secondary coverage, enter BB as part of the case number (e.g., 13-C-BB).

ASSIGNMENT 13.1 – BLUECROSS BLUESHIELD PRIMARY CMS-1500 CLAIMS COMPLETION

Objectives

At the conclusion of this assignment, the student should be able to:

1. Assign ICD-10-CM diagnosis and CPT or HCPCS level II procedure/service codes.
2. Prepare a BlueCross BlueShield insurance primary payer CMS-1500 claim.

Instructions

Complete a CMS-1500 for case studies 13-A and 13-B. Obtain a blank claim by making a copy of the CMS-1500 claim in Appendix I of the textbook. Refer to the CMS-1500 claims completion instructions (primary) in the textbook.

Donald L. Givings, M.D.   # Case Study 13-A

11350 Medical Drive ■ Anywhere NY 12345-6541 ■ (101) 111-5555

EIN: 11-1234562
NPI: 1234567890

PATIENT INFORMATION:

Name:	Monty L. Booker
Address:	47 Snowflake Road
City:	Anywhere
State:	NY
Zip Code:	12345
Telephone:	(101) 333-5555
Gender:	Male
Date of Birth:	12-25-1966
Occupation:	Editor
Employer:	Atlanta Publisher
Spouse's Employer:	

INSURANCE INFORMATION:

Patient Number:	13-A
Place of Service:	Office
Primary Insurance Plan:	BLUECROSS BLUESHIELD
Primary Insurance Plan ID #:	NXY678223434
Group #:	
Primary Policyholder:	Monty L. Booker
Policyholder Date of Birth:	12-25-1966
Relationship to Patient:	Self
Secondary Insurance Plan:	
Secondary Insurance Plan ID #:	
Secondary Policyholder:	

Patient Status   ☒ Married   ☐ Divorced   ☐ Single   ☐ Student   ☐ Other

---

DIAGNOSIS INFORMATION

Diagnosis	Code	Diagnosis	Code
1. Abnormal loss of weight		5.	
2. Polydipsia		6.	
3. Polyphagia		7.	
4.		8.	

PROCEDURE INFORMATION

Description of Procedure or Service	Date	Code	Charge
1. New patient office visit, level 2	01-19-YYYY		$100.00
2. Urinalysis, with microscopy	01-19-YYYY		$10.00
3.			
4.			
5.			

SPECIAL NOTES:
   Return visit: 3 weeks

Donald L. Givings, M.D.

11350 Medical Drive ■ Anywhere NY 12345-6541 ■ (101) 111-5555

EIN: 11-1234562
NPI: 1234567890

Case Study 13-B

PATIENT INFORMATION:

Name:	Anita B. Strong
Address:	124 Prosper Way
City:	Anywhere
State:	NY
Zip Code:	12345
Telephone:	(101) 333-5555
Gender:	Female
Date of Birth:	04-25-1959
Occupation:	Author
Employer:	Anywhere Weekly News
Spouse's Employer:	

INSURANCE INFORMATION:

Patient Number:	13-B
Place of Service:	Office
Primary Insurance Plan:	BLUECROSS BLUESHIELD
Primary Insurance Plan ID #:	XWG214556666
Group #:	
Primary Policyholder:	Anita B. Strong
Policyholder Date of Birth:	04-25-1960
Relationship to Patient:	Self
Secondary Insurance Plan:	
Secondary Insurance Plan ID #:	
Secondary Policyholder:	

Patient Status   ☒ Married   ☐ Divorced   ☐ Single   ☐ Student   ☐ Other

DIAGNOSIS INFORMATION

Diagnosis	Code	Diagnosis	Code
1. Migraine, classical		5.	
2.		6.	
3.		7.	
4.		8.	

PROCEDURE INFORMATION

Description of Procedure or Service	Date	Code	Charge
1. Established patient office visit, level 2	11-07-YYYY		$55.00
2.			
3.			
4.			
5.			

SPECIAL NOTES:
    Return visit: PRN
    Patient paid $20.00 toward today's bill.

ASSIGNMENT 13.2 – BLUECROSS BLUESHIELD PRIMARY/SECONDARY SAME PAYER CMS-1500 CLAIMS COMPLETION

Objectives

At the conclusion of this assignment, the student should be able to:

1. Assign ICD-10-CM diagnosis codes and CPT or HCPCS level II procedure/service codes.
2. Prepare BlueCross BlueShield CMS-1500 insurance claims.

Instructions

Complete CMS-1500 claims for case studies 13-C and 13-D. Obtain a blank claim by making a copy of the CMS-1500 claim in Appendix I of the textbook. Refer to the CMS-1500 claims completion instructions (Primary and Secondary when payer is the same) in the textbook.

ASSIGNMENT 13.3 – BLUECROSS BLUESHIELD SECONDARY CMS-1500 CLAIMS COMPLETION

Objectives

At the conclusion of this assignment, the student should be able to:

1. Assign ICD-10-CM diagnosis and CPT or HCPCS level II procedure/service codes.
2. Prepare a BlueCross BlueShield insurance secondary payer CMS-1500 claim.

Instructions

Complete a CMS-1500 for case study 13-E. Obtain a blank claim by making a copy of the CMS-1500 claim in Appendix I of the textbook. Refer to the CMS-1500 claims completion instructions (secondary) in the textbook.

Donald L. Givings, M.D.

Case Study 13-C

11350 Medical Drive ■ Anywhere NY 12345-6541 ■ (101) 111-5555

EIN: 11-1234562
NPI: 1234567890

PATIENT INFORMATION:

Name:	Virginia A. Love
Address:	61 Isaiah Circle
City:	Anywhere
State:	NY
Zip Code:	12345
Telephone:	(101) 333-5555
Gender:	Female
Date of Birth:	10-04-1962
Occupation:	Decorator
Employer:	Home Designs
Spouse's Employer:	Imperial Bayliners

INSURANCE INFORMATION:

Patient Number:	13-C
Place of Service:	Office
Primary Insurance Plan:	BLUECROSS BLUESHIELD
Primary Insurance Plan ID #:	XWN212567972
Group #:	123
Primary Policyholder:	Charles L. Love
Policyholder Date of Birth:	07-06-60
Relationship to Patient:	Spouse
Secondary Insurance Plan:	BLUECROSS BLUESHIELD
Secondary Insurance Plan ID #:	XMP111451111
Secondary Policyholder:	Virginia A. Love

Patient Status   [X] Married   ☐ Divorced   ☐ Single   ☐ Student   ☐ Other

DIAGNOSIS INFORMATION

Diagnosis	Code	Diagnosis	Code
1. Chronic conjunctivitis, left eye		5.	
2. Contact dermatitis		6.	
3.		7.	
4.		8.	

PROCEDURE INFORMATION

Description of Procedure or Service	Date	Code	Charge
1. Established patient office visit, level 2	07-03-YYYY		$55.00
2.			
3.			
4.			
5.			

SPECIAL NOTES:
   If conjunctivitis does not clear within one week refer to Dr. Glance.
   Return visit: PRN

Iris A. Glance, M.D. OPHTHALMOLOGIST

Case Study 13-D

66 Granite Drive ■ Anywhere NY 12345-5432 ■ (101) 111-5555

EIN: 11-6161612
NPI: 6789137892

PATIENT INFORMATION:

Name:	Virginia A. Love
Address:	61 Isaiah Circle
City:	Anywhere
State:	NY
Zip Code:	12345
Telephone:	(101) 333-5555
Gender:	Female
Date of Birth:	10-04-1962
Occupation:	Decorator
Employer:	Home Designs
Spouse's Employer:	Imperial Bayliners

INSURANCE INFORMATION:

Patient Number:	13-D
Place of Service:	Office
Primary Insurance Plan:	BLUECROSS BLUESHIELD
Primary Insurance Plan ID #:	XWN212567372
Group #:	123
Primary Policyholder:	Charles L. Love
Policyholder Date of Birth:	07-06-60
Relationship to Patient:	Spouse
Secondary Insurance Plan:	BLUECROSS BLUESHIELD
Secondary Insurance Plan ID #:	XMP111451111
Secondary Policyholder:	Virginia A. Love

Patient Status   ☒ Married   ☐ Divorced   ☐ Single   ☐ Student   ☐ Other

DIAGNOSIS INFORMATION

Diagnosis	Code	Diagnosis	Code
1. Chronic conjunctivitis, left eye		5.	
2. Conjunctival degeneration, left eye		6.	
3.		7.	
4.		8.	

PROCEDURE INFORMATION

Description of Procedure or Service	Date	Code	Charge
1. Office consultation, level 1	07-13-YYYY		$65.00
2.			
3.			
4.			
5.			

SPECIAL NOTES:
  Onset of symptoms: 07-03-YYYY.

Donald L. Givings, M.D.

11350 Medical Drive ■ Anywhere NY 12345-6541 ■ (101) 111-5555

EIN: 11-1234562
NPI: 1234567890

Case Study 13-E

PATIENT INFORMATION:

Name:	Keith S. Kutter
Address:	22 Pinewood Avenue
City:	Anywhere
State:	NY
Zip Code:	12345
Telephone:	(101) 333-5555
Gender:	Male
Date of Birth:	05-01-1955
Occupation:	Manager
Employer:	First League
Spouse's Employer:	Anderson Music

INSURANCE INFORMATION:

Patient Number:	13-E
Place of Service:	Office
Primary Insurance Plan:	AETNA
Primary Insurance Plan ID #:	FLX313007777
Group #:	
Primary Policyholder:	Keith S. Kutter
Policyholder Date of Birth:	05-01-1955
Relationship to Patient:	Self
Secondary Insurance Plan:	BLUECROSS BLUESHIELD
Secondary Insurance Plan ID #:	GPW212446868
Secondary Policyholder:	Linda Kutter
Secondary Policyholder DOB:	12-22-1956

Patient Status   ☒ Married   ☐ Divorced   ☐ Single   ☐ Student   ☐ Other

DIAGNOSIS INFORMATION

Diagnosis	Code	Diagnosis	Code
1. Muscle spasms of the back		5.	
2.		6.	
3.		7.	
4.		8.	

PROCEDURE INFORMATION

Description of Procedure or Service	Date	Code	Charge
1. Established patient office visit, level 2	09-03-YYYY		$65.00
2.			
3.			
4.			
5.			

SPECIAL NOTES:
Refer to a chiropractor.

ASSIGNMENT 13.4 – MULTIPLE CHOICE REVIEW

1. Prior to the joint venture between BlueCross and BlueShield, the BlueShield plans covered only
   a. hospital charges.
   b. physician services.
   c. prescription costs.
   d. therapy services.

2. BlueCross facilities that had signed contracts to provide services to subscribers for special rates were known as _____ hospitals.
   a. benefit
   b. member
   c. plan
   d. subscriber

3. In what year was the BlueCross BlueShield Association (BCBSA) created?
   a. 1929
   b. 1938
   c. 1977
   d. 1986

4. Which is a function of the BlueCross BlueShield Association (BCBSA)?
   a. hiring local personnel
   b. membership enrollment
   c. national advertising
   d. processing Medicaid claims

5. The difference between for-profit status and nonprofit status is that
   a. for-profit corporations pay taxes on profits generated by the corporation.
   b. for-profit corporations pay their shareholders with before-tax profits.
   c. nonprofit corporations do not have stocks, shareholders, or officers.
   d. nonprofit corporations return earned profits to stock shareholders.

6. When a policyholder moves into an area served by a different BlueCross BlueShield corporation than the policyholder previously used, the plan must
   a. guarantee transfer of membership.
   b. immediately cancel the individual's policy.
   c. locate a primary provider for the member.
   d. prohibit the member from seeking urgent care.

7. The preferred provider network (PPN) allowed rate is generally
   a. 10 percent higher than the participating provider rate.
   b. 10 percent lower than the participating provider rate.
   c. based on the Medicare Physician Fee Schedule.
   d. equal to the participating provider payment.

8. Which is an incentive for a provider to sign a PPN contract?
   a. higher reimbursement rates than those of participating providers
   b. no quality assurance or cost-containment program requirements
   c. PPN providers are not held to any managed care provisions
   d. written notification of new employer groups and hospitals

9. Small businesses are likely to select which BlueCross BlueShield coverage?
   a. fee-for-service
   b. indemnity
   c. managed care
   d. supplemental

10. An example of a benefit provided by BlueCross BlueShield basic coverage is
    a. assistant surgeon fees.
    b. mental health visits.
    c. occupational therapy.
    d. private-duty nursing.

11. The BlueCross BlueShield plan type that offers choice and flexibility to subscribers is
    a. Health Care Anywhere.
    b. indemnity coverage.
    c. major medical coverage.
    d. managed care.

12. A special accidental injury rider provides which benefit?
   a. Chronic conditions are covered if treatment is sought within the contract's established guidelines.
   b. Medical care is paid at 100 percent if treatment is received within 24–72 hours of accident or injury.
   c. Nonsurgical care is paid at 100 percent if treatment is received within the contract's established time frame.
   d. Surgical care is paid at 100 percent if treatment is received within the contract's established time frame.

13. What special handling is required for BlueCross BlueShield claims filed under the medical emergency care rider?
   a. Claims require all six procedure/service codes to be entered in Block 24D.
   b. CPT codes must reflect critical care services provided to the patient.
   c. Health insurance specialists must enter four diagnosis codes in Block 21.
   d. ICD-10-CM codes must reflect a condition that requires immediate care.

14. The outpatient pretreatment authorization plan (OPAP) is also known as
   a. preapproval.   c. precertification.
   b. preauthorization.   d. prevention.

15. What title is listed on the BlueCross BlueShield identification cards for federal employees?
   a. BlueCross BlueShield Federal Program
   b. BlueCross BlueShield National Account for Federal Employees
   c. Federal Employee Health Benefits Program
   d. Government-Wide Service Benefit Plan

16. BlueCross BlueShield Medicare supplemental plans offered by BCBS companies are also known as _____ plans.
   a. MediBlue   c. Medigap
   b. Medicare   d. MediSup

17. The BlueCard program allows members to obtain health services while in another BlueCross BlueShield service area. The patient will also
   a. pay a higher copayment or coinsurance for care.
   b. pay a higher premium for the flexible coverage.
   c. receive the benefits of the other BlueCross BlueShield contract.
   d. receive the benefits of the home plan contract.

18. Which BlueCross BlueShield program or plan would be most appropriate for a student who is attending school out of state?
   a. Away from Home Care Program   c. indemnity plan
   b. GeoBlue program   d. point-of-service plan

19. What information is entered in Block 13 of a BlueCross BlueShield CMS-1500 claim?
   a. Nothing; the box is left blank.   c. the patient's signature
   b. SIGNATURE ON FILE   d. the provider's signature

20. What information is entered in Block 29 of the BlueCross BlueShield CMS-1500 claim when the patient pays a $20.00 copayment?
   a. 0 00   c. $20.00
   b. 20 00   d. Nothing; the box is left blank.

Medicare

INTRODUCTION

This chapter familiarizes students with completion of CMS-1500 claims for Primary Medicare, Medicare as Secondary Payer (MSP), Medicare/Medigap, and Medicare/Medicaid.

NOTE:

When completing CMS-1500 claims for case studies in this workbook, enter just one diagnosis pointer letter in Block 24E.

NOTE:

When completing claims for patients who have both primary and secondary insurance coverage, enter a P (primary) next to the case number on the primary claim (e.g., 14-A-P), and enter an S (secondary) (e.g., 14-A-S) next to the case number on the secondary claim. For patients who have Medicare and Medicaid crossover coverage, add MM to the patient account number (e.g., 14-B-MM).

ASSIGNMENT 14.1 – MEDICARE PRIMARY CMS-1500 CLAIMS COMPLETION

Objectives

At the conclusion of this assignment, the student should be able to:

1. Assign ICD-10-CM diagnosis and CPT or HCPCS level II procedure/service codes.
2. Prepare a Medicare insurance primary payer CMS-1500 claim.

Instructions

Complete a CMS-1500 for case studies 14-A and 14-B. Obtain a blank claim by making a copy of the CMS-1500 claim in Appendix I of the textbook. Refer to the CMS-1500 claims completion instructions (primary) in the textbook.

Donald L. Givings, M.D.

Case Study 14-A

11350 Medical Drive ■ Anywhere NY 12345-6541 ■ (101) 111-5555

EIN: 11-1234562
NPI: 1234567890

PATIENT INFORMATION:

Name:	Alice E. Worthington
Address:	3301 Sunny Day Drive
City:	Anywhere
State:	NY
Zip Code:	12345
Telephone:	(101) 333-5555
Gender:	Female
Date of Birth:	02-16-1926
Occupation:	
Employer:	None
Spouse's Employer:	

INSURANCE INFORMATION:

Patient Number:	14-A
Place of Service:	Office
Primary Insurance Plan:	Medicare
Primary Insurance Plan ID #:	4442AA23333
Group #:	
Primary Policyholder:	Alice E. Worthington
Policyholder Date of Birth:	02-16-1926
Relationship to Patient:	Self
Secondary Insurance Plan:	
Secondary Insurance Plan ID #:	
Secondary Policyholder:	

Patient Status   ☐ Married   ☐ Divorced   ☒ Single   ☐ Student   ☐ Other

DIAGNOSIS INFORMATION

Diagnosis	Code	Diagnosis	Code
1. Breast lump, left		5.	
2. Breast pain, left		6.	
3. Family history of breast cancer		7.	
4.		8.	

PROCEDURE INFORMATION

Description of Procedure or Service	Date	Code	Charge
1. Established patient office visit, level 2	07-12-YYYY		$65.00
2.			
3.			
4.			
5.			

SPECIAL NOTES:
      Refer to Jonathan B. Kutter, M.D.

Jon B. Kutter, M.D.

Case Study 14-B

339 Woodland Place ■ Anywhere NY 12345-3214 ■ (101) 111-5555

EIN: 11-5566772
NPI: 2345675678

PATIENT INFORMATION:

Name:	Alice E. Worthington
Address:	3301 Sunny Day Drive
City:	Anywhere
State:	NY
Zip Code:	12345
Telephone:	(101) 333-5555
Gender:	Female
Date of Birth:	02-16-1926
Occupation:	
Employer:	None
Spouse's Employer:	

INSURANCE INFORMATION:

Patient Number:	14-B
Place of Service:	Office
Primary Insurance Plan:	Medicare
Primary Insurance Plan ID #:	4442AA23333
Group #:	
Primary Policyholder:	Alice E. Worthington
Policyholder Date of Birth:	02-16-1926
Relationship to Patient:	Self
Secondary Insurance Plan:	
Secondary Insurance Plan ID #:	
Secondary Policyholder:	

Patient Status   ☐ Married   ☐ Divorced   ☒ Single   ☐ Student   ☐ Other

DIAGNOSIS INFORMATION

Diagnosis	Code	Diagnosis	Code
1. Breast lump, left		5.	
2. Breast pain, left		6.	
3. Family history of breast cancer		7.	
4.		8.	

PROCEDURE INFORMATION

Description of Procedure or Service	Date	Code	Charge
1. Office consultation, level 2	07-15-YYYY		$75.00
2.			
3.			
4.			
5.			

SPECIAL NOTES:
Onset of symptoms: 07-12-YYYY. Referred by Donald L. Givings, M.D., NPI: 1234567890.

NOTE:

When assigning CPT codes for consultations, remember to use the Office or Other Outpatient, New Patient subsection of the Evaluation and Management section. Medicare and Medicaid no longer permit the reporting of codes from the Consultation subsection.

ASSIGNMENT 14.2 – MEDICARE AS SECONDARY PAYER CMS-1500 CLAIMS COMPLETION

Objectives

At the conclusion of this assignment, the student should be able to:

1. Assign ICD-10-CM diagnosis and CPT or HCPCS level II procedure/service codes.

2. Prepare a Medicare as Secondary Payer (MSP) CMS-1500 claim.

Instructions

Complete a CMS-1500 for case studies 14-C and 14-D. Obtain a blank claim by making a copy of the CMS-1500 claim in Appendix I of the textbook. Refer to the CMS-1500 claims completion instructions (secondary) in the textbook.

ASSIGNMENT 14.3 – MEDICARE/MEDIGAP CMS-1500 CLAIMS COMPLETION

Objectives

At the conclusion of this assignment, the student should be able to:

1. Assign ICD-10-CM diagnosis and CPT or HCPCS level II procedure/service codes.

2. Prepare a Medicare/Medigap CMS-1500 claim.

Instructions

Complete a CMS-1500 for case study 14-E. Obtain a blank claim by making a copy of the CMS-1500 claim in Appendix I of the textbook. Refer to the CMS-1500 claims completion instructions (secondary) in the textbook.

ASSIGNMENT 14.4 – MEDICARE/MEDICAID (MEDI-MEDI) CMS-1500 CLAIMS COMPLETION

Objectives

At the conclusion of this assignment, the student should be able to:

1. Assign ICD-10-CM diagnosis and CPT or HCPCS level II procedure/service codes.

2. Prepare a Medicare/Medicaid CMS-1500 claim.

Instructions

Complete a CMS-1500 for case studies 14-F and 14-G. Obtain a blank claim by making a copy of the CMS-1500 claim in Appendix I of the textbook. Refer to the CMS-1500 claims completion instructions (secondary) in the textbook.

Donald L. Givings, M.D.

11350 Medical Drive ■ Anywhere NY 12345-6541 ■ (101) 111-5555

EIN: 11-1234562
NPI: 1234567890

Case Study 14-C

PATIENT INFORMATION:

Name:	Rebecca Nichols
Address:	384 Dean Street
City:	Anywhere
State:	NY
Zip Code:	12345
Telephone:	(101) 333-5555
Gender:	Female
Date of Birth:	10-12-1925
Occupation:	
Employer:	Retired
Spouse's Employer:	

INSURANCE INFORMATION:

Patient Number:	14-C
Place of Service:	Inpatient hospital
Primary Insurance Plan:	BCBS
Primary Insurance Plan ID #:	667143344
Group #:	123
Primary Policyholder:	Rebecca Nichols
Policyholder Date of Birth:	10-12-1925
Relationship to Patient:	Self
Secondary Insurance Plan:	Medicare
Secondary Insurance Plan ID #:	6671AA43344
Secondary Policyholder:	Rebecca Nichols

Patient Status   ☐ Married   ☐ Divorced   ☒ Single   ☐ Student   ☐ Other

DIAGNOSIS INFORMATION

Diagnosis	Code	Diagnosis	Code
1. Rectal bleeding		5.	
2. Diarrhea		6.	
3. Abnormal loss of weight		7.	
4.		8.	

PROCEDURE INFORMATION

Description of Procedure or Service	Date	Code	Charge
1. Initial hospital visit, level 3	08-06-YYYY		$175.00
2. Subsequent hospital visit, level 3	08-07-YYYY		85.00
3. Subsequent hospital visit, level 3	08-08-YYYY		85.00
4. Subsequent hospital visit, level 2	08-09-YYYY		75.00
5. Hospital discharge, 30 minutes	08-10-YYYY		75.00

SPECIAL NOTES:
    Goodmedicine Hospital, 1 Provider Street, Anywhere Street, Anywhere NY 12345-1234. NPI: 1123456789

Lisa M. Mason, M.D. FAMILY PRACTICE   Case Study 14-D

547 Antigua Road ■ Anywhere NY 12345-8526 ■ (101) 111-5555

EIN: 11-4958672
NPI: 4567897890

PATIENT INFORMATION:

Name:	Samuel T. Mahoney Jr.
Address:	498 Meadow Lane
City:	Anywhere
State:	NY
Zip Code:	12345
Telephone:	(101) 333-5555
Gender:	Male
Date of Birth:	09-04-1930
Occupation:	
Employer:	None
Spouse's Employer:	

INSURANCE INFORMATION:

Patient Number:	14-D
Place of Service:	Office
Primary Insurance Plan:	Aetna
Primary Insurance Plan ID #:	312785894
Group #:	
Primary Policyholder:	Samuel T. Mahoney Jr.
Policyholder Date of Birth:	09-04-1930
Relationship to Patient:	Self
Secondary Insurance Plan:	Medicare
Secondary Insurance Plan ID #:	3127AA85894
Secondary Policyholder:	Samuel T. Mahoney Jr.

Patient Status [X] Married   [ ] Divorced   [ ] Single   [ ] Student   [ ] Other

DIAGNOSIS INFORMATION

Diagnosis	Code	Diagnosis	Code
1. Asthma		5.	
2. Acute upper respiratory infection		6.	
3.		7.	
4.		8.	

PROCEDURE INFORMATION

Description of Procedure or Service	Date	Code	Charge
1. Established patient office visit, level 2	10-03-YYYY		$25.00
2.			
3.			
4.			
5.			

SPECIAL NOTES:
   Dr. Mason is nonPAR with Medicare
   Onset of disease: 01-01-YYYY

Donald L. Givings, M.D.

Case Study 14-E

11350 Medical Drive ■ Anywhere NY 12345-6541 ■ (101) 111-5555

EIN: 11-1234562
NPI: 1234567890

PATIENT INFORMATION:

Name:	Abraham N. Freed
Address:	12 Nottingham Circle
City:	Anywhere
State:	NY
Zip Code:	12345
Telephone:	(101) 333-5555
Gender:	Male
Date of Birth:	10-03-1922
Occupation:	
Employer:	Retired Johnson Steel
Spouse's Employer:	

INSURANCE INFORMATION:

Patient Number:	14-E
Place of Service:	Office
Primary Insurance Plan:	Medicare
Primary Insurance Plan ID #:	6454AA54545
Group #:	
Primary Policyholder:	Abraham N. Freed
Policyholder Date of Birth:	10-03-1922
Relationship to Patient:	Self
Secondary Insurance Plan:	BCBS Medigap
Secondary Insurance Plan ID #:	NXY645454545
Secondary Policyholder:	Abraham N. Freed

Patient Status ☒ Married ☐ Divorced ☐ Single ☐ Student ☐ Other

DIAGNOSIS INFORMATION

Diagnosis	Code	Diagnosis	Code
1. Hypertension		5.	
2. Dizziness		6.	
3.		7.	
4.		8.	

PROCEDURE INFORMATION

Description of Procedure or Service	Date	Code	Charge
1. New patient office visit, level 4	03-07-YYYY		$100.00
2. EKG	03-07-YYYY		50.00
3. Venipuncture	03-07-YYYY		8.00
4.			
5.			

SPECIAL NOTES:
Return visit: 2 weeks

Donald L. Givings, M.D.

Case Study 14-F

11350 Medical Drive ■ Anywhere NY 12345-6541 ■ (101) 111-5555

EIN: 11-1234562
NPI: 1234567890

PATIENT INFORMATION:

Name:	Patricia S. Delaney
Address:	45 Garden Lane
City:	Anywhere
State:	NY
Zip Code:	12345
Telephone:	(101) 333-5555
Gender:	Female
Date of Birth:	04-12-1931
Occupation:	
Employer:	
Spouse's Employer:	

INSURANCE INFORMATION:

Patient Number:	14-F
Place of Service:	Office
Primary Insurance Plan:	Medicare
Primary Insurance Plan ID #:	4853AA75869
Group #:	
Primary Policyholder:	Patricia S. Delaney
Policyholder Date of Birth:	04-12-1931
Relationship to Patient:	Self
Secondary Insurance Plan:	Medicaid
Secondary Insurance Plan ID #:	22886644XT
Secondary Policyholder:	Self

Patient Status   ☐ Married   ☐ Divorced   ☒ Single   ☐ Student   ☐ Other

DIAGNOSIS INFORMATION

Diagnosis	Code	Diagnosis	Code
1. Rosacea		5.	
2.		6.	
3.		7.	
4.		8.	

PROCEDURE INFORMATION

Description of Procedure or Service	Date	Code	Charge
1. Established patient office visit, level 2	12-15-YYYY		$55.00
2.			
3.			
4.			
5.			

SPECIAL NOTES:
Refer patient to dermatologist
Return visit: PRN

Claire M. Skinner, M.D. DERMATOLOGY   Case Study 14-G

50 Clear View Drive ■ Anywhere NY 12345-3695 ■ (101) 111-5555

EIN: 11-5555552
NPI: 5671238901

PATIENT INFORMATION:

Name:	Patricia S. Delaney
Address:	45 Garden Lane
City:	Anywhere
State:	NY
Zip Code:	12345
Telephone:	(101) 333-5555
Gender:	Female
Date of Birth:	04-12-1931
Occupation:	
Employer:	
Spouse's Employer:	

INSURANCE INFORMATION:

Patient Number:	14-G
Place of Service:	Office
Primary Insurance Plan:	Medicare
Primary Insurance Plan ID #:	4853AA75869
Group #:	
Primary Policyholder:	Patricia S. Delaney
Policyholder Date of Birth:	04-12-1931
Relationship to Patient:	Self
Secondary Insurance Plan:	Medicaid
Secondary Insurance Plan ID #:	22886644XT
Secondary Policyholder:	Self

Patient Status   ☐ Married   ☐ Divorced   ☒ Single   ☐ Student   ☐ Other

DIAGNOSIS INFORMATION

Diagnosis	Code	Diagnosis	Code
1. Rosacea		5.	
2.		6.	
3.		7.	
4.		8.	

PROCEDURE INFORMATION

Description of Procedure or Service	Date	Code	Charge
1. Office consultation, level 3	12-18-YYYY		$85.00
2.			
3.			
4.			
5.			

SPECIAL NOTES:
  Return visit PRN
  Onset of symptoms: 12-15-YYYY

ASSIGNMENT 14.5 – MEDICARE ROSTER BILLING CLAIMS COMPLETION

Objectives

At the conclusion of this assignment, the student should be able to:

1. Assign ICD-10-CM diagnosis and CPT or HCPCS level II procedure/service codes.

2. Prepare a Medicare CMS-1500 claim for roster billing for vaccines.

 NOTE:

When assigning CPT codes for consultations, remember to use the Office or Other Outpatient, New Patient subsection of the Evaluation and Management section. Medicare and Medicaid no longer permit the reporting of codes from the Consultation subsection.

Instructions

Complete a CMS-1500 for case studies 14-H and 14-I. Obtain a blank claim by making a copy of the CMS-1500 claim in Appendix I of the textbook. Refer to the CMS-1500 claims completion instructions (roster billing) in the textbook.

Mingo River Clinic

103 Park Road ■ Anywhere NY 12345-9512 ■ (101) 111-5555

EIN: 34-6121151
NPI: 7375433213

Case Study 14-H

HICN	Name	DOB	Sex	Address	Signature
4545AA66777	Marshall, Quinn	03/01/35	M	45 Black Road Anywhere, NY 12345	*Quinn Marshall*
3378AA89961	Morales, Lucy	10/01/29	F	1841 Hillcrest Lane Anywhere, NY 12345	*Lucy A Morales*
8944AA43377	Hansberry, John	10/12/31	M	1421 Lawson Road Anywhere, NY 12345	*John Hansberry*
3312AA22121	Hershey, March	02/15/33	F	301 Deer Lane Anywhere, NY 12345	*March Hershey*
5553AA32226	Fields, Langston	05/16/28	M	8 Marble Rock Road Anywhere, NY 12345	*Langston Fields*

DIAGNOSIS INFORMATION

Diagnosis	Code	Diagnosis	Code
1. Flu vaccine		5.	
2.		6.	
3.		7.	
4.		8.	

PROCEDURE INFORMATION

Description of Procedure or Service	Date	Code	Charge
1. Flu vaccine	03-12-YYYY		$10.00
2. Administration of flu vaccine	03-12-YYYY		$ 5.00
3.			
4.			
5.			

SPECIAL NOTES:

$50 to be billed to Medicare for flu vaccine

$5 to be billed to Medicare for the administration of flu vaccine

Mingo River Clinic

Case Study 14-I

103 Park Road ■ Anywhere NY 12345-9512 ■ (101) 111-5555

EIN: 34-6121151
NPI: 7375433213

HICN	Name	DOB	Sex	Address	Signature
9983AA37777	Jones, Karen	03/01/35	F	75 Main Street Anywhere, NY 12345	*Karen Jones*
4444AA55333	Williams, Pia	08/08/28	F	17 Ski Top Lane Anywhere, NY 12345	*Pia Williams*
1111AA22333	Gooding, Maria	05/01/25	F	103 Carrier Street Anywhere, NY 12345	*Maria Gooding*
2222AA11555	Hennessy, Michael	06/10/41	M	55678 Browne Road Anywhere, NY 12345	*Michael Hennessy*
5588AA99632	White, Mary	03/03/29	F	25 Yeager Road Anywhere, NY 12345	*Mary White*
1895AA45773	Martin, Majors	05/15/31	M	1503 Williamstown Spring Road Anywhere, NY 12345	*MAJORS MARTIN*

DIAGNOSIS INFORMATION

Diagnosis	Code	Diagnosis	Code
1. Pneumonia vaccine		5.	
2.		6.	
3.		7.	
4.		8.	

PROCEDURE INFORMATION

Description of Procedure or Service	Date	Code	Charge
1. Pneumonia vaccine	05-03-YYYY		$90.00
2. Administration of pneumonia vaccine	05-03-YYYY		$ 6.00
3.			
4.			
5.			

SPECIAL NOTES:

$48 to be billed to Medicare for pneumonia vaccine.

$6 to be billed to Medicare for the administration of pneumonia vaccine.

ASSIGNMENT 14.6 – MULTIPLE CHOICE REVIEW

1. Medicare Part A coverage is available to individuals under the age of 65 who
   a. have end-stage renal disease and meet requirements.
   b. are not disabled and are willing to pay the premium.
   c. have received RRB disability benefits for one year.
   d. have received SSA disability benefits for one year.

2. Which information must be obtained about the beneficiary to confirm Medicare eligibility over the phone?
   a. date of birth
   b. mailing address
   c. marital status
   d. social security number

3. What length of time is the Medicare initial enrollment period (IEP)?
   a. 1 year
   b. 12 months
   c. 7 months
   d. 90 days

4. The Medicare "spell of illness" is also known as the
   a. benefit period.
   b. elective days.
   c. reserve days.
   d. sickness period.

5. Patients may elect to use their Medicare lifetime reserve days after how many continuous days of hospitalization?
   a. 14
   b. 45
   c. 60
   d. 90

6. For a beneficiary to qualify for Medicare's skilled nursing benefit, the individual must have
   a. enrolled in Medicare Part B in addition to Medicare Part A.
   b. had a 90-day hospitalization in an acute care facility.
   c. had at least three inpatient days of an acute hospital stay.
   d. lifetime reserve days available for nursing facility care.

7. Temporary hospitalization of a patient for the purpose of providing relief from duty for the nonpaid primary caregiver of a patient is called _____ care.
   a. boarding
   b. hospice
   c. relief
   d. respite

8. All terminally ill Medicare patients qualify for _____ care.
   a. home health
   b. hospice
   c. private-duty
   d. respite

9. Medicare Part B will cover some home health care services if the patient
   a. has been disabled more than two years.
   b. has enrolled in Medicare Advantage.
   c. does not have Medicare Part A.
   d. is terminally ill and at the end of life.

10. Federal law requires that all providers and suppliers submit claims to Medicare if they provide a Medicare-covered service to a patient enrolled in Medicare Part B. This regulation does not apply if the patient is not enrolled in Medicare Part _____.
    a. A
    b. B
    c. C
    d. D

11. Which component of the Medicare Modernization Act of 2003 was created to provide tax-favored treatment for individuals covered by a high-deductible health plan?
    a. extra coverage plans
    b. health savings accounts
    c. Medicare Part D
    d. Medicare savings accounts

12. Dr. Cummings has been practicing in town for nearly 30 years. As a courtesy to his loyal Medicare patients, Dr. Cummings does not charge the coinsurance. How can this affect Dr. Cummings's practice?
    a. It will increase the doctor's patient base because new residents will want the savings.
    b. The billing process will be smoother for the doctor's health insurance specialists.
    c. The doctor may be subject to large fines and exclusion from the Medicare program.
    d. This will only affect the doctor's bottom line; Dr. Cummings will earn less profit with this practice.

13. One of the benefits of becoming a Medicare participating provider (PAR) is
    a. faster processing and payment of assigned claims.
    b. that providers can balance-bill the beneficiaries.
    c. that there is no Advance Beneficiary Notice requirement.
    d. that there is no limit on fees or charges for services.

14. The maximum that Medicare will reimburse a nonPAR who does not accept assignment for a covered service is 80 percent of the
    a. allowed fee.
    b. limiting charge.
    c. maximum benefit.
    d. usual fee.

15. Which practitioner who submits claims for services must accept assignment?
    a. anesthesiologist
    b. orthopedic surgeon
    c. psychiatrist
    d. physician assistant

16. Dr. Taylor has instructed you, as the health insurance specialist, to obtain an Advance Beneficiary Notice (ABN) on all surgical cases in the practice just in case Medicare denies the claim. How should you handle this situation?
    a. At the next practice meeting, solicit ideas on how best to obtain signatures from each Medicare patient.
    b. Discuss the ABN with every Medicare surgical patient, and persuade the patient to sign the form.
    c. Explain to Dr. Taylor that the practice cannot do this, as Medicare considers this activity fraudulent.
    d. Print out a list of all Medicare patients in the practice and send each an ABN to sign.

17. What is entered in Block 11 of the CMS-1500 claim when a reference lab provides services to a Medicare patient in the absence of a face-to-face encounter?
    a. MSP CLAIM
    b. NONE
    c. ON FILE
    d. SAME

18. Although they may do so more frequently, how often are providers required to collect or verify Medicare as Secondary Payer (MSP) information?
    a. after a primary Medicare claim has been denied
    b. at the time of the initial beneficiary encounter only
    c. each time the beneficiary is seen by the provider
    d. each time the patient reregisters with the practice

19. Medicare can assign a claim conditional primary payer status for payment processing. Which of the following would warrant this type of conditional status?
    a. A patient who is mentally impaired failed to file a claim with the primary payer.
    b. A workers' compensation claim was denied and has been successfully appealed.
    c. The patient did not provide MSP information and the provider submits a request.
    d. The liability payer has not provided a response within 60 days of filing the claim.

20. If a service was performed on June 30, the Medicare claim must be submitted for payment and postmarked no later than
    a. December 31 of the same year.
    b. January 31 of the next year.
    c. June 30 of the next year.
    d. December 31 of the next year.

Medicaid

INTRODUCTION

This chapter familiarizes students with completion of CMS-1500 claims for primary and mother/baby Medicaid payers.

 NOTE:

When completing CMS-1500 claims for case studies in this workbook, enter just one diagnosis pointer letter in Block 24E.

 NOTE:

When completing claims for patients who have both primary and secondary insurance coverage, enter a P (primary) next to the case number on the primary claim (e.g., 15-A-P), and enter an S (secondary) (e.g., 15-A-S) next to the case number on the secondary claim.

ASSIGNMENT 15.1 – MEDICAID PRIMARY CMS-1500 CLAIMS COMPLETION

Objectives

At the conclusion of this assignment, the student should be able to:

1. Assign ICD-10-CM diagnosis and CPT or HCPCS level II procedure/service codes.
2. Prepare a Medicaid insurance primary payer CMS-1500 claim.

Instructions

Complete a CMS-1500 for case studies 15-A and 15-B. Obtain a blank claim by making a copy of the CMS-1500 claim in Appendix I of the textbook. Refer to the CMS-1500 claims completion instructions (primary) in the textbook.

Donald L. Givings, M.D.

Case Study 15-A

11350 Medical Drive ■ Anywhere NY 12345-6541 ■ (101) 111-5555

EIN: 11-1234562
NPI: 1234567890

PATIENT INFORMATION:

Name:	Sharon W. Casey
Address:	483 Oakdale Avenue
City:	Anywhere
State:	NY
Zip Code:	12345
Telephone:	(101) 333-5555
Gender:	Female
Date of Birth:	10-06-1970
Occupation:	
Employer:	
Spouse's Employer:	

INSURANCE INFORMATION:

Patient Number:	15-A
Place of Service:	Office
Primary Insurance Plan:	Medicaid
Primary Insurance Plan ID #:	22334455
Group #:	
Primary Policyholder:	Sharon W. Casey
Policyholder Date of Birth:	10-06-1970
Relationship to Patient:	Self
Secondary Insurance Plan:	
Secondary Insurance Plan ID #:	
Secondary Policyholder:	

Patient Status   ☐ Married   ☐ Divorced   ☒ Single   ☐ Student   ☐ Other

DIAGNOSIS INFORMATION

Diagnosis	Code	Diagnosis	Code
1. Excessive menstruation		5.	
2. Irregular menstrual cycle		6.	
3.		7.	
4.		8.	

PROCEDURE INFORMATION

Description of Procedure or Service	Date	Code	Charge
1. Established patient office visit, level 3	11-13-YYYY		$75.00
2.			
3.			
4.			
5.			

SPECIAL NOTES:
    Refer patient to GYN
    Return visit: PRN

Maria C. Section, M.D. OB/GYN

Case Study 15-B

11 Maden Lane ■ Anywhere NY 12345-5628 ■ (101) 111-5555

EIN: 11-6699772
NPI: 6781239012

PATIENT INFORMATION:

Name:	Sharon W. Casey
Address:	483 Oakdale Avenue
City:	Anywhere
State:	NY
Zip Code:	12345
Telephone:	(101) 333-5555
Gender:	Female
Date of Birth:	10-06-1970
Occupation:	
Employer:	
Spouse's Employer:	

INSURANCE INFORMATION:

Patient Number:	15-B
Place of Service:	Office
Primary Insurance Plan:	Medicaid
Primary Insurance Plan ID #:	22334455
Group #:	
Primary Policyholder:	Sharon W. Casey
Policyholder Date of Birth:	10-06-1970
Relationship to Patient:	Self
Secondary Insurance Plan:	
Secondary Insurance Plan ID #:	
Secondary Policyholder:	

Patient Status   ☐ Married   ☐ Divorced   ☒ Single   ☐ Student   ☐ Other

---

DIAGNOSIS INFORMATION

Diagnosis	Code	Diagnosis	Code
1. Excessive menstruation		5.	
2. Irregular menstrual cycle		6.	
3.		7.	
4.		8.	

PROCEDURE INFORMATION

Description of Procedure or Service	Date	Code	Charge
1. Office consultation, level 3	11-20-YYYY		$85.00
2.			
3.			
4.			
5.			

SPECIAL NOTES:
   Onset of symptoms: 11-13-YYYY
   Referred by Donald L. Givings, M.D., NPI: 1234567890
   Return visit: One month

NOTE:

When assigning CPT codes for consultations, remember to use the Office or Other Outpatient, New Patient subsection of the Evaluation and Management section. Medicare and Medicaid no longer permit the reporting of codes from the Consultation subsection.

ASSIGNMENT 15.2 – MEDICAID AS SECONDARY PAYER CMS-1500 CLAIMS COMPLETION

Objectives

At the conclusion of this assignment, the student should be able to:

1. Assign ICD-10-CM diagnosis and CPT or HCPCS level II procedure/service codes.

2. Prepare a Medicaid as secondary payer CMS-1500 claim.

Instructions

Complete a CMS-1500 for case studies 15-C and 15-D. Obtain a blank claim by making a copy of the CMS-1500 claim in Appendix I of the textbook. Refer to the CMS-1500 claims completion instructions (secondary) in the textbook.

ASSIGNMENT 15.3 – MEDICAID MOTHER/BABY CMS-1500 CLAIMS COMPLETION

Objectives

At the conclusion of this assignment, the student should be able to:

1. Assign ICD-10-CM diagnosis and CPT or HCPCS level II procedure/service codes.

2. Prepare a Medicaid mother/baby CMS-1500 claim.

Instructions

Complete a CMS-1500 for case study 15-E. Obtain a blank claim by making a copy of the CMS-1500 claim in Appendix I of the textbook. Refer to the CMS-1500 claims completion instructions (mother/baby) in the textbook.

ASSIGNMENT 15.4 – CHIP CMS-1500 CLAIMS COMPLETION

Objectives

At the conclusion of this assignment, the student should be able to:

1. Assign ICD-10-CM diagnosis and CPT or HCPCS level II procedure/service codes.

2. Prepare a CHIP CMS-1500 claim.

Instructions

Complete a CMS-1500 claim for case study 15-F. Obtain a blank claim by making a copy of the CMS-1500 claim in Appendix I of the textbook. Refer to the CMS-1500 claims completion instructions (primary) in the textbook.

Donald L. Givings, M.D.

11350 Medical Drive ■ Anywhere NY 12345-6541 ■ (101) 111-5555

EIN: 11-1234562
NPI: 1234567890

Case Study 15-C

PATIENT INFORMATION:

Name:	Fred R. Jones
Address:	444 Taylor Avenue
City:	Anywhere
State:	NY
Zip Code:	12345
Telephone:	(101) 333-5555
Gender:	Male
Date of Birth:	01-05-1949
Occupation:	
Employer:	
Spouse's Employer:	

INSURANCE INFORMATION:

Patient Number:	15-C
Place of Service:	Office
Primary Insurance Plan:	Aetna
Primary Insurance Plan ID #:	852963741
Group #:	
Primary Policyholder:	Fred R. Jones
Policyholder Date of Birth:	01-05-1949
Relationship to Patient:	Self
Secondary Insurance Plan:	Medicaid
Secondary Insurance Plan ID #:	55771122
Secondary Policyholder:	Fred R. Jones

Patient Status ☐ Married   ☒ Divorced   ☐ Single   ☐ Student   ☐ Other

DIAGNOSIS INFORMATION

Diagnosis	Code	Diagnosis	Code
1. Difficulty walking		5.	
2.		6.	
3.		7.	
4.		8.	

PROCEDURE INFORMATION

Description of Procedure or Service	Date	Code	Charge
1. Established patient office visit, level 3	06-19-YYYY		$75.00
2.			
3.			
4.			
5.			

SPECIAL NOTES:
  Refer patient to a podiatrist
  Return visit 3 months

John F. Walker, D.P.M. PODIATRY

546 Foothill Place ■ Anywhere NY 12345-5617 ■ (101) 111-5555

EIN: 11-9933772
NPI: 8901231234

Case Study 15-D

PATIENT INFORMATION:

Name:	Fred R. Jones
Address:	444 Taylor Avenue
City:	Anywhere
State:	NY
Zip Code:	12345
Telephone:	(101) 333-5555
Gender:	Male
Date of Birth:	01-05-1949
Occupation:	
Employer:	
Spouse's Employer:	

INSURANCE INFORMATION:

Patient Number:	15-D
Place of Service:	Office
Primary Insurance Plan:	Aetna
Primary Insurance Plan ID #:	55771122
Group #:	
Primary Policyholder:	Fred R. Jones
Policyholder Date of Birth:	01-05-1949
Relationship to Patient:	Self
Secondary Insurance Plan:	Medicaid
Secondary Insurance Plan ID #:	55771122
Secondary Policyholder:	Fred R. Jones

Patient Status   ☐ Married   ☒ Divorced   ☐ Single   ☐ Student   ☐ Other

DIAGNOSIS INFORMATION

Diagnosis	Code	Diagnosis	Code
1. Displaced closed fracture, proximal phalanx of right great toe (initial encounter)		5.	
2.		6.	
3.		7.	
4.		8.	

PROCEDURE INFORMATION

Description of Procedure or Service	Date	Code	Charge
1. Office consultation, level 2	06-23-YYYY		$75.00
2. Toe x-ray, 2 views	06-23-YYYY		50.00
3. Closed treatment of fracture, great toe	06-23-YYYY		65.00
4.			
5.			

SPECIAL NOTES:
   Onset of symptoms: 06-19-YYYY
   Referred by Donald L. Givings, M.D., NPI:1234567890

NOTE:

When assigning CPT codes for consultations, remember to use the Office or Other Outpatient, New Patient subsection of the Evaluation and Management section. Medicare and Medicaid no longer permit the reporting of codes from the Consultation subsection.

Donald L. Givings, M.D.

11350 Medical Drive ■ Anywhere NY 12345-6541 ■ (101) 111-5555

EIN: 11-1234562
NPI: 1234567890

Case Study 15-E

PATIENT INFORMATION:

Name:	Jackson, Newborn
Address:	375 Ravenwood Avenue
City:	Anywhere
State:	NY
Zip Code:	12345
Telephone:	(101) 333-5555
Gender:	Male
Date of Birth:	03-10-2011
Occupation:	
Employer:	
Spouse's Employer:	

INSURANCE INFORMATION:

Patient Number:	15-E
Place of Service:	Inpatient hospital
Primary Insurance Plan:	Medicaid
Primary Insurance Plan ID #:	77557755 (mother)
Group #:	
Primary Policyholder:	Sandy Jackson
Policyholder Date of Birth:	02-15-1985
Relationship to Patient:	Mother
Secondary Insurance Plan:	
Secondary Insurance Plan ID #:	
Secondary Policyholder:	

Patient Status ☐ Married ☐ Divorced ☒ Single ☐ Student ☐ Other

DIAGNOSIS INFORMATION

Diagnosis	Code	Diagnosis	Code
1. Healthy single liveborn infant (vaginal delivery)		5.	
2.		6.	
3.		7.	
4.		8.	

PROCEDURE INFORMATION

Description of Procedure or Service	Date	Code	Charge
1. Initial hospital care for E/M of normal newborn infant	03-10-YYYY		$150.00
2. Attendance at delivery	03-10-YYYY		400.00
3. Subsequent hospital care for E/M for normal newborn	03-11-YYYY		100.00
4.			
5.			

SPECIAL NOTES:
Inpatient care provided at Goodmedicine Hospital, 1 Provider Street, Anywhere NY 12345-1234. NPI: 1123456789
Application for infant's Medicaid ID number has been submitted.

Goodmedicine Clinic

Case Study 15-F

1 Provider Street ■ Anywhere NY 12345-1234 ■ (101) 111-2222
NPI: 3312345678   EIN: 33-1234567

Provider: Nancy J. Healer, M.D.   **EIN:** 44-1234567   **NPI:** 6789012345

PATIENT INFORMATION:

Name:	Ryan Michaels
Address:	101 Pinewood Drive
City:	Anywhere
State:	NY
Zip Code:	12345
Telephone:	(101) 111-9898
Gender:	Male
Date of Birth:	04-29-2018
Occupation:	
Employer:	
Spouse's Employer:	

INSURANCE INFORMATION:

Patient Number:	15-F
Place of Service:	Office
Primary Insurance Plan:	SCHIP
Primary Insurance Plan ID #:	BJZ06070908D
Group #:	
Primary Policyholder:	Ryan Michaels
Policyholder Date of Birth:	04-29-2011
Relationship to Patient:	Self
Secondary Insurance Plan:	
Secondary Insurance Plan ID #:	
Secondary Policyholder:	

Patient Status   ☐ Married   ☐ Divorced   ☒ Single   ☐ Student   ☐ Other

DIAGNOSIS INFORMATION

Diagnosis	Code	Diagnosis	Code
1. Acute sinusitis, frontal		5.	
2. Acute sore throat		6.	
3.		7.	
4.		8.	

PROCEDURE INFORMATION

Description of Procedure or Service	Date	Code	Charge
1. New patient office visit, level II	12-18-YYYY		$75.00
2.			
3.			
4.			
5.			

SPECIAL NOTES:
Patient paid $5.00 for today's visit.

ASSIGNMENT 15.5 – MULTIPLE CHOICE REVIEW

1. The Medicaid program is
   a. federally funded and state mandated.
   b. federally mandated and state administered.
   c. state funded and federally administered.
   d. state mandated and federally administered.

2. The Temporary Assistance to Needy Families (TANF) program provides
   a. cash assistance on a limited-time basis for children deprived of support.
   b. cash assistance to low-income families who need to purchase groceries.
   c. financial assistance for food, utilities, health care, and school expenses.
   d. temporary financial support for housing and household-related costs.

3. What is included in a couple's combined resources, according to the Spousal Impoverishment Protection legislation?
   a. automobile
   b. burial funds
   c. home
   d. summer home

4. When a patient has become retroactively eligible for Medicaid benefits, any payments made by the patient during the retroactive period must be
   a. applied toward future medical care.
   b. recorded as additional practice income.
   c. refunded to the patient by Medicaid.
   d. refunded to the patient by the practice.

5. To receive matching funds through Medicaid, states must offer what coverage?
   a. inpatient hospital services
   b. prescription drug benefits
   c. private-duty nursing care
   d. surgical dental services

6. Early and Periodic Screening, Diagnostic, and Treatment (EPSDT) services are offered for which Medicaid-enrolled population?
   a. home health patients
   b. individuals under age 21
   c. persons over the age of 65
   d. rehabilitation facility inpatients

7. Programs of All-inclusive Care for the Elderly (PACE) work to limit out-of-pocket costs to beneficiaries by
   a. limiting participants to care only from contract providers.
   b. providing only very basic medical and preventive care.
   c. requiring a flat $10 copayment for every service provided.
   d. not applying deductibles, copayments, or other cost-sharing.

8. Which is subject to Medicaid preauthorization guidelines?
   a. any minor surgery performed in the provider's procedure room
   b. medically necessary inpatient admission with documentation
   c. any extension of inpatient acute care hospital days
   d. patient hospitalization within the expected length of stay

9. Which services are exempt from Medicaid copayments?
   a. family planning services
   b. office visits
   c. outpatient urgent care
   d. prescription drug costs

10. An individual whose income is at or below 100 percent of the federal poverty level (FPL) and has resources at or below twice the standard allowed under the SSI program may receive assistance from Medicaid to pay for Medicare premiums, deductibles, and coinsurance amounts as a
    a. qualified disabled and working individual (QDWI).
    b. qualified Medicare beneficiary (QMB).
    c. qualifying individual (QI).
    d. specified low-income Medicare beneficiary (SLMB).

11. A primary care provider in a Medicaid primary care case management (PCCM) plan differs from an HMO primary care provider in that the Medicaid primary care provider is
    a. at higher risk for the cost of care provided.
    b. never permitted to authorize specialty care.
    c. not at risk for the cost of care provided.
    d. responsible for coordinating patient care.

12. A Medicaid voided claim
   a. has an additional payment to the provider.
   b. is in suspense and awaiting approval.
   c. must be corrected and resubmitted.
   d. should not have been paid originally.

13. One way the federal government verifies receipt of Medicaid services by a patient is by use of
   a. an annual audit of each state's Medicaid offices to validate expenditures.
   b. a monthly audit of all the provider's remittance advice notices and receipts.
   c. a monthly survey sent to a sample of Medicaid recipients requesting verification.
   d. a survey provided to each Medicaid recipient upon completion of treatment.

14. Medicaid reimbursement is expedited when the provider
   a. authenticates each CMS-1500 claim filed with a manual signature.
   b. enters an X in the YES box in Block 27 to accept assignment.
   c. enters the required insurance information in Blocks 11 through 11d.
   d. enters the required insurance information in Blocks 9 through 9d.

15. A Medicaid card issued for the "unborn child of . . ." is good for
   a. hospitalization services for the newborn child and the mother.
   b. medical care rendered to the mother, such as for a back strain.
   c. physician office visits for the mother for care other than prenatal.
   d. services that promote the life and health of the unborn child.

16. What is required in Block 32 if an X is entered in the YES box of Block 20?
   a. name and address of the outside laboratory
   b. name and address of the referring provider
   c. the same information as was entered in Block 31
   d. the same information as was entered in Block 33

17. Medicaid policies for eligibility are complex and vary among states; thus, a person who is eligible for Medicaid in one state
   a. is always eligible in another state.
   b. may not be eligible in another state.
   c. receives the same coverage in other states.
   d. remains eligible regardless of change in income.

18. Which is considered a valid entry in Block 24H of a Medicaid claim?
   a. the letter B, if the service was for both EPSDT and family planning
   b. the letter F, if the service provided was for family planning
   c. the number of days the Medicaid patient was treated for the current problem
   d. the number of times the Medicare patient has been treated for the problem

19. When a Medicaid patient has third-party payer coverage and a claim has been rejected, the rejection code is recorded in which block of the Medicaid CMS-1500 claim?
   a. Block 11   c. Block 22
   b. Block 19   d. Block 24H

20. When payment has been received by a primary payer, the payment amount is entered in which block of the Medicaid CMS-1500 claim?
   a. Block 19   c. Block 29
   b. Block 20   d. Block 30

TRICARE

INTRODUCTION

This chapter familiarizes students with completion of CMS-1500 claims for primary TRICARE payers.

 NOTE:

When completing CMS-1500 claims for case studies in this workbook, enter just one diagnosis pointer letter in Block 24E.

 NOTE:

When completing claims for patients who have both primary and secondary insurance coverage, enter a P (primary) next to the case number on the primary claim (e.g., 16-A-P), and enter an S (secondary) (e.g., 16-A-S) next to the case number on the secondary claim.

ASSIGNMENT 16.1 – TRICARE PRIMARY CMS-1500 CLAIMS COMPLETION

Objectives

At the conclusion of this assignment, the student should be able to:

1. Assign ICD-10-CM diagnosis and CPT or HCPCS level II procedure/service codes.
2. Prepare a TRICARE insurance primary payer CMS-1500 claim.

Instructions

Complete a CMS-1500 for case studies 16-A through 16-C. Obtain a blank claim by making a copy of the CMS-1500 claim in Appendix I of the textbook. Refer to the CMS-1500 claims completion instructions (primary) in the textbook.

Donald L. Givings, M.D.

Case Study 16-A

11350 Medical Drive ■ Anywhere NY 12345-6541 ■ (101) 111-5555

EIN: 11-1234562
NPI: 1234567890

PATIENT INFORMATION:

Name:	Jeffrey D. Heem
Address:	333 Heavenly Place
City:	Anywhere
State:	NY
Zip Code:	12345
Telephone:	(101) 333-5555
Gender:	Male
Date of Birth:	05-05-1964
Occupation:	
Employer:	US Army
Spouse's Employer:	

INSURANCE INFORMATION:

Patient Number:	16-A
Place of Service:	Office
Primary Insurance Plan:	TRICARE Select
Primary Insurance Plan ID #:	234556789
Group #:	
Primary Policyholder:	Jeffrey D. Heem
Policyholder Date of Birth:	05-05-1964
Relationship to Patient:	Self
Secondary Insurance Plan:	
Secondary Insurance Plan ID #:	
Secondary Policyholder:	

Patient Status   ☒ Married   ☐ Divorced   ☐ Single   ☐ Student   ☐ Other

DIAGNOSIS INFORMATION

Diagnosis	Code	Diagnosis	Code
1. Acute sinusitis, frontal		5.	
2. Sore throat		6.	
3.		7.	
4.		8.	

PROCEDURE INFORMATION

Description of Procedure or Service	Date	Code	Charge
1. New patient office visit, level 2	11-05-YYYY		$70.00
2.			
3.			
4.			
5.			

SPECIAL NOTES:

Donald L. Givings, M.D.

11350 Medical Drive ■ Anywhere NY 12345-6541 ■ (101) 111-5555

EIN: 11-1234562
NPI: 1234567890

Case Study 16-B

PATIENT INFORMATION:

Name:	Dana S. Bright
Address:	28 Upton Circle
City:	Anywhere
State:	NY
Zip Code:	12345
Telephone:	(101) 333-5555
Gender:	Female
Date of Birth:	08-05-1971
Occupation:	
Employer:	
Spouse's Employer:	US Navy (See duty address below)

INSURANCE INFORMATION:

Patient Number:	16-B
Place of Service:	Office
Primary Insurance Plan:	TRICARE Select
Primary Insurance Plan ID #:	567565757
Group #:	
Primary Policyholder:	Ron L. Bright
Policyholder Date of Birth:	07-12-1970
Relationship to Patient:	Spouse
Secondary Insurance Plan:	
Secondary Insurance Plan ID #:	
Secondary Policyholder:	

Patient Status   [X] Married   ☐ Divorced   ☐ Single   ☐ Student   ☐ Other

DIAGNOSIS INFORMATION

Diagnosis	Code	Diagnosis	Code
1. Chronic cholecystitis		5.	
2.		6.	
3.		7.	
4.		8.	

PROCEDURE INFORMATION

Description of Procedure or Service	Date	Code	Charge
1. Established patient office visit, level 4	06-22-YYYY		$85.00
2.			
3.			
4.			
5.			

SPECIAL NOTES:

Spouse's Employer's Address: Duty Station Address: 21 Naval Station, Anywhere NY 23456
Refer patient to Jonathan B. Kutter, M.D.

Jonathan B. Kutter, M.D.

339 Woodland Place ■ Anywhere NY 12345-3214 ■ (101) 111-5555

EIN: 11-5566772
NPI: 2345675678

Case Study 16-C

PATIENT INFORMATION:

Name:	Dana S. Bright
Address:	28 Upton Circle
City:	Anywhere
State:	NY
Zip Code:	12345
Telephone:	(101) 333-5555
Gender:	Female
Date of Birth:	08-05-1971
Occupation:	Homemaker
Employer:	
Spouse's Employer:	US Navy

INSURANCE INFORMATION:

Patient Number:	16-C
Place of Service:	Outpatient hospital
Primary Insurance Plan:	TRICARE Select
Primary Insurance Plan ID #:	567565757
Group #:	
Primary Policyholder:	Ron L. Bright
Policyholder Date of Birth:	07-12-1970
Relationship to Patient:	Spouse
Secondary Insurance Plan:	
Secondary Insurance Plan ID #:	
Secondary Policyholder:	

Patient Status   ☒ Married   ☐ Divorced   ☐ Single   ☐ Student   ☐ Other

DIAGNOSIS INFORMATION

Diagnosis	Code	Diagnosis	Code
1. Chronic cholecystitis		5.	
2.		6.	
3.		7.	
4.		8.	

PROCEDURE INFORMATION

Description of Procedure or Service	Date	Code	Charge
1. Laparoscopic cholecystectomy	06-29-YYYY		$2,300.00
2.			
3.			
4.			
5.			

SPECIAL NOTES:
Referred by Donald L. Givings, M.D., NPI: 1234567890
Onset of symptoms: 06-22-YYYY Admitted/Discharged: 6/29/YYYY
Goodmedicine Hospital, 1 Provider Street, Anywhere NY 12345-1234. NPI: 1123456789.
Spouse's Employer's Address: Duty Station
Address: 21 Naval Station, Anywhere NY 23456

ASSIGNMENT 16.2 – TRICARE SECONDARY CMS-1500 CLAIMS COMPLETION

Objectives

At the conclusion of this assignment, the student should be able to:

1. Assign ICD-10-CM diagnosis codes and CPT or HCPCS level II procedure/service codes.
2. Prepare a TRICARE secondary CMS-1500 claim.

Instructions

Complete the CMS-1500 claim for case studies 16-D and 16-E. Obtain a blank claim by making a copy of the CMS-1500 claim in Appendix I of the textbook. Refer to the textbook CMS-1500 claims completion instructions when payer is the same for primary and secondary health insurance coverage.

Donald L. Givings, M.D.

Case Study 16-D

11350 Medical Drive ■ Anywhere NY 12345-6541 ■ (101) 111-5555

EIN: 11-1234562
NPI: 1234567890

PATIENT INFORMATION:

Name:	Odel M. Ryer, Jr.
Address:	484 Pinewood Ave.
City:	Anywhere
State:	NY
Zip Code:	12345
Telephone:	(101) 333-5555
Gender:	Male
Date of Birth:	01-28-1969
Occupation:	
Employer:	US Air Force
Spouse's Employer:	Paws and Tails

INSURANCE INFORMATION:

Patient Number:	16-D
Place of Service:	Office
Primary Insurance Plan:	AETNA
Primary Insurance Plan ID #:	464444646B
Group #:	
Primary Policyholder:	Rose M. Ryer
Policyholder Date of Birth:	04-01-1970
Relationship to Patient:	Spouse
Secondary Insurance Plan:	TRICARE Select
Secondary Insurance Plan ID #:	464444646
Secondary Policyholder:	Odel M. Ryer, Jr.

Patient Status   [X] Married   [ ] Divorced   [ ] Single   [ ] Student   [ ] Other

DIAGNOSIS INFORMATION

Diagnosis	Code	Diagnosis	Code
1. Heartburn		5.	
2.		6.	
3.		7.	
4.		8.	

PROCEDURE INFORMATION

Description of Procedure or Service	Date	Code	Charge
1. Established patient office visit, level 2	04-12-YYYY		$55.00
2.			
3.			
4.			
5.			

SPECIAL NOTES:

Return visit: PRN

Primary insurance paid: $44.00.

Donald L. Givings, M.D.

Case Study 16-E

11350 Medical Drive ■ Anywhere NY 12345-6541 ■ (101) 111-5555

EIN: 11-1234562
NPI: 1234567890

PATIENT INFORMATION:

Name:	Annalisa M. Faris
Address:	394 Myriam Court
City:	Anywhere
State:	NY
Zip Code:	12345
Telephone:	(101) 333-5555
Gender:	Female
Date of Birth:	04-04-2008
Occupation:	Full-Time Student
Employer:	US Marines (Father)
Spouse's Employer:	Borders Publishing (Mother)

INSURANCE INFORMATION:

Patient Number:	16-E
Place of Service:	Inpatient hospital
Primary Insurance Plan:	BLUECROSS BLUESHIELD
Primary Insurance Plan ID #:	323233333X
Group #:	
Primary Policyholder:	Mari L. Faris
Policyholder Date of Birth:	06-21-1995
Relationship to Patient:	Mother
Secondary Insurance Plan:	TRICARE Prime
Secondary Insurance Plan ID #:	621334444
Secondary Policyholder:	Nacir R. Faris
Secondary Policyholder DOB:	10-12-1996

Patient Status	☐ Married	☐ Divorced	☒ Single	☒ Student	☐ Other

DIAGNOSIS INFORMATION

Diagnosis	Code	Diagnosis	Code
1. Chills with fever		5.	
2. Lethargy		6.	
3. Loss of appetite		7.	
4. Loss of weight		8.	

PROCEDURE INFORMATION

Description of Procedure or Service	Date	Code	Charge
1. Initial hospital visit, level 3	06-02-YYYY		$200.00
2. Subsequent hospital visit, level 3	06-03-YYYY		85.00
3. Subsequent hospital visit, level 2	06-04-YYYY		75.00
4. Discharge day management, 30 minutes	06-04-YYYY		75.00

SPECIAL NOTES:
Goodmedicine Hospital, 1 Provider Street, Anywhere NY 12345. NPI: 1123456789.
Father's Employer's Address: Duty Station Address: 555 Regiment Way, Anywhere NY 12345
Patient was discharged 06/04/YYYY but not seen
Primary insurance paid: $344.00

ASSIGNMENT 16.3 – STANDARD TIME AND MILITARY TIME

Objectives

At the conclusion of this assignment, the student should be able to:

1. Explain the difference between standard time and military time.

2. Convert standard time to military time, and convert military time to standard time.

Overview

Military time is a method of expressing time that is used by the military, emergency services (e.g., law enforcement, firefighting, paramedics), hospitals, and other entities. In the practice of medicine, military time is generally used for documentation of care in the patient record. The difference between *standard time* and military time is how hours are expressed. Standard time uses numbers 1 through 12 to identify each of the 24 hours in a day; military time uses the hours that are numbered from 0100 to 2400 (e.g., midnight is 2400, 1:00 AM is 0100, 1:00 PM is 1300, and so on). Standard time and military time express minutes and seconds in the same way. When converting from standard to military time and vice versa, the minutes and seconds do not change. Standard time requires the use of AM and PM to clearly identify the time of day. Because military time uses a unique two-digit number to identify each of the 24 hours in a day, the designation of AM or PM is unnecessary. The following table summarizes the relationship between regular and military time.

Standard Time		Military Time	Standard Time		Military Time
12:00	AM	2400	12:00	PM	1200
12:30	AM	2430	12:30	PM	1230
1:00	AM	0100	1:00	PM	1300
1:30	AM	0130	1:30	PM	1330
2:00	AM	0200	2:00	PM	1400
2:30	AM	0230	2:30	PM	1430
3:00	AM	0300	3:00	PM	1500
3:30	AM	0330	3:30	PM	1530
4:00	AM	0400	4:00	PM	1600
4:30	AM	0430	4:30	PM	1630
5:00	AM	0500	5:00	PM	1700
5:30	AM	0530	5:30	PM	1730
6:00	AM	0600	6:00	PM	1800
6:30	AM	0630	6:30	PM	1830
7:00	AM	0700	7:00	PM	1900
7:30	AM	0730	7:30	PM	1930
8:00	AM	0800	8:00	PM	2000
8:30	AM	0830	8:30	PM	2030
9:00	AM	0900	9:00	PM	2100
9:30	AM	0930	9:30	PM	2130
10:00	AM	1000	10:00	PM	2200
10:30	AM	1030	10:30	PM	2230
11:00	AM	1100	11:00	PM	2300
11:30	AM	1130	11:30	PM	2330

Instructions

Complete each statement below.

1. The patient was admitted to Goodmedicine Hospital at 1900 for chest pain on 2/06/YY, which is _____ in standard time.

2. The patient was discharged on 12/06/YY at 6:00 PM, which is _____ in military time.

3. Nora Jeffrey was treated in the emergency department for abdominal pain on 8/24/YY. Mrs. Roberts was treated by the physician at 8:00 AM and discharged at noon; these times correspond to _____ and _____ in military time, respectively.

4. During Frankie Martin's encounter, Dr. Fox was told that Frankie takes vitamins every morning at 7:00 AM and a sleep aid at 8:00 PM; these times correspond to _____ and _____ in military time, respectively.

5. Dr. York's schedule of patient appointments for Monday includes the following:
   a. Dallas Richardson at 1330
   b. Mark Miller at 1100
   c. Sally Dunn at 0800
   d. Cindy Gates at 1430
   e. Joan Harvey at 0930
   f. Billy Johnson at 1000

   Enter the last name of each patient in the order Dr. York will see them, according to military time:

   _____

ASSIGNMENT 16.4 – MULTIPLE CHOICE REVIEW

1. The conversion of CHAMPUS to TRICARE was the result of a(n)
   a. act of legislation that was passed in 1967 at the request of the military.
   b. need to limit the amount of money paid for military dependents' care.
   c. reorganization of each branch of the U.S. uniformed services.
   d. successful CHAMPUS Reform Initiative (CRI) demonstration project.

2. Lead agents of selected military treatment facilities (MTFs) hold what rank?
   a. captain
   b. commander
   c. lieutenant
   d. major

3. The entire health care system of the U.S. uniformed services is known as the
   a. CHAMPUS Reform Initiative (CRI).
   b. Department of Defense Health System.
   c. Military Health System (MHS).
   d. TRICARE Demonstration Project.

4. The organization responsible for coordinating and administering the TRICARE program is the
   a. Military Health System.
   b. TRICARE Management Activity.
   c. U.S. Department of Defense.
   d. U.S. Office of Health Affairs.

5. The term *sponsor* is used to describe
   a. active duty, retired, or deceased military personnel.
   b. beneficiaries of military personnel.
   c. dependents of military personnel.
   d. remarried former spouses of military personnel.

6. Claims are submitted to the TRICARE
   a. Management Activity.
   b. Program Integrity Office.
   c. regional contractors.
   d. service centers.

7. TRICARE plans are primary to
   a. employer-sponsored HMOs.
   b. liability insurance claims.
   c. Medicaid.
   d. workers' compensation.

8. TRICARE nurse advisors are available 24/7 to assist with
   a. preauthorizations and referrals for health care services.
   b. providing information to beneficiaries about TRICARE.
   c. rendering emergency care to TRICARE beneficiaries.
   d. treatment alternatives and recommendations for care.

9. The entity responsible for the prevention, detection, investigation, and control of TRICARE fraud, waste, and abuse is the
   a. Military Health System.
   b. Program Integrity Office.
   c. TRICARE Management Activity.
   d. TRICARE Service Center.

10. Which TRICARE option is a fee-for-service plan?
    a. CHAMPUS
    b. TRICARE
    c. TRICARE Prime
    d. TRICARE Select

11. In which TRICARE option are active military personnel required to enroll?
    a. CHAMPUS
    b. TRICARE
    c. TRICARE Prime
    d. TRICARE Select

12. A military treatment facility (MTF) *catchment area* is
    a. also known as a TRICARE Region, and is managed by lead agents.
    b. defined by code boundaries within a 40-mile radius of an MTF.
    c. an area where health care services are not available to military personnel.
    d. an area that contains civilian health care professionals to render care.

13. If a TRICARE Prime beneficiary seeks care from a facility outside of the treatment area without prior approval, the point-of-service option is activated. This will result in what cost(s) to the beneficiary?
    a. a coinsurance payment of 50 percent for each service or treatment and no deductible
    b. an annual deductible plus 50 percent or more of visit or treatment fees
    c. beneficiary payment for all services out-of-pocket
    d. the same annual deductible as TRICARE Extra and Standard

14. Which TRICARE option has costs that vary based on sponsor's military status, and includes an annual outpatient deductible and cost shares (or percentages) for covered services?
    a. CHAMPUS
    b. TRICARE
    c. TRICARE Prime
    d. TRICARE Select

15. TRICARE outpatient claims will be denied if they are filed more than
    a. one year after the patient's discharge.
    b. one year after the date of service.
    c. six months after the date of service.
    d. 30 days after the date of service.

16. If the physician's charges for care of a TRICARE beneficiary, as the result of an accidental injury, are $500 or higher, the insurance specialist must submit a
    a. DD Form 2527 that was completed by the patient.
    b. DD Form 2527 that was completed by the provider.
    c. DD Form 2642 that was completed by the patient.
    d. DD Form 2642 that was completed by the provider.

17. TRICARE has established a good-faith policy for assigned claims to protect the provider when
    a. a claim submitted to TRICARE contains charges for a noncovered service.
    b. a patient presented an ID card and it turned out to be invalid.
    c. the health insurance specialist entered an incorrect charge on the claim.
    d. the provider has abused the TRICARE program and is under investigation.

18. Supplemental health care programs (SHCPs) are available through military associations and
    a. private third-party payers.
    b. government programs.
    c. state disability plans.
    d. workers' compensation.

19. The Civilian Health and Medical Program of the Department of Veterans Affairs (CHAMPVA) is a comprehensive health care program for which the _____ shares costs of covered health care services and supplies with eligible beneficiaries.
    a. Department of Defense
    b. Department of Health and Human Services
    c. Department of the Interior
    d. Department of Veterans Affairs

20. When the TRICARE patient has been referred by a military treatment facility, attach a(n) _____ to the CMS-1500 claim.
    a. DD Form 2527
    b. DD Form 2161
    c. DD Form 2642
    d. MTF referral form

Workers' Compensation

INTRODUCTION

This chapter familiarizes students with completion of CMS-1500 claims for primary workers' compensation payers.

 NOTE:

When completing CMS-1500 claims for case studies in this workbook, enter just one diagnosis pointer letter in Block 24E.

ASSIGNMENT 17.1 – WORKERS' COMPENSATION PRIMARY CMS-1500 CLAIMS COMPLETION

Objectives

At the conclusion of this assignment, the student should be able to:

1. Assign ICD-10-CM diagnosis and CPT or HCPCS level II procedure/service codes.
2. Prepare a workers' compensation insurance primary payer CMS-1500 claim.

Instructions

Complete a CMS-1500 for case studies 17-A and 17-B. Obtain a blank claim by making a copy of the CMS-1500 claim in Appendix I of the textbook. Refer to the CMS-1500 claims completion instructions (primary) in the textbook.

Donald L. Givings, M.D.

Case Study 17-A

11350 Medical Drive ■ Anywhere NY 12345-6541 ■ (101) 111-5555

EIN: 11-1234562
NPI: 1234567890

PATIENT INFORMATION:

Name:	Sandy S. Grand
Address:	109 Darling Road
City:	Anywhere
State:	NY
Zip Code:	12345
Telephone:	(101) 333-5555
Gender:	Female
Date of Birth:	12-03-1972
Occupation:	Personal trainer
Employer:	Starport Fitness Center
Address:	257 Treadmill Way
City:	Anywhere
State:	NY
Zip Code:	12345
SSN:	425991188

INSURANCE INFORMATION:

Patient Number:	17-A
Place of Service:	Office
WC Insurance Plan:	Workers Trust
FECA #:	987654321
WC Claim #:	CLR545701
WC Policyholder:	Starport Fitness Center
Address:	257 Treadmill Way
City:	Anywhere
State:	NY
Zip Code:	12345
Relationship to Patient:	Employer

Patient Status   ☐ Married   ☐ Divorced   ☒ Single   ☐ Student   ☐ Other

DIAGNOSIS INFORMATION

Diagnosis	Code	Diagnosis	Code
1. Wrist fracture, closed, left (initial encounter)		5.	
2. Fall from chair (initial encounter)		6.	
3. Fall at work (office building)		7.	
4.		8.	

PROCEDURE INFORMATION

Description of Procedure or Service	Date	Code	Charge
1. New patient office visit, level 4	02-03-YYYY		$100.00
2.			
3.			
4.			
5.			

SPECIAL NOTES:

Patient's SSN is 425-99-1188: Date of injury: 02-03-YYYY

Employer's phone number: (101) 333-6565. Case manager's name is June Ward.

Donald L. Givings, M.D.

11350 Medical Drive ■ Anywhere NY 12345-6541 ■ (101) 111-5555

EIN: 11-1234562
NPI: 1234567890

Case Study 17-B

PATIENT INFORMATION:

Name:	Marianna D. Holland
Address:	509 Dutch Street
City:	Anywhere
State:	NY
Zip Code:	12345
Telephone:	(101) 383-8761
Gender:	Female
Date of Birth:	11-05-1977
Occupation:	Hairstylist
Employer:	Hair Etc.
Address:	8731 Miracle Mile
City:	Anywhere
State:	NY
Zip Code:	12345

INSURANCE INFORMATION:

Patient Number:	17-B
Place of Service:	Office
WC Insurance Plan:	Workers Shield
FECA #:	654321987
WC Claim #:	BA678802
WC Policyholder:	Hair Etc.
Address:	8731 Miracle Mile
City:	Anywhere
State:	NY
Zip Code:	12345
Relationship to Patient:	Employer

Patient Status   ☒ Married   ☐ Divorced   ☐ Single   ☐ Student   ☐ Other

DIAGNOSIS INFORMATION

Diagnosis	Code	Diagnosis	Code
1. Open wound of right ring finger (initial encounter)		5.	
2. Injured by hair cutting scissors (initial encounter)		6.	
3. Injured at work (hair salon)		7.	
4.		8.	

PROCEDURE INFORMATION

Description of Procedure or Service	Date	Code	Charge
1. New patient office visit, level 3	05-12-YYYY		$80.00
2.			
3.			
4.			
5.			

SPECIAL NOTES:

Patient may return to work 5/16/YYYY.

Employer's phone number: (101) 383-6700. Case manager's name is Julie Kindle.

Patient's SSN is 521-15-0429. Date of injury: 05-12-YYYY

ASSIGNMENT 17.2 – WORKERS' COMPENSATION INTAKE FORM

Introduction

A workers' compensation intake form is completed for each new patient who seeks care for a work-related accident so that appropriate services are provided.

Objectives

At the conclusion of this assignment, the student should be able to:

1. Determine the patient information necessary for workers' compensation third-party billing.

2. Accurately complete insurance verification forms.

Instructions

1. Review case study 17-A for patient Sandy S. Grand, and complete the workers' compensation intake form.

2. Review case study 17-B for patient Marianna D. Holland, and complete the workers' compensation intake form.

3. Enter only the data included on each case study. (Some data may not be available at the patient's first office visit and would need to be entered at a later time.)

Case Study 17-A
Workers' Compensation Intake Form
Dr. Donald L. Givings, M.D. ■ 11350 Medical Drive ■ Anywhere NY 12345-6541 ■ (101) 111-5555
Today's Date:
Patient Name:
Patient Number:
Date of Injury:
Claim Number:
Type of Injury/Body Part:
Employer Name:
Address:
Insurance Company:
Phone Number:
Fax Number:
Claim Adjuster:
Treatment Authorized:
Completed by:
Notes:

Case Study 17-B	
Workers' Compensation Intake Form	
Dr. Donald L. Givings, M.D. ▪ 11350 Medical Drive ▪ Anywhere NY 12345-6541 ▪ (101) 111-5555	
Today's Date:	
Patient Name:	
Patient Number:	
Date of Injury:	
Claim Number:	
Type of Injury/Body Part:	
Employer Name:	
Address:	
Insurance Company:	
Phone Number:	
Fax Number:	
Claim Adjuster:	
Treatment Authorized:	
Completed by:	
Notes:	

ASSIGNMENT 17.3 – MULTIPLE CHOICE REVIEW

1. The Division of Coal Mine Workers' Compensation administers and processes claims for the
   a. Coal Mine Workers' Compensation Program.
   b. Federal Employees' Compensation Act Program.
   c. Federal Employment Liability Act.
   d. Longshore and Harbor Workers' Compensation Program.

2. Federal and state laws require employers to maintain workers' compensation coverage to meet minimum standards, covering a majority of employees for work-related illnesses and injuries
   a. only for companies that have a history of occupational deaths.
   b. for employers who are able to afford coverage.
   c. if the employee was not negligent in performing assigned duties.
   d. for companies with high-risk occupations only.

3. The Black Lung Program is also called the
   a. Coal Mine Workers' Compensation Program.
   b. Longshore and Harbor Workers' Compensation Program.
   c. Merchant Marine Act.
   d. Office of Workers' Compensation Programs.

4. The Mine Safety and Health Administration (MSHA) is similar in purpose and intent to the
   a. Energy Employees Occupational Illness Compensation Program.
   b. Federal Occupational Illness Compensation Program.
   c. Longshore and Harbor Workers' Compensation Program.
   d. Occupational Safety and Health Administration (OSHA).

5. Material Safety Data Sheets (MSDS) contain data regarding
   a. chemical and hazardous substances used at a worksite.
   b. how to implement an effective safety program at work.
   c. medicinal and therapeutic substances used at a worksite.
   d. the yearly number of occupational injuries and illness.

6. How long must records of employee vaccinations and accidental exposure incidents be retained?
   a. 10 years   c. 7 years
   b. 20 years   d. 5 years

7. The Federal Employment Liability Act (FELA) and the Merchant Marine Act were designed to
   a. develop a compensation fund for occupational injuries and deaths.
   b. increase the salaries of persons in certain high-risk occupations.
   c. offer medical and health care benefits to federal employees.
   d. provide employees with protection from employer negligence.

8. Which agency is responsible for handling appeals for denied workers' compensation claims?
   a. Occupational Safety and Health Administration
   b. Office of Workers' Compensation Programs
   c. State Insurance Commissioner
   d. State Workers' Compensation Commission

9. In which scenario would an employee be eligible for workers' compensation benefits?
   a. An angry worker was injured in the warehouse while trying to attack a coworker.
   b. An employee broke an ankle while walking with a coworker during their lunch hour.
   c. An employee was injured in an accident while driving to the bank to deposit the employer's checks.
   d. The employee was injured in a fall after drinking too much alcohol at a dinner meeting.

10. Workers' compensation survivor benefits are calculated according to the
    a. degree of risk that was involved in the employee's occupation.
    b. employee's earning capacity at the time of illness or injury.
    c. number of survivors in the household under the age of 18.
    d. period of time the employee was disabled before death.

11. A patient was treated by his primary care physician on 01/25/YY for a wrist fracture that occurred on the
    job. On 02/02/YY, the patient was evaluated for symptoms of severe high blood pressure and a recheck of
    the wrist fracture. Where should the provider document treatment from the visit on 02/02/YY?
    a. Both services should be recorded in the patient's medical record.
    b. Both services should be recorded in the workers' compensation record.
    c. Only the fracture recheck is to be recorded in the workers' compensation record.
    d. Only the visit from 01/25/YY is to be recorded in the workers' compensation record.

12. The First Report of Injury form is completed by the
    a. employer.   c. provider.
    b. patient.   d. witness.

13. The treating physician's personal signature is required
    a. if the patient has requested report copies.
    b. on all original reports and photocopies.
    c. only on original reports.
    d. only on photocopied reports.

14. After the claim has been acknowledged, the information that must be included on all correspondence to the employer, payer, billings, and the Commission Board is the
    a. file/case number assigned to the claim.
    b. patient's employee number.
    c. patient's Social Security number.
    d. treating physician's provider EIN number.

15. What information is entered in Block 11b of the worker's compensation CMS-1500 claim?
    a. Y4 and payer claim number
    b. date of injury
    c. employer
    d. Social Security number

16. Which of the following can be a designated state workers' compensation fiscal agent?
    a. a private, commercial insurance company
    b. the Office of Workers' Compensation Programs
    c. the state's compensation board
    d. the state's Department of Labor

17. Workers' compensation plans that allow an employer to set aside a state-mandated percentage of capital funds to cover employee compensation and benefits are
    a. combination programs.
    b. commercial insurance.
    c. self-insurance plans.
    d. state-funded plans.

18. If a patient fails to alert the provider that an injury was work-related, and then changes his mind later and tries to receive workers' compensation benefits, the claim will most likely be
    a. denied by the workers' compensation payer, and the patient will have to appeal.
    b. held in suspense for an indefinite period of time until documentation is reviewed.
    c. paid by workers' compensation beginning with the date of the most recent treatment.
    d. paid out-of-pocket by the patient first, then reimbursed by workers' compensation.

19. Which box is marked in Block 6 of the workers' compensation CMS-1500 claim?
    a. Child
    b. Other
    c. Self
    d. Spouse

20. Which box is marked in Block 1 of the workers' compensation CMS-1500 claim if the patient is a federal employee?
    a. FECA
    b. Medicaid
    c. Medicare
    d. Other

NOTES

NOTES

NOTES

NOTES

NOTES

NOTES

NOTES

NOTES

NOTES